First World War
and Army of Occupation
War Diary
France, Belgium and Germany

30 DIVISION
90 Infantry Brigade
Manchester Regiment
18th Battalion
8 November 1915 - 20 February 1918

WO95/2339/3

The Naval & Military Press Ltd
www.nmarchive.com
Published in association with The National Archives

Published by

The Naval & Military Press Ltd

Unit 10 Ridgewood Industrial Park,

Uckfield, East Sussex,

TN22 5QE England

Tel: +44 (0) 1825 749494

www.naval-military-press.com

www.nmarchive.com

This diary has been reprinted in facsimile from the original. Any imperfections are inevitably reproduced and the quality may fall short of modern type and cartographic standards.

© **Crown Copyright**
Images reproduced by permission of The National Archives, London, England, 2015.

Contents

Document type	Place/Title	Date From	Date To
Heading	WO95/2339-3		
Heading	24th Division 90th Infy Bde 18th Bn Manchester Regt Nov 1918-Feb 1918		
Heading	30th Division 18th Manchester Vol I Nov 15		
Heading	War Diary Of 18th Service Battalion Manchester Regiment. From 8th. November. 1915. To 30th November. 1915. Volume 1		
Heading	30th Div. 18th Manchester Vol 2		
War Diary	Boulogne	08/11/1915	09/11/1915
War Diary	Coulon Villers	10/11/1915	19/11/1915
War Diary	Cardonette	19/11/1915	27/11/1915
War Diary	Canaples	28/11/1915	30/11/1915
Heading	War Diary Of 18th Service Battalion Manchester Regt. From 1st December 1915 To 31st December 1915 Volume		
War Diary	Canaples	01/12/1915	16/12/1915
War Diary	Canaples	17/12/1915	31/12/1915
Heading	18th Manchester Vol 3 Jan		
War Diary	Canaples	01/01/1916	05/01/1916
War Diary	Talmas	06/01/1916	06/01/1916
War Diary	La Houssoye	07/01/1916	08/01/1916
War Diary	Suzanne	09/01/1916	21/01/1916
War Diary	Subsector AL	22/01/1916	31/01/1916
Heading	War Diary Of 18th Service Battn. Manchester Regt From February 1st 1916 To February 29th 1916		
War Diary	Subsector ZI	01/02/1916	29/02/1916
Miscellaneous	98th Infantry Brigade 30th Division 10th Corps 2nd Feb- 1916		
Miscellaneous			
Heading	War Diary Of 18th Service Battalion Manchester Regiment From 1 March 1916 To-31 March 1916. Vol 5		
War Diary	Y I Subsector	01/03/1916	19/03/1916
War Diary	Bois Des Tailles	20/03/1916	31/03/1916
War Diary	90th Infy 30th, 13th 8th March 1916		
Miscellaneous	90th Infy 30th 8th March 1916		
Heading	War Diary Of 18th (S) Bn. Manchester Regt. From 1st April 1916 To 30th April 1916 Vol 6		
War Diary	Frechen Court	01/04/1916	10/04/1916
War Diary	Poulainville	11/04/1916	11/04/1916
War Diary	Picquigny	12/04/1916	29/04/1916
War Diary	Corbie	30/04/1916	01/05/1916
War Diary	Bray	02/05/1916	02/05/1916
War Diary	Suzanne	03/05/1916	07/05/1916
War Diary	In Trenches	08/05/1916	14/05/1916
War Diary	In Suzanne	15/05/1916	18/05/1916
War Diary	In Trenches	19/05/1916	25/05/1916
War Diary	Suzanne	26/05/1916	31/05/1916
Miscellaneous	18th Service Battalion Manchester Regiment. Appendix I	01/05/1916	01/05/1916

Miscellaneous	18th Service Battalion. Manchester Regiment. Appendix 2	08/05/1916	08/05/1916
Miscellaneous	Report On Hostile Raid On "Y" Sector On Night Of 12/13th May 1916 Appendix 3	12/05/1916	12/05/1916
Miscellaneous	Intelligence Report.	13/05/1916	13/05/1916
Miscellaneous	Appendix "A" Report On Action Of Lewis Guns.	14/05/1916	14/05/1916
War Diary	Appendix "B" Report On Communications.	14/05/1916	14/05/1916
Miscellaneous	90th. 30th. 13th. May 1916. Appendix 2	18/05/1916	18/05/1916
Miscellaneous	18th Service Battalion Manchester Regiment. Appendix 4	25/09/1916	25/09/1916
Heading	War Diary Of 18th Service Battalion The Manchester Regiment. From June 1st 1916 To June 30th 1916		
War Diary	Suzanne	01/06/1916	01/06/1916
War Diary	Billon Wood	02/06/1916	12/06/1916
War Diary	Etinehem	13/06/1916	18/06/1916
War Diary	Saisseval	19/06/1916	26/06/1916
War Diary	Etinehem Camp	27/06/1916	30/06/1916
Miscellaneous	18th Service Battalion Manchester Regiment. Appendix I		
Operation(al) Order(s)	18th. Service Battalion Manchester Regiment. Operation Order No. 13 Appendix 3	11/06/1916	11/06/1916
Miscellaneous	To Officer Commanding.	18/06/1916	18/06/1916
Operation(al) Order(s)	18th Bn. Manchester Regiment Operation Order No. 15. Lieut. Colonel By W.L. Smith.	26/06/1916	26/06/1916
Miscellaneous			
Miscellaneous	Reference Operation Order No. 15	26/06/1916	26/06/1916
Miscellaneous	18th Bn. Manchester. Regiment. Supplement No.1 To Operation Order No. 15 Lieut. Col. W. A. By Smith.	27/06/1916	27/06/1916
Miscellaneous	18th Bn. Manchester Regiment. Supplement Order No 2 to Operation Order No. 15 By Lieut. Col. W.A. Smith.		
Miscellaneous			
Operation(al) Order(s)	18th Service Battalion Manchester Regiment. Operation Order No. 16		
Miscellaneous	Memorandum on the Organisation of Specialists		
Heading	War Diary Of 18th (S) Bn. Manchester Regt. For July 1916		
War Diary	War Diary Of 18th (Service) Battalion The Manchester Regt. From 1st July 1916 To 31st July 1916		
War Diary	Montauban	01/07/1916	02/07/1916
War Diary	Happy Valley	03/07/1916	11/07/1916
War Diary	Bois Des Celestins	12/07/1916	13/07/1916
War Diary	Bois Des Celestine Daours	14/07/1916	17/07/1916
War Diary	Daours-Bois Des Celestins	18/07/1916	18/07/1916
War Diary	Happy Valley	19/07/1916	21/07/1916
War Diary	Mansel Copse.	22/07/1916	24/07/1916
War Diary	German Trenches	24/07/1916	24/07/1916
War Diary	Old German Front Line	26/07/1916	26/07/1916
War Diary	Mansel Copse	27/07/1916	29/07/1916
Miscellaneous	To D.A.G. 3rd Echelon. Vol 9	07/08/1916	07/08/1916
Miscellaneous	G.O.C. 90th Infantry Brigade App. KI		
Heading	Operations July 8th To 11th Trones Wood App K 2		
Miscellaneous	To G.O.C. 90th Infantry Brigade. App K2	14/07/1916	14/07/1916
Miscellaneous	Appendix K 2	08/07/1916	08/07/1916
Miscellaneous	To Brigade Major, 90th Infantry Brigade.	20/07/1916	20/07/1916
Miscellaneous	Ref Order No. To O.C. Coys		
Miscellaneous	To O.C. A.B.C. & D. Coys.	07/07/1916	07/07/1916

Miscellaneous	To Lieut. B.B. Salmon.	07/07/1916	07/07/1916
Miscellaneous	To O.C. Company.	07/07/1916	07/07/1916
Operation(al) Order(s)	18th Bn. Manchester Regiment. Operation Order No. 17, By Colonel W.A. Smith. App 2	07/07/1916	07/07/1916
Miscellaneous	Appendix K 3		
Operation(al) Order(s)	18th Service Battalion Manchester Regiment Order No. 18 Major P. Godlee. Appendix K3	13/07/1916	13/07/1916
Operation(al) Order(s)	18th Service Battalion Manchester Regiment Order No. 19 Major H.B.O. Williams Appendix K 4		
Miscellaneous	Appendix K 4		
Miscellaneous	Appendix K 5		
Operation(al) Order(s)	18th Service Bn. Manchester Regiment. Operation Order No. 20. By Major H.B.O. Williams.	19/05/1916	19/05/1916
Miscellaneous	Appendix K 6		
Heading	Casualties App K 6 30.7.16	30/07/1916	30/07/1916
Miscellaneous	18th Service Battalion Manchester Regiment.	31/07/1916	31/07/1916
Miscellaneous	18th Service Battalion Manchester Regiment.		
Miscellaneous	18th Service Battalion Manchester Regiment.	04/08/1917	04/08/1917
Miscellaneous	Operation Order No. By Major H.B.O. Williams Commanding Muriel		
Miscellaneous	Sheet 2 S 30 A 6/4	29/07/1916	29/07/1916
Miscellaneous	Operation Order No. 2 18th Bn. Manchr Regt.	29/07/1916	29/07/1916
Miscellaneous	K 7		
Miscellaneous	18th Bn. Manchester Regt.	18/07/1916	18/07/1916
Miscellaneous	Congratulatory Messages.		
Miscellaneous	Appendix "A" Load For Carrying Parties.		
Miscellaneous	Appendix "B"		
Heading	17th Manchester Vol 4. 30th Div.		
Miscellaneous	Appendix C		
Heading	18th Manchester Rgt 30 Vol III		
Heading	90th Brigade 30th Division. 1/18th Battalion Manchester Regiment August 1916		
War Diary	Mansel Copse	01/08/1916	02/08/1916
War Diary	Airaines	03/08/1916	04/08/1916
War Diary	Busnes	05/08/1916	10/08/1916
War Diary	Le Hamel Essars	11/08/1916	28/08/1916
War Diary	Le Hamel Essars	27/08/1916	31/08/1916
Miscellaneous	16th Service Battn. Manchester Regiment Operation Order No. By Major H.B.C. Williams August 10th 1916 Appendix 1	10/08/1916	10/08/1916
Heading	War Diary Of The 18th Service Battalion The Manchester Regiment For The Month Of September 1916. (Volume XI.)		
War Diary	Le Hamel & Essars	01/09/1916	02/09/1916
War Diary	Trenches	03/09/1916	07/09/1916
War Diary	Le Touret	08/09/1916	12/09/1916
War Diary	Hingette	13/09/1916	13/09/1916
War Diary	Trenches	14/09/1916	15/09/1916
War Diary	Hingette	16/09/1916	16/09/1916
War Diary	Bellerive	17/09/1916	20/09/1916
War Diary	Flesselles	21/09/1916	30/09/1916
Operation(al) Order(s)	18th. Bn. Manchester Regiment. Operation Order No. 21. By Lieut. Colonel H.B.O. Williams. Appendix S.I.		
Miscellaneous	Operation Order By Lieut. Col. H.B.O. Williams Commanding 18th Battalion Manchester Regiment. Appendix S.2.		

Miscellaneous	Operation Order No. 23 By Lieut. Col. H.B.O. Williams Commanding 18th (S) Battalion Manchester Regiment. Appendix S.3.		
Operation(al) Order(s)	Operation Order No. 24 By Lieut. Col. H.B.O. Williams Commanding 18th Battalion Manchester Regiment. Appendix S.4.		
Operation(al) Order(s)	Operation Order No. 25 By Lieut. Col. H.B.O. Williams Commanding 18th Battalion Manchester Regiment. Appendix S.5.		
Operation(al) Order(s)	Operation Order No. 25 By Lieut. Col. H.B.O. Williams Commanding 18th Battalion Manchester Regiment. Appendix S.6.		
Miscellaneous	Entraining State. 18th Service Battalion Manchester Regiment. Appendix S7	00/09/1916	00/09/1916
Operation(al) Order(s)	Operation Order No. 26 By Lieut. Col. H.B.O. Williams Commanding 18th (S) Battalion Manchester Regiment.	19/09/1916	19/09/1916
Operation(al) Order(s)	Operation Order No. 27 By Lieut. Col. H.B.O. Williams Commanding 18th (S) Battalion Manchester Regiment. Appendix S.8	20/09/1916	20/09/1916
Heading	War Diary Of 18th Service Battalion The Manchester Regiment. From October 1st 1916 To October 31st 1916		
War Diary	Flesselles	01/10/1916	03/10/1916
War Diary	Buire	04/10/1916	05/10/1916
War Diary	Fricourt Camp	06/10/1916	09/10/1916
War Diary	Trenches	10/10/1916	19/10/1916
War Diary	Marl Borouch Wood	20/10/1916	21/10/1916
War Diary	Ribemont	22/10/1916	26/10/1916
War Diary	Sus-St Leger	27/10/1916	29/10/1916
War Diary	Bellacourt	30/10/1916	31/10/1916
Operation(al) Order(s)	Battalion Operation Order X.B.	03/10/1916	03/10/1916
Operation(al) Order(s)	Operation Order No. 28. By Lieut. Col. H.B.O. Williams Commdg. 18th. (S). Battalion. Manchester Regiment.	06/10/1916	06/10/1916
Heading	War Diary October 1916 Appendix X2		
Operation(al) Order(s)	Operation Order No.28. By Lieut. Col. H.B.O. Williams Commdg. 18th (S) Battalion Manchester Regiment.	06/10/1916	06/10/1916
Operation(al) Order(s)	Operation Order No. 29. By Lieut. Col. H.B.O. Williams Commdg. 18th Service Battalion Manchester Regiment.	09/10/1916	09/10/1916
Miscellaneous	To O.C All Coys		
Operation(al) Order(s)	Operation Order No. 28. By Lieut. Colonel. H.B.O. William., Commanding. 18th Service Battalion Manchester Regiment.	09/10/1916	09/10/1916
Operation(al) Order(s)	Operation Order No. 28. By Lieut. Colonel. H.B.O. Williams., Commanding. 18th Service Battalion Manchester Regiment.	09/10/1916	09/10/1916
Miscellaneous	Operation Order No. X 3		
Heading	War Diary October 1916 X3		
Heading	Operation October 12-16 1916		
Miscellaneous	Operation Order No.	12/10/1916	12/10/1916
Miscellaneous		11/10/1916	11/10/1916
Miscellaneous	Report On Operations October 10th-13th 1916	10/10/1916	10/10/1916
Heading	War Diary October 1916 X6		

Miscellaneous	Operation Order No. Y.k.7		
Heading	War Diary October 1916 Appendix X5		
Miscellaneous	Operation After Orders.	12/10/1916	12/10/1916
Operation(al) Order(s)	Operation Order No. 29. By N Col. H.B.C. Williams Commanding 18th Manchester Regt.	21/10/1916	21/10/1916
Miscellaneous	Operation After Orders.	12/10/1916	12/10/1916
Heading	War Diary Of 18th Service Battalion The Manchester Regiment. From 1st November 1916 To 30th November 1916		
War Diary	Bellacourt	01/11/1916	05/11/1916
War Diary	Trenches	06/11/1916	11/11/1916
War Diary	Bailleulval	12/11/1916	17/11/1916
War Diary	Trenches	18/11/1916	23/11/1916
War Diary	Bellacourt	24/11/1916	30/11/1916
Miscellaneous	Operation Order No. 30. By Lieut. Colonel H.B.O. Williams Commanding 18th Service Battalion. Manchester Regiment. Appendix VI	04/11/1916	04/11/1916
Operation(al) Order(s)	Operation Order No. 31. By Major C.E. Lembcke. Commanding 18th Service Battalion. Manchester Regiment. Appendix N2	11/11/1916	11/11/1916
Operation(al) Order(s)	Operation Order No. 32. By Major C.E. Lembcke Commanding 18th Service Battalion. Manchester Regiment. Appendix N3.	17/11/1916	17/11/1916
Miscellaneous	Operation Order No 33. By Major C.E. Lembcke. Commanding 18th Service Battalion. Manchester Regiment. Appendix N4	24/11/1916	24/11/1916
Operation(al) Order(s)	Operation Order No. 34. By Major C.E. Lembcke. Commanding 18th Service Battalion. Manchester Regiment. Appendix N5	29/11/1916	29/11/1916
Heading	War Diary Of 18th Service Battalion The Manchester Regiment. From 1st December 1916. To 31st December 1916 Volume XIV		
War Diary	Trenches	01/12/1916	06/12/1916
War Diary	Bailleulval & Basseux	07/12/1916	12/12/1916
War Diary	Trenches	13/12/1916	18/12/1916
War Diary	Bellacourt	19/12/1916	23/12/1916
War Diary	Trenches	24/12/1916	30/12/1916
War Diary	Bailleulval & Basseul	31/12/1916	31/12/1916
Operation(al) Order(s)	Operation Order No. 35. By Lieut. Col. H.B.O. Williams. Commanding. 18th (S) Battalion, Manchesters Regt.	05/10/1916	05/10/1916
Operation(al) Order(s)	Operation Order No. 36. By Lieut. Col. H.B.O. Williams Commanding 18th (S) Battalion Manchester Regiment.	11/12/1916	11/12/1916
Operation(al) Order(s)	Operation Order No. 37. By Lt. Col. H.B.O. Williams Commanding 18th (S) Battalion Manchester Regt.	17/12/1916	17/12/1916
Operation(al) Order(s)	Operation Order No 38. By Lt. Col. H.B.O. Williams Commanding 18th (S) Battalion Manchester Regt.	23/12/1916	23/12/1916
Miscellaneous	O.C. All Companies.	23/12/1916	23/12/1916
Miscellaneous			
Operation(al) Order(s)	Operation Order No. 40. By Major. Col. Lembcke. Commanding 18th Battn. Manchester Regiment.		
Heading	War Diary Of 18th Service Battalion Manchester Regiment. From 1st January 1917 To 31st January 1917 Volume XV		
War Diary	Bailleulval	01/01/1917	04/01/1917

War Diary	Sus St Leger	05/01/1917	30/01/1917
War Diary	Doullens & Sus	31/01/1917	31/01/1917
Operation(al) Order(s)	Operation Order No. 41. By Major C.E. Lembcke. Commanding 18th Battn. The Manchester Regiment.	04/01/1917	04/01/1917
Heading	War Diary For The Month Of February 1917 18th Service Battalion The Manchester Regiment.		
War Diary	Doullens & Sus. St. Leger	01/02/1917	04/02/1917
War Diary	Doullens & Halloy	05/02/1917	09/02/1917
War Diary	Doullens & Beaurepaire Fm	10/02/1917	22/02/1917
Miscellaneous	Appendix T1	01/02/1917	01/02/1917
Operation(al) Order(s)	Operation Order No. 42.		
Heading	War Diary For The Month Of March 1917 18th. Service Battalion The Manchester Regiment.		
War Diary	Doullens & Beaurepaire	01/03/1917	11/03/1917
War Diary	Pommera	12/03/1917	17/03/1917
War Diary	Monchiet	19/03/1917	20/03/1917
War Diary	In The Line	21/03/1917	31/03/1917
Operation(al) Order(s)	Operation Battalion Order No 42 By Captain T.J. Kelly Commanding 18th Battalion The Manchester Regiment.	12/03/1917	12/03/1917
Miscellaneous	To Captain C.J. Homewood	17/03/1917	17/03/1917
Operation(al) Order(s)	Operation Order No. 46 By Lieut. Col. C.E. Lembcke Commanding 18th. Bn. Manchester Regt.	18/03/1917	18/03/1917
Miscellaneous			
Operation(al) Order(s)	Operation Order No. 49. By Lt Col. C.E. Lembcke Commanding 18th Bn. Manchester Regt.	21/03/1917	21/03/1917
Operation(al) Order(s)	Operation Order No. 49. By Lieut. Col. C.E. Lembcke Commanding 18th Bn. Manchester Regt.	29/03/1917	29/03/1917
Heading	War Diary For The Month Of April 1917 18th Service Battalion-The Manchester Regiment. Volume 18		
War Diary	Basseux	01/04/1917	04/04/1917
War Diary	Bois Leux Au Mont	05/04/1917	08/04/1917
War Diary	Area S. Of Mercatel	09/04/1917	11/04/1917
War Diary	Hindenburg System S.W. Of Heninel	11/04/1917	12/04/1917
War Diary	Bienvillers Au Bois	14/04/1917	18/04/1917
War Diary	Neuville Vitasse Area	19/04/1917	22/04/1917
War Diary	Trenches S.E. of Heninel	23/04/1917	23/04/1917
War Diary	Neuville Vitasse Area	24/04/1917	24/04/1917
War Diary	Trenches S.E. Of Neuville Vitasse.	25/04/1917	28/04/1917
War Diary	Croisette	29/04/1917	30/04/1917
Operation(al) Order(s)	Operations Order No. 48 By Lieut. Col. C.E. Lembcke Commanding 18th Battalion The Manchester Regiment.	03/04/1917	03/04/1917
Miscellaneous	90th Infantry Brigade.	14/04/1917	14/04/1917
Miscellaneous	18th Battalion Manchester Regt.		
Operation(al) Order(s)	Operation Order No. 49. By Lieut. Col. C.E. Lembcke, Commanding 18th Battalion The Manchester Regiment.	18/04/1917	18/04/1917
Operation(al) Order(s)	Operation Order No. 50. By Lieut. Col. C.E. Lembcke, Commanding 18th Battalion The Manchester Regiment.	19/04/1917	19/04/1917
Miscellaneous	90th Infantry Brigade.	26/04/1917	26/04/1917
Operation(al) Order(s)	Operation Order No. 51. By Lieut. Col. C.E. Lembcke Commanding 18th (S) Battalion. The Manchester Regiment.	26/04/1917	26/04/1917
Heading	War Diary For The Month Of May 1917. 18th Service Battalion The Manchester Regiment. Volume XIX		
War Diary	Croisette	01/05/1917	03/05/1917
War Diary	Le Quesnoy	04/05/1917	25/05/1917
War Diary	Hazebrouck Area	26/05/1917	31/05/1917

Operation(al) Order(s)	Operation Order No. 52. By Lieut. Colonel. C.E. Lembcke Commanding 18th (S) Battalion The Manchester Regiment.	02/05/1917	02/05/1917
Operation(al) Order(s)	Operation Order No. 53. By Lieut. Col. C.E. Lembcke Commanding 18th (S) Battalion The Manchester Regiment.	19/05/1917	19/05/1917
Operation(al) Order(s)	Operation Order No. 54. By Lieut. Colonel. C.E. Lembcke Commanding 18th (S) Battalion The Manchester Regiment.	21/05/1917	21/05/1917
Operation(al) Order(s)	Operation Order No. 56. By Lieut. Colonel.C.E. Lembcke Commanding 18th (S) Battalion The Manchester Regiment.	23/05/1917	23/05/1917
Operation(al) Order(s)	Operation Order No. 57. By Lieut. Colonel.C.E. Lembcke Commanding 18th (S) Battalion The Manchester Regiment.	24/05/1917	24/05/1917
Heading	Operation Order No. 58. By Lieut. Colonel C.E. Lembcke Commanding 18th (Service) Battalion The Manchester Regiment.	30/05/1917	30/05/1917
Heading	War Diary For The Month Of June 1917. 18th Service Battalion-The Manchester Regimen. Volume. XX		
War Diary	Lumbres	01/06/1917	06/06/1917
War Diary	Hipshoek	07/06/1917	09/06/1917
War Diary	Toronto Camp	10/06/1917	15/06/1917
War Diary	Trenches	16/06/1917	22/06/1917
War Diary	Nordausques	23/06/1917	29/06/1917
War Diary	Dickebusch Area	30/06/1917	30/06/1917
Operation(al) Order(s)	Operation Order No. 59 By Lieut. Colonel. C.E. Lembcke Commanding 18th (S) Battalion. The Manchester Regiment.	03/06/1917	03/06/1917
Operation(al) Order(s)	Battalion Operation Order No. 60. By Lieut. Colonel C.E. Lembcke. Commanding 18th (S) Battalion The Manchester Regiment.	08/06/1917	08/06/1917
Operation(al) Order(s)	Battalion Operation Order No. 61. By Lieut Colonel C.E. Lembcke. Commanding 18th (S) Battalion The Manchester Regiment.	14/06/1917	14/06/1917
Operation(al) Order(s)	Operation Order No. 62. By Lieut. Colonel. C.E. Lembcke. Commanding 18th (S) Battalion The Manchester Regiment.	27/06/1917	27/06/1917
Miscellaneous	Operation Order.	28/06/1917	28/06/1917
Heading	War Diary For The Month Of July 1917 18th (Service) Battalion. The Manchester Regiment. Volume XXI		
War Diary	Dickebusch Huts	01/07/1917	07/07/1917
War Diary	Louches	08/07/1917	17/07/1917
War Diary	Wippenhoek Area	18/07/1917	24/07/1917
War Diary	Chateau Segard	24/07/1917	27/07/1917
War Diary	Line.	28/07/1917	31/07/1917
Miscellaneous	Copy Of Telegram Received From 30th. Division Headquarters.	05/07/1917	05/07/1917
Operation(al) Order(s)	Battalion Operation Order No. 64. By Lieut. Colonel C.E. Lembcke. Commanding 18th (S) Battalion. The Manchester Regt.		
Operation(al) Order(s)	Battalion Operation Order No. 66. By Lieut. Colonel. C.E. Lembcke, Commanding 18th (Service) Battalion The Manchester Regiment.	16/07/1917	16/07/1917

Operation(al) Order(s)	Operation Order No. 67. By Lieut. Colonel. C.E. Lembcke. Commanding 18th (S) Battalion. The Manchester Regiment.	21/07/1917	21/07/1917
Operation(al) Order(s)	Operation Order No. 68. By Lieut. Colonel. C.E. Lembcke Commanding 18th (Service) Battalion The Manchester Regiment.		
Operation(al) Order(s)	Operation Order No. 67. By Lieut. Colonel. C.E Lembcke Commanding 18th (Service) Battalion The Manchester Regiment.	23/07/1917	23/07/1917
Miscellaneous	Report On Operation Of July 26th 1917.	26/07/1917	26/07/1917
Operation(al) Order(s)	Operation Order No. 69.	28/07/1917	28/07/1917
Miscellaneous	To Headquarters, 90th Infantry Brigade.	03/08/1917	03/08/1917
Heading	War Diary For The Month Of August 1917. 18th Service Battalion. Manchester Regiment. Volume XXII.		
War Diary	Line.	01/08/1917	04/08/1917
War Diary	Terdeghem.	05/08/1917	07/08/1917
War Diary	Strazeele	08/08/1917	10/08/1917
War Diary	Berthen Area	11/08/1917	21/08/1917
War Diary	Parrain Farm Camp.	23/08/1917	29/08/1917
War Diary	Messines	30/08/1917	31/08/1917
Operation(al) Order(s)	Operation Order No. 69 By Lieut. Colonel. C.E Lembcke Commanding 18th (S) Battalion The Manchester Regt.		
Miscellaneous	Amendment To Battalion Operation Order.	09/08/1917	09/08/1917
Operation(al) Order(s)	Operation Order No. 70 By Lieut. Colonel. C.E. Lembcke. Commanding 18th (S) Battalion. The Manchester Regiment.	09/08/1917	09/08/1917
Operation(al) Order(s)	Operation Order No. 92 By Major. T.J. Kelly. M.C Commanding 18th (S) Battn. The Manchester Regiment.		
Operation(al) Order(s)	Battalion Operation Order No. 72 By Major T.J. Kelly M.C. The Manchester Regiment.	28/08/1917	28/08/1917
Heading	War Diary For The Month Of September 1917 18th Service Battalion The Manchester Regiment.		
War Diary	Messines Area	01/09/1917	02/09/1917
War Diary	Dranoutre	03/09/1917	22/09/1917
War Diary	Chinese Wall	23/09/1917	30/09/1917
Operation(al) Order(s)	Operation Order No. 95. By Lieut. Colonel. C.E. Lembcke. Commanding 18th (S) Battn. The Manchester Regiment.		
Operation(al) Order(s)	Operation Order No. 96. By Lieut. Colonel. C.E. Lembcke. Commanding 18th (S) Battn. The Manchester Regiment.	10/09/1917	10/09/1917
Operation(al) Order(s)	Battalion Operation Order No. 97. By Lieut. Colonel. C.E. Lembcke Commanding 18th (S) Battalion The Manchester Regiment.	15/09/1917	15/09/1917
Operation(al) Order(s)	Battalion Operation Order No. 98. By Lieut. Colonel. C.E. Lembcke Commanding 18th (S) Battalion The Manchester Regiment.	20/09/1917	20/09/1917
Heading	War Diary For The Month Of October 1917 18th (Service) Battalion-The Manchester Regiment. Volume XXVI		
War Diary		01/10/1917	01/10/1917
War Diary	Kemmel Chateau Area	02/10/1917	05/10/1917
War Diary	Daylight Corner	05/10/1917	12/10/1917
War Diary	In The Line	13/10/1917	17/10/1917

War Diary	Vroilandhoek Camp	18/10/1917	26/10/1917
War Diary	Vroilandhoek	27/10/1917	30/10/1917
War Diary	In The Line	31/10/1917	31/10/1917
Operation(al) Order(s)	Operation Order No. 99. By Lieut. Colonel. C.E. Lembcke Commanding 18th (S) Battalion. The Manchester Regiment.	30/09/1917	30/09/1917
Operation(al) Order(s)	Battalion Operation Order. By Lieut. Colonel. C.E. Lembcke. Commanding 18th (S) Battalion. The Manchester Regiment.	09/10/1917	09/10/1917
Operation(al) Order(s)	Operation Order No. 101. By Major. T.J. Kelly M.C. Commanding 18th Service Bn The Manchester Regiment.	15/10/1917	15/10/1917
Operation(al) Order(s)	Operation Order No. 102. By Major. T.J. Kelly M.C. Commanding 18th Service Bn The Manchester Regiment.	16/10/1917	16/10/1917
Operation(al) Order(s)	Operation Order No. 103. By Major. M.C.Theobald D.S.O. Commanding 18th Service Bn The Manchester Regiment.	28/10/1917	28/10/1917
Miscellaneous	Issued To Orderly At		
Heading	War Diary For The Month Of November 1917 18th Service Battalion The Manchester Regiment. Volume 25		
War Diary	Saint Jean	08/11/1917	24/11/1917
War Diary	In The Line	01/11/1917	07/11/1917
War Diary	Swan Chateau	26/11/1917	26/11/1917
War Diary	Swan Chateau	09/11/1917	30/11/1917
Operation(al) Order(s)	Operation Order No. 104. By Major M.C.W. Theobald, D.S.O. Commanding 18th (S) Battalion. The Manchester Regiment.	03/11/1917	30/11/1917
Operation(al) Order(s)	Battalion Operation Orders. By Major. M.C.W.Theobald, D.S.O. Commanding 18th (S) Battalion, The Manchester Regiment.	05/11/1917	05/11/1917
Operation(al) Order(s)	Operation Order No. 106. By Major M.C.W.Theobald, D.S.O. Commanding 18th (S) Battalion. The Manchester Regiment.	07/11/1917	07/11/1917
Operation(al) Order(s)	Operation Order No. 107. By Major. M.C.W.Theobald. D.S.O. Commanding 18th (Service) Battalion The Manchester Regiment.	27/11/1917	27/11/1917
Heading	War Diary For The Month Of December 1917 18th Service. Battalion. The Manchester Regiment. Vol 26		
War Diary	Swan Chateau	01/12/1917	09/12/1917
War Diary	Polderhoek Sector	11/12/1917	17/12/1917
War Diary	Alberta Camp	18/12/1917	31/12/1917
Operation(al) Order(s)	Operation Order No. 108. By Major H.C.W.Theobald. D.S.O. Commanding 18th (Service) Batt, The Manchester Regiment.	10/12/1917	10/12/1917
Miscellaneous	Headquarters, 21st Infantry Brigade.	16/12/1917	16/12/1917
Miscellaneous	Operation Orders. By Major T.J. Kelly. M.C. Commanding V.W.E.	15/12/1917	15/12/1917
Operation(al) Order(s)	Operation Order No. 109. By Lieut. Colonel. H.C.W.Theobald. D.S.O. Commanding 18th (Service). Battalion., The Manchester Regiment.	23/12/1917	23/12/1917
Operation(al) Order(s)	Operation Order No. 110. By Lieut. Col. H.C.W.Theobald. D.S.O. Commanding 18th. Batt. Manchesters Regt.	27/12/1917	27/12/1917

Operation(al) Order(s)	Operation Order No. 111 By Major T.J. Kelly M.C. Commanding 18th Batt. Manchester Regt.	29/12/1917	29/12/1917
Heading	18th Manchester Regiment. January 1918		
Heading	War Diary For The Month Of January 1918 18th Service Battalion. The Manchester Regiment Volume XXVII		
War Diary	Forrester Camp	01/01/1918	06/01/1918
War Diary	Ebblinghem	06/01/1918	08/01/1918
War Diary	Vaire-Sous-Corbie	09/01/1918	14/01/1918
War Diary	Nesle	15/01/1918	19/01/1918
War Diary	Libermont	20/01/1918	25/01/1918
War Diary	Behericourt	26/01/1918	26/01/1918
War Diary	Chauny	27/01/1918	28/01/1918
War Diary	In The Line	29/01/1918	31/01/1918
Operation(al) Order(s)	Operation Order No. 111. By Major T.J. Kelly M.C. Commanding 18th (S) Battalion. The Manchester Regiment.	03/01/1918	03/01/1918
Operation(al) Order(s)	Operation Order No. 113. By Major T.J. Kelly M.C. Commanding 18th (S) Battalion. The Manchester Regiment.		
Operation(al) Order(s)	18th Battalion Manchester Regt. Operation Order No. 114	12/01/1918	12/01/1918
Operation(al) Order(s)	18th Service Battalion Manchester Regiment. Operation Order No. 115	13/01/1918	13/01/1918
Operation(al) Order(s)	18th (S) Battn. Manchester Regiment. Operation Order No. 116	18/01/1918	18/01/1918
Operation(al) Order(s)	18th (S) Battn. Manchester Regiment. Operation Order No. 117	25/01/1918	25/01/1918
Miscellaneous	18th. Service Battalion Manchester Regiment. Operation Order 118	26/01/1918	26/01/1918
Miscellaneous	18th (S) Bn. Manchester Regt.	29/01/1918	29/01/1918
Heading	18th Manchester Regiment. February 1918		
Heading	War Diary For The Month Of February 1918 18th Service Battalion The Manchester Regiment. Volume XXVIII Vol 28		
War Diary		01/02/1918	20/02/1918
Operation(al) Order(s)	18th Bn. Manchester Regt. Operation Order No. 121	08/02/1918	08/02/1918
Operation(al) Order(s)	18th (S) Bn. Manchester Regt. Operation Order No. 122	09/02/1918	09/02/1918
Operation(al) Order(s)	18th (S) Bn. Manchester Regt. Operation Order No. 123	10/02/1918	10/02/1918
Operation(al) Order(s)	18th (S) Bn. Manchester Regt. Operation Order No. 124	16/02/1918	16/02/1918

W095/23391/3

18th Manchester
Pt. I
D/
7634

30th November

Nov 15
Dec 18

C O N F I D E N T I A L.

WAR   DIARY.

OF

18th. SERVICE BATTALION. MANCHESTER REGIMENT.

From 8th. November. 1915.   to 30th. November. 1915.

(Volume /).

18th Manchester
Vol 2
131/7834

Sheet 1

Army Form C. 2118

WAR DIARY
INTELLIGENCE SUMMARY
(Erase heading not required.)

18th (Service) Bn The Manchester Regt

Place	Date	Hour	Summary of Events and Information	Remarks and references to Appendices
BOULOGNE	6.11.15	9.0 P.M.	Arrived from LARK HILL SALISBURY. Marched to OSTROHOVE Rest Camp at BOULOGNE. Route March. Entrained for PONT REMY at 2 A.M. 10.11.15	
BOULOGNE	9.11.15			
COULONVILLERS	10.11.15	11.0 A.M.	Arrived at PONT REMY. Marched from BOULOGNE for PONT REMY & COULON VILLERS (11 mls)	
"	11.11.15		at COULONVILLERS – Cleaning Billets, inspecting clothing & accoutrements. Route March 4½ mls	
"	12.11.15		– Rifle firing, Bayonet fighting. Route March 5¼ miles	
"	13.11.15		do do do 6½ do	
"	14.11.15		Church Parade or Divine Service	
"	15.11.15		Bugle Route March	
"	16.11.15		do Practise in loading wagons Rifle firing & under Company arrangements	
"	17.11.15		Marched from COULONVILLERS & VIGNACOURT. Billeted for night at VIGNACOURT	
			VIGNACOURT & CARDONETTE	
CARDONETTE	19.11.15		At CARDONETTE – Cleaning Billets, Inspection of Rifles, clothing &c	
"	20.11.15		do Route Marches under Company arrangements	
"	21.11.15		do Parade for Divine Service	
"	22.11.15		do Practise in loading wagons. Route marches by ½ Battalions. Entrenchment in afternoon	
"	23.11.15		do Practice with Smoke Helmets with Tl gas. Enemy training	
"	24.11.15		do (Bugle) Route March. Route training & Company training in afternoon	
"	25.11.15		do Coy Training Battalion & under Company & arrangement Col Kent A.E. TOWNSEND and Sgt PERKINS and Pte BAGNALL injured by bomb during inoculation Company. Route March. Field Cooking. French Orders. Gas helmet practice. 2nd "	
"	26.11.15		A.E. TOWNSEND died from injuries received from bombing practice on 25".11.15"	
"	27.11.15		do Bombing Practice. Major Collins (Col Dull & Memorial Closs at 11 a.m.)	
MARLES	28.11.15		Marched from CARDONETTE to CANAPLES via COISY, BERTANGLES, FLESSELLES	
"	29.11.15		At CANAPLES. Cleaning Billets. Ration Rations to follow under Training & Rifle firing under Company arrangements	
"	30.11.15		do French Orders & Ration Cooking by under Company arrangements	

1875 |Wt. W593/826 1,000,000 4/15 J.B.C. & A. A.D.S.S./Forms/C. 2118.

CONFIDENTIAL

WAR DIARY OF

18TH SERVICE BATTALION MANCHESTER REGT

FROM 1ST DECEMBER 1915.

TO 31ST " "

(Volume   .)

WAR DIARY
or
INTELLIGENCE SUMMARY

Army Form C. 2118

SHEET 2

Instructions regarding War Diaries and Intelligence Summaries are contained in F.S. Regs., Part II. and the Staff Manual respectively. Title Pages will be prepared in manuscript.

(Erase heading not required.)

18th (Service) Bn. The Manchester Regt

Place	Date 1915	Hour	Summary of Events and Information	Remarks and references to Appendices
CANAPLES	DEC 1		Company work. Bathing Parade. Route Marches	
"	" 2		do	
"	" 3		do	
"	" 4		Wood cutting &c	
"	" 5		Church Parade. Wood cutting &c	
"	" 6		Wood cutting. Hurdle making &c	
"	" 7		Marched to PUCHEVILLERS (10 miles)	
"	" 8		Regtl HQ & "C" Coy marched to ENGLEBELMER. B&D Coys to MESNIL. Hurdle making to HEDAUVILLE	
			HQ & ENGLEBELMER "A" Coy in trenches with 2/Royal Irish Regt. "B" Coy in trenches with 1/Bord. James Rifles	Regtl HQ MESNIL handed over HEDAUVILLE
"	" 9		do	do
"	" 10		" "C" do	B Coy at MESNIL
"	" 11		HQ & A Coy do	do
"	" 12		do	B Coy at MESNIL
"	" 13		do	do
"	" 14		do	do
"	" 15		Headquarters A & C Coys at ENGLEBELMER. B & D Coys at MESNIL. Employed at HEDAUVILLE	
"	" 16		Marched to PUCHEVILLERS	
"	" 17		Marched to CANAPLES	
CANAPLES	" 18		Cleaning Clothing Equipment. Improving Billets	
"	" 19		Building latrines & kitchens. Drying Room. making footpath. Improving Billets generally	
"	" 20		Practice in trench digging, resisting dug out building &c. By day and by night	
"	" 21		Rifle Grenade Fusillade on 30ft & 150 to 30 yards range	
"	" 22		Bayonet fighting continues (see behind instruct) moderate. Effort entrenchments	
"	" 23		Musketry in practice with 5 rds on 300 yards & 30 yards range	
"	" 24		Practice with wire breakers & illuminating bombs. Instruction of Lewis Gunners	
"	" 25		training under Brigade bombing officers in grenade throwing by men of N.R.	
"	" 26			
"	" 27			
"	" 28			
"	" 29			
"	" 30			
"	" 31			

18th Manchester
Vol: 3

Sheet 3

Army Form C. 2118

WAR DIARY
or
INTELLIGENCE SUMMARY
(Erase heading not required.)

18th Service Batt^n The Manchester Reg^t

Place	Date 1916	Hour	Summary of Events and Information	Remarks and references to Appendices
CANAPLES	Jan. 1		Idling in trenches & improving billets. Machine gun sections training under brigade arrangements	
"	" 2		Divine service	
"	" 3		Idling in trenches, company drill, lectures on gas helmets	
"	" 4		Building, Machine order parade under Adjutant. Bombers practising at BERTEAUCOURT	
"	" 5		Parades under company arrangements, cleaning billets, loading stores, &c.	
TALMAS	" 6		Marched to TALMAS (5½ miles)	
LA HOUSSOYE	" 7		Marched from TALMAS to LA HOUSSOYE (10 miles)	
"	" 8		Headquarters and "A" & "B" Coys to ETINEHEM; "C" & "D" Coys to CHIPILLY (12 miles)	
SUZANNE	" 9		Marched in evening to SUZANNE (5 miles)	
"	" 10		The battalion took over A1 subsector of line from 9th ROYAL SCOTS and NORTHANTS YEOMANRY (DRAGONS WOOD only). "A" Coy in night in DRAGONS WOOD; "B" in VAUX WOOD; "D" in BATTLE DUGOUTS, each coy sending a platoon to the trenches at MOULIN DE FARGNY, which is on extreme left in SUBSECTOR A2. "C" Battalion in reserve	
"	" 11			
"	" 12			
"	" 13		Two men killed today, one at MOULIN DE FARGNY, two others wounded. 11005 Pte Brown "D" coy killed today; one man wounded FARGNY MILL today	
"	" 14		one N.C.O killed today at ECLUSIER CROSSROADS	
"	" 15		LT R. S. ENGLAND went to hospital today with cartilage of the knee	
"	" 16		In the line, no casual casualties	
"	" 17		"	
"	" 18		"	LT BUCHANAN + half M.G section 11th SOUTH LANCS attached S to reinforce infantry of SUBSECTOR A1
"	" 19		"	
"	" 20		One man dies in hospital from wounds received 19/1/16	
"	" 21		In the line. LT BUCHANAN 11th SOUTH LANCS. sent to hospital today sick	

WAR DIARY or INTELLIGENCE SUMMARY

Army Form C. 2118

Sheet 4

18th Service Batt'n The Manchester Regt

Place	Date	Hour	Summary of Events and Information	Remarks and references to Appendices
SUBSECTOR A1	Jan 22		In the line, no casualties	
	"23		Divine Service, C.E. and R.C. VAUX CHURCH	
	"24		One man wounded to-day	
	"25		No casualties	
	"26		Two men wounded to-day	
	"27		Half M.G. section, 11th SOUTH LANCS ceased to be attached to battalion from this date, going to SUBSECTOR A2. One man wounded	
	"28		Heavy bombardment of SUBSECTOR A1 today. One man killed and eight wounded. This evening 2nd Lt BLENKIRON took patrol of 20 other ranks to ascertain whether FRENCH had withdrawn in the night. The Officer with 10490 Lce Cpl SQUIBBS, "D" Coy, & 9943 Pte WHITWORTH, "A" Coy approached	
		9.0 PM	wire entering village of FRISE where they were heard talking in French. Patrol waited 5 hours as the three had not returned came back to VAUX. The three were posted as missing next day.	
		9.15 PM	German attempted to cut wire in front of No 11 truck, but were repeated by machine gun, bomb & rapid rifle fire. One wounded German was captured. "We had 5 N.C.O's men wounded to-day	
	"29		Heavy shelling continued. One man killed and 7 wounded	
	"30		A missing man was found dead in old dressing station at VAUX	
	"31		A missing N.C.O. was found dead in same shell hole as other man WILTON	at VAUX

LIEUT. COLONEL,
18th Service (3rd City) Batt., Manchester Regiment.

Confidential.
War Diary
of
18th Service Battn Manchester Regt

From   February 1st 1916.
To.   February 29th 1916.

Volume ( )

Sheet 5

Army Form C. 2118

WAR DIARY
or
INTELLIGENCE SUMMARY
(Erase heading not required.) 18th Service Battn The Manchester Regt

Place	Date 1916	Hour	Summary of Events and Information	Remarks and references to Appendices
SUBSECTOR Z1	Feb 1		Draft of 25 men from 25th (Reserve) Battn Manchr Regt arrived. Reports to companies. Two men wounded.	
	" 2		Lt Col FRASER, Lt KNOWLES, & Lt POWELL + 18 other ranks proceeded from VAUX N.W end of FRISE, where the party split up into three sections of six each under an officer. Three strands of wire had been cut when a sentry challenged. The sentry was shot by Lt KNOWLES & thereupon fire was opened on the party from 30 rifles, & after throwing 25 grenades, throwing in a heavy burst rapid fire we withdrew without casualty out of the 5 men accounted to party from the 25th (Reserve) Battn Manchester Regt.	
	" 3		Lt COL W.A. FRASER, Lt W.P. KNOWLES, Lt J.P. CUNLIFFE + 4 other ranks while making a reconnaissance of the RIVER SOMME were fired upon by a strong body of the enemy, firing signal bombs with the bomb one scout missing. Three men wounded. "B" coy suffered heavy casualties in VAUX by shell fire, six men being killed and 15 wounded	
	" 4		One man wounded today	
	" 5		One man wounded today	
	" 6		One man killed today	
	" 7		One N.C.O. Killed and one man wounded today	
	" 8		One N.C.O. wounded today	
	" 9		Nothing to report	
	" 10		A German rifle and box of high explosive fuses on wire, in front of MOULIN DE FARGNY launcher	
	" 11		Nothing to report	
	" 12		Services for Church of England and R.C. troops were celebrated today in the Phosphate mine at VAUX which since Feby 5th has been occupied by all the troops in the village except the orderly room staff + headquarter servants. One man killed today. 2 w/ L/S E.KAVANAGH, C.A.S. TIMMS, & A. COOPER from the 14th BATT Manchester Regt & 200 other ranks from the 25th (Reserve) Batt. Manchester Regt joined today. 2nd Lt KAVANAGH is posted to "C" Coy and the other two officers to "D" Coy.	
	" 13			

Sheet 6

Army Form C. 2118

WAR DIARY
or
INTELLIGENCE SUMMARY
(Erase heading not required.)

Instructions regarding War Diaries and Intelligence Summaries are contained in F. S. Regs., Part II. and the Staff Manual respectively. Title Pages will be prepared in manuscript.

Place	Date	Hour	Summary of Events and Information	Remarks and references to Appendices
SUZZECTOR Z1	Feb 14		One man wounded	
	" 15		Nothing to report	
	" 16		2nd Lt H.A. POWELL & four other ranks today entered the northern end of FRISE which is occupied by the enemy, and entered a building used as a guardroom. They brought away with them 16 German hand grenades.	
	" 17		Lt COL BAIRD, 5 Officers, and 21 other ranks of the 8th ARGYLL and SUTHERLAND HIGHLANDERS (T) arrives today	
	" 18		Nothing to report	
	" 19		Lt COL BAIRD, 5 Officers, and 21 other ranks of 8th ARGYLL and SUTHERLAND HIGHLANDERS left the outpost today.	
	" 20		Nothing to report. Draft of 4 N.C.O's & men from 25th Manchester Regt comes today	
	" 21		Nothing to report	
	" 22		2nd Lt SALMON and 2nd Lt TWIST joined today from 25th Battn Manchester Regt. Extract from orders of this date :— "Will you please convey my appreciation of this good work to Lt Powell his N.C.O's and men" (Signed) W. N. CONGREVE Lt GEN. Commanding 13th Corps	

SCOUTS

"G.O.C. 90th INFANTRY BRIGADE wishes to take this opportunity of congratulating Lts KNOWLES and POWELL and the scouts of the 18th Manchester Regt on their excellent work during the last few weeks

(Signed) H. F. MONTGOMERY.
Brigade major

Sheet 7

Army Form C. 2118

WAR DIARY
or
INTELLIGENCE SUMMARY
(Erase heading not required.)

Place	Date	Hour	Summary of Events and Information	Remarks and references to Appendices
SUBSECTOR Z.1	Feb 23		Nothing to report	
	" 24		Nothing to report	
	" 25		Nothing to report	
	" 26	3.0 A.M.	A strong fighting patrol of enemy appeared on our wire in front of KNOWLES POINT, where "B" Coy had a listening patrol of 2 N.C.Os and 8 men. Our patrol sent in several volleys bursts of rapid fire and threw bombs then withdrew to DUCK POST without Casualties. A search party found that one German had been badly wounded and dragged away. But his equipment was found near the wire.	
	" 27	8.30 P.M.	A party of Germans estimated at 60 strong attacked KNOWLES POINT. Warning of the attack was given by scouts who had been sent out in front to protect a working party. The enemy were met by hand grenades & heavy rifle fire. 2 L⁺ NELSON who was in command sent back for reinforcements. These were brought up by 2ⁿᵈ L⁺ SALMON and L⁺ KELLY, who took command. A Lewis gun was also taken up and the enemy retired, leaving two men dead on our wire. They were seen to take back a number of wounded. Our casualties were three men killed and nine wounded. A scout (CORPORAL BROOKS) was captured. and taken towards FRISE in charge of one man. He managed to conceal a MILLS grenade in his lining & his jerking & on the two approached a front of Germans he stunned his guard with a blow from the bomb & then running the fuse threw it amongst the front, and escaped.	

Sheet 8

Army Form C. 2118

WAR DIARY
or
INTELLIGENCE SUMMARY

(Erase heading not required.) 18th Battn The Manchester Regt

Instructions regarding War Diaries and Intelligence Summaries are contained in F. S. Regs., Part II. and the Staff Manual respectively. Title Pages will be prepared in manuscript.

Place	Date	Hour	Summary of Events and Information	Remarks and references to Appendices
SUBSECTOR 21	Feb 28		Nothing to report	
	" 29		Nothing to report	

G Tipton
Major for Lt Col
Commanding 18th Manchester Regt

Army Form W. 3121.

Brigade: 90th Infantry
Unit:
Division: 30th
Corps:
Date of Recommendation: 2nd Feb 1916

Schedule No.	Unit	Regtl. No.	Rank and Name	Action for which commended	Recommended by	Honour or Reward	(To be left blank)
	18th Manch. R.	10893	Sergt. Tomlinson J. (Signalling Section)	During the bombardment of A1 Sr Sector on the 28th and 29th January 1916, who demonstrated at great risk under the heavy shell fire by day and by night, keeping the wires between Bn HdQrs & that of the Coys, Coy OC Pns to Regt of gnts in open, stating by shells and so was explained. Sergt Tomlinson went out but so Regt HdQrs & gave attention, and simply repaired all the damages that had been caused. My notes to Regt. Monograd of Village. Comr. writes my notes to Regt. Missions during those two days at BOIS DE VAUX and VAUX VILLAGE.	Watson Lt Col Comdg 18th Manch R	D.C.M. from Brig Genl 90th Inf Bde	Approved 2
	18th Man. R.	10835	Sergt. Potts B.W. (Machine Gun Section)	At MOULIN DE FARGNY, on the night of the 12/13th January 1916, when a heavy rifle and M.G. fire was directed upon No.1 & 2 Lewis guns the making a rapid gun movement difficult. He set the machine gun of the parapet repeatedly during the night and drew off the GERMAN trenches since Bott the enemy. Since a most moonlight night and he was fully exposed to the enemy. Immediately after his brought off the rifle, and supported the firing he brought off a GERMAN gun that the GERMAN rifle fire, and saw the fire of a fresh line of the craft of the CHAPEAU DE GENDARME. He accompanied in Co.nouse by the bombing	(signature) Lt Col Comdg 18th Man R	D.C.M.	Approved 2
	18th Manch. R.	10813	Sergt Hill F.H.C.	Sn command 2nd bombing of Bn during this bombardment upon MOULIN DE FARGNY, he in person attacked on a sap, by his skillful handling rallied his men who were beaten back and drove off the enemy, and obtained a prisoner.		D.C.M.	

Regt.		No.	Rank	Name		Act	Award
18th Manch. R. (18th Service Battalion the Manchester Regiment)		10239	Sergt.	CLEGG, S. (Squire GLF 19)	During the bombardment of VAUX VILLAGE on the night of 15th/16th November, 1916, he learnt with the greatest bravery and dangerous work. Keeping together men in a safety refundated, dying on 2018 the day under the heaviest shell fire gathered regarding much B.F. of danger, he did not desist until every wounded man was in safety.		D.C.M.

Confidential

WAR DIARY

OF

18TH SERVICE BATTALION

MANCHESTER REGIMENT

FROM 1. MARCH 1916

To -
    31 MARCH 1916

(VOLUME   )

Army Form C. 2118

Sheet 9

WAR DIARY
or
INTELLIGENCE SUMMARY

(Erase heading not required.) 18th (Service) Batt" The Manchester Regt

Instructions regarding War Diaries and Intelligence Summaries are contained in F.S. Regs., Part II. and the Staff Manual respectively. Title Pages will be prepared in manuscript.

Place	Date	Hour	Summary of Events and Information	Remarks and references to Appendices
Y1 SUBSECTOR	1916 March 29	12.25 A.M.	KNOWLES POINT, held by LT T.J. KELLY with a party of 16 men & a Lewis gun, was attacked by the enemy. The bombers reached our wire & threw several bombs but then drew back owing to our heavy bombing beyond. We replied effectively with bombs, rifle and machine gun fire and the enemy retired before the arrival of reinforcements. The wire was badly cut. The enemy left a few bombs & bomb cutters behind. No casualties. Extract from to-day's orders:- "Commander-in-Chief awards MILITARY CROSSES to LT W.P. KNOWLES and 2nd LT H.A. POWELL and D.C.M. to Corporal (now Sergeant) A.J.B. BROOKE, all 18th MANCHESTER REGT. Please convey CORPS and DIVISIONAL Commanders congratulations. The Brigadier General takes this opportunity of congratulating LT KNOWLES 2nd LT POWELL & Corporal (now Sergt) BROOKE on their well-earned rewards and on the skill, courage and initiative shown Major F. Lupton as Commanding Officer during the absence of Lt Col W.A. Fraser feels sure that all ranks will join with him in congratulating Lt KNOWLES, 2nd Lt POWELL and Sergt BROOKE on the honours they have gained for themselves and the 18th Manchester Regt."	

Army Form C. 2118

Sheet 10

WAR DIARY
or
INTELLIGENCE SUMMARY

(Erase heading not required.) 1/8th (Service) Battn 1/o Manchester Regt

Instructions regarding War Diaries and Intelligence Summaries are contained in F. S. Regs., Part II. and the Staff Manual respectively. Title Pages will be prepared in manuscript.

Place	Date	Hour	Summary of Events and Information	Remarks and references to Appendices
Y.1 SUBSECTOR	March 2		Nothing to report	
	" 3		— do —	
	" 4		No man wounded	
	" 5		A heavy burst of fire from FRISE lestfarmor at KNOWLES POINT to suppose that an attack was imminent and S.O.S. signal was sent up. A reconnaissance, however, showed that all was clear. One man wounded.	
	" 6		Nothing to report	
	" 7		2nd Lt POWELL was severely wounded owing to accidental discharge of a revolver by a brother officer in "B" Coy mess. Machine gun emplacement at KNOWLES POINT was struck by a shell, four of team being killed & one severely wounded. Three others wounded. LT COL W.A. FRASER returned from leave today & assumes command	
	" 8		2nd Lt J.L. NELSON was killed instantly in the DUCK POST by the accidental discharge of a rifle. Four men & one wounded in VAUX WOOD by a shell falling on dug-out. Nothing to report.	
	" 9		Nothing to report.	
	" 10		Nothing to report. (the garrison of which retires according to orders)	
	" 11	6.0 P.M.	After heavily shelling KNOWLES POINT and DUCK POST the enemy occupies LODGE WOOD in force. A number of men also appears in front of the blockhouse at the DUCK POST. Artillery fire was at once obtained and the machine guns of the subsector were contentrated in the wood. Scouts sent out at intervals between the shelling reported that the enemy had but retired. Flares were sent for our artillery	

WAR DIARY or INTELLIGENCE SUMMARY

Army Form C. 2118

Sheet 11

Place	Date Hour	Summary of Events and Information	Remarks and references to Appendices
Y/1 SUBSECTOR	March 11 1916	attack, Lt KNOWLES leading the first line, Lt KELLY the 2nd and 3rd, and 2nd Lt STATHAM the third. It was then found that the bridge over the arm of the SOMME between the DUCKPOST and LODGE WOOD had been removed.	
	March 12 7.0 P.M	After several scouting parties had ascertained that the enemy still held LODGE WOOD our artillery heavily shelled the position and at this hour an infantry attack was launched, Lt KNOWLES to the right attack, & 2nd Lt KAVANAGH the left attack, and Lt CUNLIFFE in in support with two LEWIS guns. Lt KELLY was also in support with the second line but this was not called upon as the enemy retired. The wire was then heavily shelled and it was decided to postpone reducing it until daylight. Lt Col W.H. FRASER went to hopeful look out & Major G. Lupton took conveyance of the battalion. A reconnaissance at dawn showed that the enemy had completely evacuated KNOWLES POINT and LODGE E, leaving behind a great quantity of stores — (two bags Queens shells nibs Equipment clothing tools etc. — and the dead men belonging to the 1st PIONEER BATTALION, 13 Infantry Division, 14 Army Corps.	
	March 13		

Army Form C. 2118

WAR DIARY
or
INTELLIGENCE SUMMARY
(Erase heading not required.) 1/8 Service Battalion The Manchester Regt

Place	Date	Hour	Summary of Events and Information	Remarks and references to Appendices
Sheet 12 1/1 SUBSECTOR	1916 March 13		There were again had the enemy suffered heavy casualties from our rifle & telegraph fire. Our casualties. No report here 2nd. MAJOR WM. SMITH assumes command of the battalion today.	
	March 14		Three men wounded today.	
	" 15		Today LT HARRISON and 30 Other ranks "A" Coy from DRAGONS WOOD relieved LT KELLY and 30 other ranks "B" Coy in VAUX.	
	" 16 " 17 " 18		Nothing to report.	
			do.	
			Draft of 41 other ranks from 23rd Mayjube Regt arrives today. MAJOR G. LUPTON left battalion today for 30th	
	" 19		Two men wounded. DIVISIONAL SCHOOL. Capt. LYNDE and LT WATSON proceeded on leave. The battalion was relieved today by the 8th Batt EAST SURREY REGT and marched by half-companies to the BOIS DES TAILLES. The casualties of the battalion were: "A" Coy, 8 killed, 2 died of wounds, 6 wounded, 1 missing. "B" Coy, 1 officer killed, 1 officer wounded, 14 other ranks killed, 4 died of wounds, 26 wounded, one missing, "C" Coy, 8 other ranks killed, 5 died of wounds, 12 wounded, "D" Coy, 1 officer missing, 1 other rank killed, 12 wounded, 1 missing. Total 103 killed, wounded and missing.	
BOIS DES TAILLES	20		Draft of Platoon and Coy drill to syllabus.	

1875 Wt. W593/826 1,000,000 4/15 J.B.C. & A. A.D.S.S./Forms/C. 2118.

Sheet 13

Army Form C. 2118

WAR DIARY
or
INTELLIGENCE SUMMARY

(Erase heading not required.) 18th (Service) Batt. The Manchester Regt.

Place	Date 1916	Hour	Summary of Events and Information	Remarks and references to Appendices
BOIS DES TAILLES	March 21		Drill, route march, and training according to syllabus.	
	" 22		do	
	" 23		do War learned that the General Officer commanding in chief had granted the military cross to 2nd Lt. P.A. BLYTHE and the D.C.M. to 10355 Pte A. BANCROFT, "C" Coy, for gallantry displayed on March 8th when they along with three other men entered under heavy fire in an attempt to rescue five men from a dug-out in VAUX WOOD which had been smashed in by shell.	
	24		do	
	25		do	
	26		do	
	27		parties at COPSE F and TRIGGER WOOD.	
	28		Same as 27. Except C+D Coys who provided working	
	29		Batt moved from Bois des Tailles to Billets at FRECHENCOURT Except 3 Platoons of D Coy billeted at PONT NOYELLES. No.19 Batt Kings Liverpool Regt relieved the Batt at Bois des Tailles.	
	30		The Batt provided a working party of 100 men under Capt. D. BERRY to work on	
	31		the new Railway being constructed at FRECHENCOURT.	

Walsh T Major
Commanding 18th Bn. Manchester Regt.

Army Form W. 3121.

Brigade. 30th **Division.** 13th **Corps.** **Date of Recommendation.** 8th March 1916

Appendix 2

Schedule No. (To be left blank)	Unit	Regtl. No.	Rank and Name	Action for which commended	Recommended by	Honour or Reward	(To be left blank)
	19th (S) Bn MANCHESTER REGT.		Lieut Percy Arthur Blythe	On the 8th March 1916 during a German bombardment of VAUX WOOD & during the the wood was inspected by Lieut Blythe, the manner being completed. Lieut Blythe then proceeded & collected a small party of men & proceeded to dig them out, working himself with his hands, and carried until they were all recovered and taken into a place of safety, together and three dead. During the whole of this time H.E. Shells were falling all round them. 107 Shells falling in close proximity to them in the space of 55 minutes.		Victoria Cross	
RAMC No Y/c 19th Manch Regt			Captain William Harold BUTLER	The complete disregard of danger and devotion to duty of Capt Butler has repeatedly come under my notice during the last 3 weeks in the following instances:— (1) During the bombardment of VAUX VILLAGE on the 25th January and the 11th Feby 1916, Capt Butler was indefatigable in his attendance on the wounded, frequently putting them in his dugout under heavy shell fire. (2) During the severe bombardment of NEW DRAGOON'S FARM BY MILL in January & Feby 1916, Capt Butler's Aid Post was perpetually fired on through being in dangerous proximity to 4 posts of the Battery and whilst in dugout proceeded to the dugout of the Officer Killed & Wounded, which lay 400 yds from the complete time of the communication trenches by shell fire, the men are	W.W. Fraser Lieut Col Comman'g 19th Bn Manch Regt	Military Cross	

Army Form W. 3121.

Schedule No. (to be left blank)	Unit	Regtl. No.	Rank and Name	Action for which commended	Recommended by	Honour or Reward	(To be left blank)

Brigade. 30th   Division. 131th   Corps.   Date of Recommendation. 31 March 1916

Rank and Name: (Continued)

Action for which commended:
instance of a wounded man having been left unattended by him.
(3) On the 9th of March 1916, during the bombardment of VAUX WOOD, Capt. B. Utley on learning that 5 men were buried in a dug-out, immediately proceeded to the scene, assisted at their rescue, helped to carry them into a place of safety and attended to them under heavy shell fire; no less than 10(?) shells falling in the immediate neighbourhood in less than 1 hour.

W.T. Turner
Lieut Col.
Commanding 19th (S) Bn Manch Regt.

C.B. Morris(?) Brig. Gen(?)
Cmdg(?) 30 Div(?)

18 Manchrs
Vol 6

Confidential

War Diary
of
18th (S) Bn. Manchester Regt.

from

1st April 1916.
to
30th April 1916

(Volume 6)

Sheet 14

Army Form C. 2118

WAR DIARY
or
INTELLIGENCE SUMMARY

(Erase heading not required.) 18th (Serve) Batt The Manchester Regt

Place	Date 1916	Hour	Summary of Events and Information	Remarks and references to Appendices
FRECHEN-COURT	April 2		Divine Service was held at FRECHENCOURT for A.B.+C Coys and one Platoon of "D" Coy and at PONT NOYELLES for three remaining Platoons of No 4 Coy.	
	3		The Battalion was engaged under direction of R.E. in constructing a new railway which links up the chief villages in this part of the department of THE SOMME held by British troops	
	4			
	5			
	6		Specialists — machine gunners, bombers, grenadiers (trained) under their own officers.	
	7			
	8			
	9			
	10			
POULAINVILLE	11		Marched to POULAINVILLE, 7 miles	
PICQUIGNY	12		Marched to PICQUIGNY, 9 miles	
	13		Platoon and company training in accordance with Brigade training Scheme. Specialists under their own officers at headquarters.	
	14		Coy of 58 O.R. was formed.	
	15		Capt. HOBKIRK returned to ENGLAND to do Divine Service for Coy E, R.C. and Nonconformists	
	16			
	17		Training as on 13th – 15th	
	18			
	19		Lt Col. GODLEE returned to battalion from Divisional Staff work for training.	

Sheet 15

Army Form C. 2118

WAR DIARY
or
INTELLIGENCE SUMMARY

(Erase heading not required.) 18th (Service Batt'n) The Manchester Regt.

Instructions regarding War Diaries and Intelligence Summaries are contained in F.S. Regs., Part II. and the Staff Manual respectively. Title Pages will be prepared in manuscript.

Place	Date 1916	Hour	Summary of Events and Information	Remarks and references to Appendices
PICQUIGNY	April 20		Extract from today's orders:- The appointment of Lt Col W.A. SMITH, 20th Batt'n THE KING'S (LIVERPOOL) REGT to the permanent command of the 18th MANCHESTER REGT is now approved.	
"	" 21		Battalion training in fields near PICQUIGNY - SOUES road. Lt A.A. HARRISON 4th Batt'n THE MANCHESTER REGT and 19 O.R. from 25th (Reserve) Batt'n THE MANCHESTER REGT joined today. The three highest to "C" Coy	
"	" 22		Battalion training in trenches at AILLY-SUR-SOMME. CAPT WOODLAND, Coy E and R.C. Batt'n won 100 yds, half mile	Acting Lt Col Manchester Regt
"	" 23		Divine service for Col E and R.C. Batt'n. 90th Brigade sports held at PICQUIGNY and some runs in brigade horse show.	
"	" 24		Battalion took part in brigade training	
"	" 25		do.	
"	" 26		Coys at disposal of company commanders. Bathing morning	
"	" 27		do	
"	" 28		Battalion training. 2nd Lt D H ROBERTS joined for duty S of AILLY French attack 2nd Lt D WILCOX do to A Coy	
"	" 29		do B —	
CORBIE	30		Batt'n marches to CORBIE. CAPT F WOLFENDEN joined for duty	

1875 Wt. W593/826 1,000,000 4/15 J.B.C. & A. A.D.S.S./Forms/C. 2118.

Army Form C. 2118

WAR DIARY
or
INTELLIGENCE SUMMARY

(Erase heading not required.) 18th (S) Bn: Manchester Regt.

Vol 7

Instructions regarding War Diaries and Intelligence Summaries are contained in F.S. Regs., Part II. and the Staff Manual respectively. Title Pages will be prepared in manuscript.

Sheet 16

Place	Date	Hour	Summary of Events and Information	Remarks and references to Appendices
CORBIE	May 1	4 pm	C.O. inspected Billets. Bn: moved to BRAY in Bus reserve to 54th Bde.	
BRAY	" 2	7.30 pm	"SUZANNE" in possession to go to Bde Y sector.	See Appendix 1.
SUZANNE	" 3		Bn: in Billets. Supplied working parties night + day.	
	" 4		" 2:0 am Bn: stood to arms until 3:30 am. French S.06 Somme heavily bombarded.	
	" 5		Also 16th March. R in Y3 Sub-sector. Same time SUZANNE heavily shelled.	
	" 6		It was ascertained afterwards that the French trenches had been raided. Two O.Rs slightly wounded.	
	" 7		Bn: in Billets. Working parties supplied by night + day. Reinforcements; 17 O.R. joined for duty.	
In Trenches	" 8	7.0 pm	Bn: took over Trenches in Y3 Subsector. 2nd Lt "16F March. R. Relief completed at 11.30 pm.	See Appendix 2.
"	" 9		Major J.S. WHITEHEAD 17th March. R took temporary command of Bn: during absence on leave of Lt Col. N.A. SMITH. Casualties 1 O.R. slightly wounded.	
"	" 10		Trenches heavily bombarded and much damaged done by hostile shells + minenwerfer Casualties Killed 1 O.R. Wounded 16 O.Rs.	
"	" 11		Trenches again bombarded much damage done during bombardment several men taking cover in a disused mine shaft were buried through a trench mortar shell striking the entrance to shaft. A party under 2nd Lt. B.B. SALMON kept trying to release them when a jerk of Trench of mud fall took place burying some of his party. 2nd Lt. B.B. SALMON behaved with great gallantry. Casualties Wounded 2 O.Rs. Missing	D/B GREAT BANKS
"	" 12		Trenches again bombarded during the day time.	
"	" 13	1.0 am	Heavy hostile bombardment accompanied by an infantry attack. Killed Capt. L. HENSHAW wounded Capt. D. BERRY. Killed 5 Brunt of attack borne by C + D Coys who were in the Capt. HENSHAW "C" Coy, Capt. "S.E. NOTTAM "D" Coy.	

1875 Wt. W593/826 1,000,000 4/15 J.B.C. & A. A.D.S.S./Forms/C. 2118.

Army Form C. 2118

WAR DIARY
or
INTELLIGENCE SUMMARY
(Erase heading not required.)

Sheet 17   18th Bn. Manchester Regt

Place	Date	Hour	Summary of Events and Information	Remarks and references to Appendices
In Trenches	May 13 cont	10 am	The following O.Rs were specially noted for great coolness & courage throughout. No 10683 Pt MARSDEN. E and No 10762 Pt BROWNE C.E.	
"	" 14		Day comparatively quiet. Working parties busy repairing damaged trenches.	
"	"	8.30 pm	Relieved by 18th Bn Manch R. Bn returned to 90th / Bde.	
In Suzanne	" 15		In Billets. Working parties under RE's day & night	
"	" 16		" "	
"	" 17		" "	Maj G.E. HOARE proceeded to Base for permanent duty there
"	" 18		" "	
In Trenches	" 19	8.30 pm	Relieved 18th Manch R in Y3 sub-sector.	
"	" 20		Comparatively quiet. Trenches repaired during day. Wire strengthened at night.	
"	" 21		Our Artillery heavily bombarded enemy (Bosche) trenches, doing considerable damage.	
"	" 22		Enemy retaliated. Quiet. Casualties 1 O.R wounded.	
"	" 23		Very quiet. 2) Two shells fell near PETRIE AV no damage done. 2nd Lt TURPIN and 47 O.Rs joined Bn from Base	
"	" 24		" " Casualties. Wounded 1 O.R	
"	" 25		Bn relieved by 17th Manch R commencing 8.0 pm on their return to SUZANNE &	For details see Appendix 4
Suzanne	" 26		Return to 90th Inf Bde. " " " In Billets. Working parties under RE's day & night. Bayonet fighting, gas Attack drill carried out by Coys	
"	" 27		" " Casualties 10 R wounded	
"	" 28		" "	
"	" 29		" "	
"	" 30		" "	
"	" 31		" " Casualties 1 O.R wounded	

Arkwright Lt Col
Comm'd'g 18th S.Bn. Manchester Regt.

SECRET.   Copy No. 1. Appendix 1.   (WD)   Order No. 7.

18th SERVICE BATTALION MANCHESTER REGIMENT.

Reference, M I N S. Sheet 17.   1st May, 1916.

1.	The Battalion will move to BRAY today.
2. STARTING POINT.	Junction of the RUE FAIDHERIE and the PLACE.
3. ADVANCE GUARD. 2nd Lt. Wallwork. 1 sect. "B" Coy.	Will move about ½ mile in advance of the Battalion by the Northern road to BRAY. Points 102, 108 & 105.
4. MAIN BODY. Order of march. "A" Coy. "B" Coy. less 1 sect. "C" Coy. "D" Coy. less 1 sect.	Will pass starting point at 4 p.m. and follow route taken by Advance Guard
5. REAR GUARD. 1 sect. "D" Coy.	In rear of the transport.
6.	After passing the BOIS DES TAILLES, 70 yards interval will be preserved between platoons. The head of the column will not pass that point before 7 p.m. Transport will have an interval of 70 yards between sections of 2 vehicles.

R.J.O. Haworth Lieut.
Acting Adjutant.
18. Service Battalion,
Manchester Regiment.

Issued by Orderly at 1. P.m.
Copy no. 1 File.
" " 2 "A" Coy.
" " 3 "B"
" " 4 "C"
" " 5 "D" Coy.
" " 6 M.O.
" " 7 Q.M.
" " 8 Transport Officer.
" " 9 Lewis Gun Officer.
" " 10 War Diary.

SECRET.   Copy No .... "Appendix 2   ORDER No.9.

18th. SERVICE BATTALION. MANCHESTER REGIMENT.

8 MAY 1916

Reference :- Trench Map. MARICOURT.

The Battalion will relieve the 16th. Manchester Regiment in Y3.
SUB-SECTOR. commencing at 7.pm.

STARTING POINT.   North end of EAST. St. SUZANNE.

ORDER of MARCH.   C, A, D, B. 1st. Company will pass Starting Point at
                    6.30.pm. 5 minutes interval between platoons.

DISPOSITION.   Trenches A23/1, A23/2, and A29/6. "C" Company.
                    Trenches A23/3, A23/4. "D" Company.
                    Counter-Attack Company. "A" Company.
                    FARGNY RAVINE (Reserve) "B" Company.
                    2 Platoons in S. Works. 2 Platoons Battalion Headquarters
                    O.C. Coys will be under the orders of the C.O. 16th.
                    Manchr. Regt until the relief of the whole Sub-Sector
                    is complete. They will be informed of this from
                    Headquarters.
                    There is to be no mention of the word "RELIEF" over the
                    telephone. O.C. Coys will report completion of relief
                    by saying "Rations arrived".

AIRCRAFT.   If enemy aircraft or observation balloons are up at the
                    time of starting, Platoons must move through the trenches
                    via SUZANNE AVENUE.

GUIDES.   Guides will meet Platoons at Sentry Post. SUZANNE ROAD.

OFFICERS' VALISES. Officers' valises must be in Q.M. Stores at 5.pm.

................................Lieut,
                                 Acting Adjutant.
                        18th. S. Bn. Manchester Regiment.

Issued by Orderly at ...12.15pm..
Copy No. 1. Filed.
        2. A. Company.
        3. B. Company.
        4. C. Company.
        5. D. Company.
        6. Transport Officer.
        7. Lewis Gun Officer.
        8. Medical Officer.
        9. Signalling Officer.
        10. Quartermaster.
        11. War Diary.

Appendix 3. (W.D)

REPORT ON HOSTILE RAID ON 'Y' SECTOR.
on night of 12/13th May 1916.

Compiled from reports of Battalions concerned and statement
of prisoners taken.

The raid was made by men of the 63rd Regiment to the number of
120-150 with 3 Officers or possibly more; these were picked men,
volunteers and distinct from the garrison of the trenches;
they had been billeted in COMBLES and arrived the night of 11/12th
May.
For the attacks on our Saps, Sections of 12 were told off with
2 N.C.Os. to each Section. Each man's objective and duties were
clearly defined; the raid had been practised beforehand and the
men had been shown a map of our trenches made from Aeroplane
photographs; prisoner states that 2 Machine Guns were to have
supported the raiding party but failed to advance.
The object of the raid was to obtain prisoners and if possible
Machine Guns.

HOSTILE ACTION.
The attack was prepared for by bombardment by artillery and
Minenwerfer which had considerable effect on our wire for two
days; Artillery was quieter on the 12th inst. but towards
evening sniping and rifle grenade fire were active, no doubt to
keep down our observers. An enemy wiring party was observed at
10.30.p.m. presumably opening paths through their wire. Later
M.G. fire swept Y.2 and intense bombardment was preceded by
4 reddish lights and 5 Minenwerfer into A.29/4.
The intense bombardment of our entire front, support and
communication trenches and Battalion H.Q. started at 1.a.m. and
a barrage was put round BUZANCE; it seems that the enemy's plan
was to make a sudden and immediate attack on Saps A.29/4, A29/6
and A29/2 (13, 14 and 15) and an attack after heavy bombardment
on the left of Y.3; this latter attack did not begin till 1.40.a.m.
The parties which attacked the Saps tied white handkerchiefs to
our wires to mark their way back.

OUR OWN ACTION.
Y.2. Subsector. The telephone wires to the front from Battalion
H.Q. were broken; red rockets were seen near A.29/4 H.Q. and
S.O.S. wired to Battery, who immediately put up a barrage fire.
Reinforcements were asked for (by lamp signal) by FARCHY MILL
and A.29/4 and sent up; communications were kept up with Y.3 H.Q.
Almost immediately after heavy bombardment started, a number of
Germans entered 29/4 Sap (13) and worked half way down but were
bombed out; the presence of miners and carriers at work in the
Sap head complicated matters.
About 2.20.a.m. a short spell of slackening of Artillery fire
was followed by requests from Front Line (by lamp) for increased
rate of fire, which was effective. Shortly after 3.a.m. the
bombardment slackened, and about 3.30.a.m. the situation was
normal.
Casualties:- Other Ranks 2 killed, 12 wounded, 3 wounded and
remaining at duty.

Y.3 Subsector. The S.O.S. Signal (see Appendix B) was
answered by rapid fire from the supporting battery who had
already begun a slow retaliatory fire.
The attack on A.29/6 Sap (14) was at once beaten off by rifle
and M.G. fire.

2.

Round A.23/2 Sap (15) the wire had been badly damaged by previous bombardments and this was being repaired; a sudden attack was made, the Sap head bombed, and 4 men taken prisoners, on of whom broke away on reaching the German wire and made his way back.

The Main Attack was delivered on A.23/2 (15 Trench) where it was beaten down by rifle and M. G. fire, and especially on A.23/3 and A.23/4 at 1.40.a.m. The enemy advanced three times against A.23/3 but were driven back in crossing the crest from the valley in front of Y. WOOD by rifle and M. G. fire; our M. G. situated E. of PERONNE Road was very effective. On the extreme right of A.23/4 the attack was pressed further home : three Germans reached our line, one being killed, the other two wounded and taken prisoners. The action was over by 3.a.m. and the situation became normal.

Casualties:- Officers-killed 1, Wounded 2. Other Ranks - Killed 5, Wounded 26, Missing 9 (3 known to be prisoners).
(No casualties from rifle fire.)

The work of the Artillery was prompt and excellent and much appreciated by all ranks. One prisoner reported that our Artillery was very effective, especially the 18 pounder batteries.

14.5.16.

BRIGADIER GENERAL
COMMANDING 90TH INFANTRY BRIGADE.

INTELLIGENCE REPORT.

Made from Statement of WILLY SCHADE Prisoner of War taken in raid on trenches in A.23.a and A.23.b on night of 12/13th May.1916.

A. **ORDER OF BATTLE.**
   The 63rd Regiment occupy the line from A.17.a to CURLU.
   To the North is the 62nd Regiment and to the South the 11th Division.
   The line from CHAPEAU DE GENDARME to PERONNE Road is held by 3 Companies.
   One Company from CHAPEAU DE GENDARME to A.29b.93.96.
   One Company from A.29.b.81.97 to A.23.d.10.57.
   One Company from A.23.d.10.57 to PERONNE Road.
   A raiding party is attached to the Regiment.
   Before the raid this party had been in billets in CURMAS.
   They hold the line with 1 man to 10 metres of trench in daytime and 4 men at night.

B. (1). Our Artillery has little effect on the German Dug-outs which are from 10 to 15 metres deep.
   Our 18 pounders are very effective.
   (2). Minenwerfer.
   The Minenwerfer are of ordinary pattern, throwing a bomb of 180 (German) pounds. Prisoner states that they have a range of 3 kilometres, but this is probably exaggerated.
   (4). Aeroplanes.
   The Germans possess excellent maps of our trenches made from Aeroplane photographs.

C. Working parties on the mining (reported in F.) work continuously throughout the 24 hours and the work is being pushed forward rapidly.

D. (1) Batteries.
   77 mm. Battery at B.13.a.7.5. This Battery is across the railway at the W. end of the cutting.
   There are two anti-aircraft guns in the same place (9.7 calibre).
   15 cm. Battery. from B.13.b.75.73 to B.13.b.78.93 on E side of road running N. from MAUREPAS Station.
   12 cm. Battery at B.9.c.82.03. on N.E. edge of wood.
   Battery at H.3.a.20.93 on E. of road running on E. side of HEM Wood.
   Battery at H.6.c.67.70 E. of HEM Church. Dugouts under Church itself.
   O.P. in last house but one in CURLU. (Prisoner denies existence of O.P. in CURLU Church.)
   (2). Machine Guns at:-
          A.29.b 93.72.
          A.29.b 56.94.
          A.23.b 70.00.
          A.23.c 87.66.
          A.23.a 99.15.
          A.23.a 96.20.
          A.23b 12.39.
   (3) Trench Mortars at:-
          A.23.d 90.15.
          A.23.b 85.06.

APPENDIX A.

REPORT ON ACTION OF LEWIS GUNS.

The front attacked is covered by 10 LEWIS GUNS, 5 having covered emplacements allotted to them as "Battle Positions", the other 5 in open emplacements with a definite line of fire detailed in case of attack.

On the left the enemy was plainly observed in front of A.29, 3 and 4 and were quickly dispersed by the fire of the guns in those trenches and also by one of our guns which, by arrangement with the O.C., of the Subsector on our immediate left, occupies a position just North of the PERONNE Road from which place the entire front of A.29, 2, 3 and 4 is excellently covered. This gun did splendid work.

The guns on the right of Y.2 and Y.3 Subsectors maintained steady bursts of fire throughout the attack, doing valuable work in preventing any possible advance of the enemy in large numbers.

Each gun fired approximately 800 rounds, a regular supply of loaded magazines being kept up by Nos. 3, 4 and 5 by the Company Reserve at Company H.Q. At the conclusion of the raid the guns had almost full strength of loaded magazines at each position, namely 24.

Stoppages. Several cases of hard extraction were met with; this may have been due to the heating of the guns as all of the teams report that their guns got extremely hot.
In two cases bolts were changed and extractors were found to be weak, but the same trouble developed again very quickly.
On the whole however, the guns worked very well.

2.

F. **MINING.**
There is extensive mining about the MARICOURT - PERONNE Rd.
6 shafts have been sunk and they are already 30 to 40 metres
long, going out in all directions. (The prisoner did not
give the depth of the shafts). He also denies the existence
of mining in front of A.23.2 or A.23.3.

H. **GENERAL.**
The Works S. of the PERONNE Road are evidently at the head
of the mine reported in para. F. The prisoner admits the
existence of a large number of dug-outs in this place.

The prisoner could read a map correctly and knew the ground
thoroughly and could easily discern any point of the map.
He knew our trenches thoroughly from the aeroplane maps.

E Fearnside Capt for

14.5.16.
BRIGADIER GENERAL,
COMMANDING 90TH INFANTRY BRIGADE.

APPENDIX 'B'.

REPORT ON COMMUNICATIONS.

1. **WIRE.**
All forward lines from Battalion Hqtrs to Company Hqtrs in the line were immediately cut - those in Y.3. in 14 places; one of the lines from Battalion to Brigade was cut but sufficient lines held to ensure direct communication between Battalions and Brigade.

2. **VISUAL.**
Lamp Signals were used with good effect from Forward Companies in Y.2 and from Right Company of Y.3. It was most useful in communicating between Y.3 Hqtrs and their Supporting Battery; a message was sent by lamp from Y.3 Hqtrs to A/85 who passed it on to B/149 the Supporting Battery.
The chief difficulty about Visual Signalling was the smoke from shells, which in two cases obscured the signal. Hence it is imperative that a message such as "S.O.S. Y.3" should be repeated until counter barrage is actually begun. The contours of the ground render direct Visual Signalling from such points as Battalion Hqtrs to Supporting Battery difficult in this Sector, and further work is needed on Visual Stations which have only recently been established in Y.3 Left.

3. **RUNNERS.**
Very good work was done by runners, notably on the left of Y.3 where they formed the only means of communications.

4. **ROCKETS.**
Rocket Signals were unsatisfactory. In no case was a complete series of 5 rockets observed. In one case one rocket failed to ignite and in another the rocket merely squibbed over the parapet.
Unless they can be kept very dry they are not of much value.
It is proposed to carry out further tests.

14.2.16.

Army Form W. 3121.

Schedule No. (to be left blank)	Unit	Brigade.	Regtl. No.	30H. Division.	Rank and Name	13H. Corps.	Action for which commended	12. May 1916. Date of Recommendation.	Recommended by	Honour or Reward	(To be left blank)
	12th Bn. Manchester Regiment.				2/Lieut. Bernard Enoch SALMON.		During Enemy bombardment of Y3 sub sector about 2.30 a.m. on the 10th May, 2 trench mortar shells fell on a Mine shaft in which several men of his Company were sheltering. The mine shaft was blown in & most of the men were buried. 2/Lieut. Salmon as soon as he heard of the incident at once organised and led a rescue party, amongst whom were Privates H. Allen and G.H. Greathawks and entered the Mine. Storey also another shell fire party, bringing with it his rescue party. Notwithstanding this he extricated himself I was. personally responsible for the rescue of one Corporal and one private. During the period of rescue (incurred by this the heavy shelling continued) he continued his exertions till the order to cease by his Company Commander at 10 a.m. Pte. Allen was unfortunately killed. 2/Lieut. Salmon has previously distinguished himself by his personal courage and example & was recommended for the Military Cross on 5th March 1916.		Brig. General Sir Bart, 14th Manchester Regt.	Military Cross.	

Army Form W. 3121.

Schedule No. (to be left blank)	Unit	Regtl. No.	Rank and Name	Action for which commended	Recommended by	Honour or Reward	(To be left blank)
	18th Bn Manchester Regiment	11215	Private George Henry GREATBANKS	For the excellent service and courage displayed by him in assisting the party with which he & Corporal Gill Pte Allen (killed) on the early morning of the 10th May 1916. to rescue two comrades who had been buried during the bombardment of the trenches by Minenwerfer shells. Though assisting in the rescue of Corporal Gill and Pte. S.A. Lewis Greatbanks still he laboured to work of rescue — having to be sent for rest. —	Lt Col. Noel W Kemp-Ganbys 18 Manchester Regt.	Military Medal	awarded 2
	18th Bn Manchester Regiment	10683	Private Edwin MARSDEN	During the enemy's raid of the bombardment during the raid on 4/3 — it was found this a fast supply of bombs was urgently needed on the Rifle Road. In spite of a continuous severe fire on the communication trenches leading to the Grenade store, Pte Marsden volunteered to bring up a supply of bombs, and this he successfully carried out. Later afterward Pte Marsden to the men of his Platoon — his previous coolness and courage on this occasion proved a fine example to his comrades.	Lt Col Kemp-Ganbys Comndg 18th Bn Manchester Regt.	Military Medal	awarded 2

Date of Recommendation. 12 May 1916.
90th Brigade. 30th Division. 13th Corps.

Army Form W. 3121.

Schedule No.: (blank)
Unit: 12th Bn. Manchester Regiment
Regtl. No.: 10612
Rank and Name: Private Conrad Ernest BROOKE
Brigade: 20th
Division: 7th
Corps: 12/
Date of Recommendation: 18 May 1916.

Action for which commended:

During the early portion of the attack on the enemy trenches on the night 12/13 May 1916 of Y/2 Sector - the Fauck Saw [Saar] of which, he was a member, was attached to a party of enemy Bombers who had sapped out toward the enemy emplacement - the Sub Sections of [these?] Saws had [?] to act on one of the 7 men comprising the team were wounded. He remaining three with Pte. Brooke continued to serve it until it [?] jammed. To avoid capture they moved the gun to another position on the trenches and whilst 2 of the team were putting the gun in order, Pte. Brooke took his Rifle & advanced towards the enemy bombing party. Three 2 of the enemy & thus under cover rescued the S.A.A. & Bomb supply of the Saw, and brought and took prisoner one of the enemy Bombers (Musketier SCHADE). He then also under heavy fire proceeded to Company Headquarters, fetched up a further supply of S.A.A. and continued to fire his Lewis Gun whilst any of the line had been gained.

Recommended by: [signature] Lieut. Commander 12th Bn. Manchester Regiment.

Honour or Reward: Distinguished Conduct Medal.

Appendix 2

SECRET.   Copy No. 11.   Appendix 4.   Order No. 11.

18TH SERVICE BATTALION MANCHESTER REGIMENT.

25th May 1916.

1. RELIEF.   The 16th Batt. Manchester Regiment will commence
                      relieving the 18th Batt. Manchester Regiment at 8 p.m.
                      to-night.

2. ORDER OF RELIEF.   Companies will be relieved in the following order:-
                      A. D. B. C.
                      Platoons as relieved will march into billets in SUZANNE.
                      An interval of at least 100 yards must be maintained
                      between platoons.

3. REPORTS.   O.C. Companies will report to Battle Headquarters by
                      runner when their Companies are relieved and will also
                      report to Headquarters, SUZANNE when their Companies are
                      in billets stating hour of arrival.

4. TRANSPORT.   2 Limbered wagons will be at Hillside Headquarters at
                      8.30 p.m. to collect all Officers baggage and Company
                      boxes.

5. ROUTE.   All platoons being relieved from the trenches will
                      use PETRIE AVENUE.

                                                        2nd Lieut.
                                                        Acting Adjutant,
                                                        18th Service Battalion,
                                                        Manchester Regiment.

Issued by Orderly at 11.30 am
Copy No. 1 Filed.
       2 "A" Coy.
       3 "B" "
       4 "C" "
       5 "D" "
       6 Transport Officer.
       7 Lewis Gun Officer.
       8 Medical Officer
       9 Signalling Officer.
      10 Quartermaster.
      11 War Diary

Confidential

War Diary
= of =
18th (Service) Battalion,
The Manchester Regiment.

From June 1st 1916.
to June 30th 1916.

18. Manchester
Vol 8
June

Army Form C. 2118

WAR DIARY or INTELLIGENCE SUMMARY

(Erase heading not required.)

Sheet 18 18th S. Bn. The Manchester Reg.

Place	Date	Hour	Summary of Events and Information	Remarks and references to Appendices
SUZANNE	June 1st		In Billets. 2 Coys working under RE during morning. Batt marched to camp at BILLON WOOD to be in reserve to 21st Inf. Bde. 1.0pm SUZANNE shelled. Casualties 2 O.R's wounded	For details see appendices
BILLON WOOD	2nd "		2 Coys by day + 2 by night working under RE. Awards were granted to Officers + men of the Bn. for courage + coolness during a hostile attack on the night 12/13 May as follows:-	
	3rd "		2nd Lt. B.B. SALMON, Military Cross, No.10612 Pte C.E. BROOKE "D" Coy D.C.M. and No.11215 Pte GREATBANKS "C" Coy and 10683 Pte E. MARSDEN "D" Coy both Military Medal.	✗ See appendices 2
	4th "		Appointment: 2nd Lt. MILES BRUNTON appt Adjt + promoted Lieut. to date from 17/2/16. 2 Coys by day + 2 by night work under RE. 2nd Lt. J.P. KNOWLES appd I.O. Officer	
	5th "		"	
	6th "		" Awards to following extract from the Gazette of 16th March. R.) awarded Military Cross, two also Appendix 2	
			d/d 2/3/6/16 Capt. W.H. BUTLER R.A.M.C (attd 18th March R) awarded Military Cross, two also Appendix 2 for devotion to duty in attending to wounded during the bombardment of YPOX on 30 by 12 and after days. D.C.M awarded to No. 10835 Sgt F.W. POTTS. Military Medal to No. 10239 Sgt S. CLEBB ✗	
	7th "		2 Coys by day + 2 by night working under RE. The following officers joined for duty. 2nd Lt J.F. MOTLER, 2nd Lt G.H. DOUGHTY, and 2nd Lt A.C. CLOUGH	
	8th "		"	
	9th "		"	
	10th "		"	
	11th "		"	
	12th "	6.30pm	The 20th Bn. Kings L'pool Regt relieved the Bn at BILLON WOOD, latter went into Billets at ETINEHEM Appendix 3 as 30th Div. Reserve.	
ETINEHEM	13th "		Supplied working parties night and day. do	
	14th "		Armies in France adopted Time as decreed by French Govt. 1 O.R. wounded	

1875 Wt. W593/826 1,000,000 4/15 J.B.C. & A. A.D.S.S./Forms/C. 2118.

SHEET 19

Army Form C. 2118

WAR DIARY
or
INTELLIGENCE SUMMARY. 18th (S) Bn. Manchester Regt.
(Erase heading not required.)

Place	Date	Hour	Summary of Events and Information	Remarks and references to Appendices
ETINEHEM	June 15		C.O. inspected billets. Supplied working parties for RE + Div. Batt. organised into specialist platoons. 1 OR wounded accidentally.	App. 4
"	16		Fatigues	
"	17		do	
"	18		Batt. marched from ETINEHEM to SAISSEVAL, by train from HEILLY to AILLY SUR SOMME, to Training.	
SAISSEVAL	19		Training. 1 OR wounded accidentally.	App. 4a
"	20		Training. 1 OR wounded accidentally.	
"	21		Training. Draft of 48 OR joined for duty. 2nd Lt. S.J. BROWN, 2nd Lt. J.S. PARTINGTON, 2nd Lt. H.P. CRICHTON	
"	22 23 24 25		} Training	
"	26		do. CAPT. W.F.ROUTLEY + 2nd Lt. S. FERNYHOUGH joined for duty. Batt. marched from SAISSEVAL by train from AILLY SUR SOMME to HEILLY, thence marching to ETINEHEM CAMP.	App. 5

Army Form C. 2118

WAR DIARY
or
INTELLIGENCE SUMMARY

(Erase heading not required.)

SHEET 20

16th (S) Bn. Manchester Regt

Place	Date	Hour	Summary of Events and Information	Remarks and references to Appendices
ETINEHEM CAMP	27		Numerous Fatigue parties found. Capt BOOLEE appts as 2⁰ in Command & proceeds major with effect from May 19	
"	28		Fatigue parties do do	
"	29	9.25 am	2 3 OR wounded by bomb explosion.	M.A. 6
"	30		Batt? proceed to Assembly Trenches	

P. Yester - Maj. for O.C.

Appendix 1 to War diary

Operation

1st June, 1916.

1. **OBJECT.** In accordance with 90th Brigade Operation Order No. ..
   19th Batt. Manchester Regiment will leave BRUAY
   to-day and march to camp at ...., to be in reserve
   to 91st Infantry Brigade, at ..S.B9/5.
   Starting Point, ...

2. **ORDER OF MARCH.** A,B,C,D Coys. "A" Coy. head of column to pass Starting
   Point at 4.15 p.m. remainder will follow at intervals of
   5 minutes between platoons.
   Battalion to be clear of .... by 5.35 p.m.

3. **ROUTE.** S.B9/5, .. 7 central, thence due N. to .... then by
   the ......

4. **GUIDES.** 1 per platoon will be provided.

5. **REPORTS.** Arrival in camp to be reported by O.C. Companies to
   Battalion Headquarters.

6. **TRANSPORT.** This will move independently by .... route. M.O. and
   Regtl. carts to move to ..... at 4.30 p.m.

Miles Brown
2nd Lieut.
Acting Adjutant,
19th Service Battalion,
Manchester Regiment.

Issued by Orderly at 12 noon
Copy No. 1 Miles.
    2 "A" Coy.
    3 "B"
    4 "C"
    5 "D"
    6 Transport Officer.
    7 Quartermaster.
    8 Lewis Gun Officer.
    9 Medical Officer.
    10 Signalling Officer.
    11 War Diary.

SECRET.   Copy No. 11   Operation Order No.13.

Appendix 3

18th. SERVICE BATTALION. MANCHESTER REGIMENT.

Ref. ALBERT 1/40,000. Combined Sheet.   11th. June. 1916.

1. **INTENTION.** In accordance with 90th. Infantry Brigade Operation Order No.21 the 20th. Kings Liverpool Rgt. will relieve the 18th. Manchester Regt tomorrow 12th inst., The latter will move to billets at ETINEHEM. *and will be in reserve to the 90th Infy Bde*

2. **ROUTE** (Unless otherwise ordered). N. side of ~~tramline~~ tramline to BRONFAY FARM. Thence by F29d (Central), to L15b4/8, thence to L15d/2/4 and L15c3/7 (Crucifix) thence to ETINEHEM via L20a. (Central) to L25b. (Central).

3. **ORDER OF MARCH.** A, B, C, D by platoons at 3 minute intervals as relieved.

4. **TRANSPORT.** Will follow in rear of last platoon, except wagon with cooking utensils which will proceed independantly as soon as loaded.

5. **REPORTS.** O.C. Coys. will report to Headquarters when their Coys have been relieved at BILLON WOOD and also when they are present in Billets.

                                              Lieut.
                                              Adjutant.
                    18th. S. Bn. Manchester Regiment.

Issued by Orderly at 5.30 a.m
Copy No. 1. Filed.
    2. "A" Coy.
    3. "B" Coy.
    4. "C" Coy.
    5. "D" Coy.
    6. Transport Officer.
    7. Quartermaster.
    8. Lewis Gun Officer.
    9. Medical Officer.
   10. Signalling Officer.
   11. War Diary.

SECRET.

To:- Officer Commanding.,
           ....Company.

Ref:- Copy of 90th.Infantry Brigade Attack Orders G198 herewith.

Para 1.   Battalion will form up as follows:- A & B Coys. in Assembly trench in rear of 17th.Manchr.Regt. "A" on the right "B" on the left, "C"C& "D" in Assembly trench in rear of 2nd.R.S.F. on L of Support Av. C on right, D on left.(see diagram B attached).

Para 2.   Formation when advancing. Coys will move in line of ½ platoons in file(see diagram C attached) B.Coy.leading.

Para 3.   Carrying parties, B Coy will detail two platoons to carry up materials from Div.Forward Dump at CAMBRIDGE COPSE.to Brigade dump DUKE St. and 2 platoons to carry up materials from Brigade forward dump to KEEP A.(Diagram A), and afterwards help the Coy. of 2nd.R.S.F. to consolidate For materials to be carried see Bde Order. A Coy. 4 platoons will carry S.A.A,Grenades etc., from Bde Dump to KEEP A. This Coy will detail one Officer to be in charge of Bde. Dump. Route to be followed by Carrying parties, a straight line from DUKE St. to nearest point of Railway track E of the Rd. from TALUS BOISE and thereby the side of the trench running from MONTAUBAN to Railway track at A3.b.4/1. D Coy will detail one platoon as carrying party as stated in para 2 Bde Order G198.

Para 4.   The Battalion Runners as under:-
9906.L/Cpl.G.Nicholl. "A"Coy. 10458.L/Cpl.Spenceley W.H.
11137.Pte Bray S.   "B"Coy.   9823.Pte Bannister H.P. "A"Coy
10407. " Hicks B.M. "C"Coy.   9913. " Payne R.   "
10235. " Butterworth A. "B"Coy9827. " Cowx W.   "
10746. " Whiteley E.A."D"Coy. 10814." Grimshaw W.   "D"Coy
and three Company Runners per Company will report to the Adjutant immediately on arrival at the training ground.

18th.June.   (Sd).Miles Brunton.,Lieut.,
                                             Adjutant.,
                              18th.Bn.Manchester Regiment.

SECRET.   COPY No. 13

18th. Bn. MANCHESTER REGIMENT OPERATION ORDER No. 15.
BY.
LIEUT. COLONEL. W. A. SMITH.

Ref:- Map. MONTAUBAN 1/20000 Combined sheets 57.d.S.E, 57.c.S.W., 62.d.
N.E., 62.c.N.W., and LONGUEVAL 1/10000. 57.c.S.W.3.Edition
2.B., and plan of MONTAUBAN.

26th.6.1916.

1.	On a date to be announced later the 90th. INFANTRY BRIGADE will take part in an offensive against the enemy positions.
2. OBJECTIVE.	The objective of the 90th. BRIGADE will be MONTAUBAN.
3. FLANK.	The 55th. INFANTRY BRIGADE of the 18th. DIVISION will assault the west end of the village on the left of the 90th. INFANTRY BRIGADE.
4. FRONT LINE TRENCHES and R. FLANK.	The 21st. INFANTRY BRIGADE advancing at Zero, will first capture the enemy's 1st. & 2nd. line trenches, from the point where the road running North to MONTAUBAN cuts the GLATZ REDOUBT at A.3.c.8/6 to the road running from TALUS BOISE to the W. end of MONTAUBAN. The 89th. INFANTRY BRIGADE will hold the line from the right of the 21st. BRIGADE to the E. end of DUBLIN TRENCH.
5. ADVANCE OF 90th. INFANTRY BRIGADE.	The 90th. INFANTRY BRIGADE will advance from the position of Assembly at 60 minutes after Zero, and pass through the 21st. INFANTRY BRIGADE and assault MONTAUBAN.
6. FORMATION FOR ATTACK.	The 17th. Bn. Manchester Regiment will lead the R. of the attack, the 16th. Bn. Manchester Regiment will lead the L. of the attack. The 2nd. R.S.F. will be in Support. The 18th. Bn. Manchester Regt. will be in BRIGADE RESERVE.
7. PLACE OF ASSEMBLY.	Assembly trenches S. of CAMBRIDGE COPSE on both sides of SUPPORT AVENUE. B "B" Coy. (less 2 platoons) & "C" Coy. (from Right to Left) on the right of the 2nd. R.S.F. to the East of SUPPORT Av. "A" Coy. (less 2 platoons) & "D" Coy. (less 2 platoons) in the trench in rear of the 2nd. R.S.F. to the West of SUPPORT Av. These positions will be taken up during the night previous to the assault (Y. night) at an hour to be announced later.
8. POSITION OF Bn. H.Q.	To be announced later.
9. ORDER OF ADVANCE.	"C" Coy will advance at a distance of 600 behind the R. Coys. of 2nd. R.S.F. in line of ½ platoons in file at 40 paces interval. B "D" Coy. (less 2 platoons) at a distance of 100 from "C" Coy. in the same formation. Both Companies will file to their left after the 2nd. R.S.F. have advanced and leave the trench in their tracks.

3.

12. TRENCH BRIDGES.	Trenches will be crossed by bridges laid by Battalions in front.
13. DEFENCE OF MONTAUBAN.	KEEPS and DEFENCES will be organised as shewn in plan of MONTAUBAN already issued. The 16th.Bn.Mchr.Rgt.holding front junction of trenches at point S.27.c.69/60. (exclusive) along N. edge of village to point S.27.b.93/42. and then S.E. to road at S.27.b. 99/22. (exclusive). The 17th Bn.Mchr.Rgt from S.27.b.99/22. (inclusive) to point where CHIMNEY TRENCH joins NORD ALLEY. and R.S.F. one Coy. in KEEP "A" remainder in S.TRENCH. Lieut Col.WALSH,2nd.R.S.F. will be O.C.MONTAUBAN DEFENCES.
14. COMMUNI-CATION.	Central Signal Station will be formed by Brigade Signal Officer at S.W. corner of CAMBRIDGE COPSE in SUPPORT AVENUE connected with COPSE "B" for the Assembly Trenches. The Battalion Signalling Section after the advance will lay a line from the N.end of the FLECHE, SAP A.9/4. to Advance Battalion Headquarters. Other Battalions will have Stations at the junction of SOUTHERN TRENCH and VALLEY TRENCH and at point where TRAIN ALLEY enters MONTAUBAN. Visual Signalling in Advance Divisional Station will be at A.14.l.7/3. off W.AVENUE,which can communicate with Advance Brigade Headquarters. The ground sheet will be laid at Bn.H.Q. Flares will be issued to each Battalion to shewn position to Aircraft of the Front Line of Attack, to be fired (by order of an Officer only) in batches of 3 at once, 15 seconds interval between batches.
15. RUNNERS.	3 Battalion Runners per Coy. to report to Bn.H.Q., this number will be increased to 4 in the event of a Company going into close action with the enemy. Runners to report to Bn.Signalling Officer at time of Assembly.
16. COMMUNI-CATION TRENCHES.	Up traffic. SUPPORT AVENUE, TRAIN ALLEY. Down traffic. VALLEY TRENCH WEST AVENUE.
17. PRISONERS.	In all cases to be handed over to 2nd.R.S.F. No escort to exceed in number 10% of prisoners, slightly wounded men to be used as escort when possible.
18. EQUIPMENT OF CASUALTIES.	Rifles,S.A.A, bombs,wire cutters and equipment must be collected from Casualties and dumped near Bn.H.Q. Wounded men capable of walking must take equipment to the Dressing Station, but no S.A.A. bombs or wire-cutters which should be handed over.
19. LEWIS GUNNERS.	The 1st.Lewis Gun Sections of "A" & "D" Coys and Sgt Pot's will be under the Bn. Lewis Gun Officer, and will advance in rear of "D" Coy. The Reserve Lewis Gunners of 16th. & 17th.Bn.Mchr.Rgt. will also join this party.
20. STRENGTH.	Only 5 Officers per Coy will go into action, the remainder together with the 2nd.-in-Command will remain with the Regimental Transport.
21. DISTINGU-ISHING MARKS.	All except runners will wear a yellow patch on the back of the pack, selected men will also wear a metal disc,bright side to be shewing above yellow patch. Officers and N.C.O.s will carry Vigilant mirrors. Men carrying wire-cutters will wear white patch on the shoulder strap.

2.

10. BRIGADE RESERVE.

On reaching the ravine S. of MONTAUBAN, "C"Coy. will entrench astride the Railway from A.3.B.63/37. to A.3.d.21/90.

~~"B"~~ "D"Coy.(less 2 platoons) will occupy that part of TRAIN ALLEY between the junction of ALT TRENCH and the track from TALUS BOISE to MONTAUBAN.

BATTALION HEADQUARTERS will be at the junction of TRAIN ALLEY and ALT TRENCH.

11. CARRYING PARTIES.

"A"Coy.

1. 2 platoons to report to O.C. 201st.Field Coy.R.E., at COPSE "F" at 6.0.pm on "Y" night, for the purpose of carrying stores as directed by O.C.Field Coy. On completion of duty will rejoin "D"Coy.

2. 2 platoons to carry S.A.A.,etc., from BRIGADE Forward Dump in DUKE St. to KEEP "A". (For details of load see Appendix 1.) This party will advance as far as DUKE St. in line of ½ platoons at 40 paces interval 400 in rear of the L.Coys. of 2nd.R.S.F. On completion of carrying duties will rejoin the Battalion.

~~"B"Coy.~~ "D"

1. 2 platoons to carry consolidation materials from BRIGADE Reserve Dump to KEEP "A", this party will draw their loads when assembling, and advance on the L. of and in the same formation as "A" Coy, but will keep in touch with the Coy. of 2nd.R.S.F. occupying KEEP "A" and act under the orders of the O.C. that Company, as regards further carrying, or assisting in consolidation.
(For details of loads see Appendix "A".).
When no longer required at KEEP "A" this party will join the Battalion.

2. 1 platoon to carry S.A.A. from DIVISIONAL Forward Dump to BRIGADE Forward Dump DUKE St. to report to BRIGADE Bombing Officer at 6.0pm. on "Y"night, and act under his orders, on completion of duty to rejoin Battalion.

3. 1 Officer and ½ platoon to carry water from LE FLECHE to MONTAUBAN, to report to Staff Captain. 90th.INFANTRY BRIGADE at 6.0pm. on "Y"night and to return to Battalion on completion of duty.

4. ½ platoon to carry Ammunition for 90th.Stokes Mortar Battery, and will meet guide from 90th. Stokes Mortar Battery in SUPPORT AVENUE at S.W. corner of CAMBRIDGE COPSE at 1½ hours before Zero.

~~"D"Coy.~~ B

1. Two (weak) platoons to carry ammunition etc, for 90th.BRIGADE M.G.Coy. to report to O.C. 90th.Bde. M.G.Coy in trenches immediately S. of CAMBRIDGE COPSE when Battalion takes position of Assembly. A proportion of these will accompany 4 Machine Guns to MONTAUBAN in rear of 16th.& 17th.Bn.Manchester Regt. After reaching destination they will rejoin the Battalion at the place mentioned in para. 10. Remainder of M.G.Coy. with remainder of "D"Coy. carrying party will be under the orders of O.C. 18th.Bn.Mchr Regt. and remain with BDE Reserve.

2. One N.C.O. and 15 men to load ammunition at the DIVISIONAL Dump "U" Works, further orders for this party will be issued later.

"C"Coy.

1. Will have one platoon organised for carrying if required.

4.

22. **WATER.** Bottles must be full at the time of advance and must not be drawn upon without necessity. Water in MONTAUBAN must not be used until tested.

23. **RATIONS.** If situation permits rations will be brought up nightly to MONTAUBAN by Transport. If this is impossible they will be obtained from the Reserve Dump in NAPIER REDOUBT Yard at MARICOURT. Carrying parties to be organised from Bn.H.Q. if possible.
For rations to be carried on the man see Appendix "B", these are not to be consumed without the orders of an Officer. All reinforcements must bring rations for the next day.

24. **GAS.** The gas helmet will be worn rolled up under the steel helmet.

25. **OIL BOTTLES.** O.C.Coys will see that all oil bottles are full before advancing and that all have pull-throughs and flannelette. Rifles must be frequently cleaned if used.

26. **MEDICAL.**
   1. AID POSTS at Bn.H.Q. marked with a Red Cross.

   2. COLLECTING STATIONS marked by Red Cross inside a circle.
      A. S.end of TALUS BOISE A.15.a.3/0.
      B. PERONNE Rd. A.20.b.6/9.

   3. ADVANCE DRESSING STATION at BILLON FARM.

Stretcher Bearers should avoid using trenches where possible. Lying down cases to be taken to a Collecting Station. Walking cases will be collected at L.10.c.1/1. on BRAY-BRONFAY Rd.

27. **DOCUMENTS ETC.,** No documents or maps likely to assist enemy to be taken N. of PERONNE Rd. but all Officers must have Field Message Books with envelopes and the MONTAUBAN & LONGUEVAL maps.

28. **INTELLIGENCE.** Two N.C.O.s (L/Cpl.Nichol & L/Cpl.Spenceley) will act, when necessary, as Intelligence men under the orders of Intelligence Officer.

Issued to Orderly........pm.
Copy No. 1. File.
    2. C.O.
    3. 2nd-in-Command.
    4. Adjutant.
    5. L.G.O.
    6. Intelligence Officer.
    7. "A"Coy.
    8. "B"Coy.
    9. "C"Coy.
  10. "D"Coy.
  11. Transport Officer.
  12. Quartermaster.
  13. War Diary.
  14. Medical Officer.

LIEUT.
ADJUTANT,
18th Bn. Mchr. Rgt.

Reference OPERATION ORDER No.15. dated 26th.6.1916. for "D"Company read "B"Company and for "B"Company read "D"Company throughout.

27th.June.1916.

............Lieut,
Adjutant.,
18th.Bn.Manchester Regiment.

SECRET.   Copy No. 14

18th.Bn.MANCHESTER REGIMENT.Supplement No.1. to OPERATION ORDER No.15.
                              BY.
                    LIEUT.COL. W. A. SMITH.

                                                27th.June,1916.

1. REBOMBARDMENT.   Should it be necessary to rebombard any portion
                    of the line to be attacked the rebombardment
                    means:-

                        Bombardment starts.   0.0.
                        Intensive.   0.25.
                        Infantry Assault.   0.30.

2. CARRYING   After the 1st.bombardment has been completed will
   PARTIES.   come and go to MONTAUBAN by the Communication
                    Trenches, moving on top of and beside the trench.
                    In the event of coming under fire they will get
                    into the trench and continue to move as fast as
                    possible.   There will always be an Officer or
                    responsible N.C.O. in rear of each carrying party.
                    As far as possible the loads of casualties will be
                    picked up and taken on.
                    Carrying parties must not halt on account of hostile
                    fire.

3. DRESS OF   All Infantry Officers will wear puttees and
   OFFICERS.   equipment.

                                        ....LIEUT.,
                                                              ADJUTANT.,
                                        18th.Bn.MANCHESTER REGIMENT.

Issued to Orderly at...3.15....pm.

Copy No.1.File.
     No.2. C.O.
     No.3. 2nd-in-Command.
     No.4. Adjutant.
     No.5. L.G.Officer.
     No.6. Intelligence Officer.
     No.7. "A"Coy.
     No.8. "B"Coy.
     No.9. "C"Coy.
     No.10."D"Coy.
     No.11.Transport Officer.
     No.12.Quartermaster.
     No.13.Medical Officer.
     No.14.War Diary.

war diary

Copy No..... 12

18th.Bn.MANCHESTER REGIMENT.
SUPPLEMENTARY ORDER No... to OPERATION ORDER No.15.
BY
LIEUT. COL. W. A. SMITH.

Military Map 1916.
Ref:-Sht. Combined Sheet 1/40,000.

1.   90th.INFY BDE. will move to Assembly Trenches to-night.

2.STARTING Cross Roads MINDEN, L.22.c.8/2.
  POINT

3.ORDER OF 16th.Bn.Manchester Regt.
  MARCH.   2nd.R.Scots Fus. (2 Companies).
  Lt.Col.   { Battalion Headquarters.   } L.Col.
  W. A. SMITH. 18th.Bn.Manchester Regt. { "A"Coy.(less 2 platoons). }
                                        { "D"Coy.(less 2 platoons). }

             17th.Bn.Manchester Regt.
  Lt.Col.   18th.Bn.Manchester Regt. { "B"Coy.(less 2 platoons). } L.Col.
  C.HUTCHILL   { "C"Coy.   }
             2nd.R.Scots Fus. (2 Companies).

             Less 1 Sergt and 16 Lewis Gunners and Lewis Guns in the
             case of each Coy. These numbers to include the 1st.L.G.
             Team in each Company.

4.TIME.   "A"Coy. (less 2 platoons). { pass starting point
             "D"Coy. (less 2 platoons). { at 7.30.pm.
             "B"Coy. (less 2 platoons). and "C"Coy. pass Starting Point
             at 8.10.pm.

5.ROUTE.   MAMETZ-BRAY Rd. to point 87.(i.e. L.14.c.8/1) then N.E.
             through L.14.d., L.14.b., L.15.a., BUNNY Rd to L.15.b.7/7,
             then S.E. to L.16.c.7/2, then E. to L.17.d.6/1.

6.   The BDE. will then form into two columns; 1.Column under
             Lt.Col.PETRIE,D.S.O. 16th.Mchr Rgt, 2 Coys R.S.F. and 2 Coys
             ("A" & "D")18th.Mchr.Rgt. 2.Column under Col. JOHNSON,
             17th.Mchr Rgt, 2 Coys ("B" & "C") 18th.Mchr.Rgt, 2 Coys
             2nd.R.S.F.
                    These columns will march from here on parallel
             routes as shown on special maps already known to guides to
             ASSEMBLY TRENCHES.

7.PRECAUTIONS. A distance of 300ˣ will be maintained between Coys.
             throughout the march unless there is danger of loosing
             touch, when O.C.Coys may decide to close up.

8.   On reaching line running E. & W., S. of BILLON WOOD
             through A.25.D.Central, Columns will close to Column of
             route, and continue the march at 10.40.pm.

9.GUIDES.   2nd.Lieut.B.B.DAWSON. will act as guide to "A" & "D"Coys.
             and will march in front of "A"Coy. The N.C.O.guides of
             "D"Coy will be attached to "A"Coy.
             2nd.Lieut.C.F.TURNER. will act as guide to "B" & "C"Coys
             and will march in front of "B"Coy, and the N.C.O.guides
             of "C"Coy will be attached to "B"Coy.
             All these guides will rejoin their Coys on arrival at
             ASSEMBLY TRENCHES.
             Connecting files will be dropped by leading Coys when
             there is any risk of loosing touch.
             There must be absolute silence and no smoking.

2.

10. 2nd.Lieut. DOUGHTY and 6 men of "C"Coy will leave camp at
    ....p.m. and proceed by the ordinary trench route and report
    to Lieut GIBSON in SUPPORT Av. at the S.E.corner of the
    GAID at 9.0.pm. to assist in guiding Coys to their trenches,
    and in distributing materials for the carrying parties.

11. 2 platoons "A"Coy under 2nd.Lieut. ROBB... will leave camp
    at 4.30.p.m. to report to O.C.221st.F.Coy., R.E. at their
    dump at BRAY at 5.30.pm. On arrival at ASSEMBLY TRENCHES
    they will rejoin their Coy, but will advance in the attack
    along with detachments of 221st.F.Coy., ... 50? in rear of
    the rear Coys of the 2nd.R.W.F. to ...... AT MONTAUBAN, and
    be under the orders of O.C. R.E. ... When not required
    they will rejoin the Battalion.
    The 221st.F.Coy. R.E., will assemble between the R of the
    16th.Mchrs. and SUPPORT Av. and the O.C. of the party must
    arrange to keep in touch with the B.E. before and during
    the advance.

12. All troops of 90th.INF. BDE must be N. of PERONNE RD. by
    1..a.m. tomorrow.

13. 1 Sgt. and 14 Lewis Gunners per Coy under Bn.Lewis Gun
    Officer, will proceed in 2 parties by FRICHEUX-BRAY Rd. to
    Rt. 27 L.14.b. to B.OEUF FARM, where handcarts will be
    unloaded, detachments carrying guns and accessories, via
    BILLON WOOD, BILLON Av. and SUPPORT Av. to their positions
    in ASSEMBLY TRENCHES. O.C."C"Coy will detail an N.C.O. guide
    to accompany this party.
    (see para 19 Operation Order No.15).
    The Lewis Gun Officer will select a suitable spot near
    B. OEUF FARM for leaving the handcarts and will leave two
    men to look after them with orders to remain until relieved.
    "B" & "C"Coys teams will form the 1st.party and will pass
    cross roads ETINEHEM L.25.a.7/7 at 8.30.pm.
    "A" & "D" Coys teams will form the 2nd.party and will pass
    the cross roads ETINEHEM L.25.a.7/7 at 9.45.pm.

14. POSITION   On extreme R. of ASSEMBLY TRENCH allotted to "B" & "C"Coys.
    IN ASSEMBLY On the arrival of the Companies later, "B" & "C"Coys
    TRENCHES for teams will rejoin their Companies.
    L.GUN TEAMS.

15. 2 platoons of "B"Coy under 2nd.Lieut.D.WILCOX will report to
    O.C.90th.BDE.M.GUN.Coy at 2..0.p.m. today.

16. Sub para 5. of para 11. of Operation Order No.15. is
    cancelled.
    "D"Coy will detail a whole platoon to carry ammunition for
    Stokes Mortar Battery, to report ..... BARN HALL, BRAY
    .....pm.
    Sub para 6 of para 11. Operation Order No.15 is cancelled.

17. STORES.   S.A.A. & Grenades.
    Forward stores at Junction of ...... Av. and MINE St.
    Reserve store in SUPPORT Av. Sth E. of R.E. Av.

18. PIONEERS.   Pioneers will carry axes and saws and a few other useful
    tools.

19. Rations for tomorrow and following day besides Iron Rations
    will be carried.

20. Gas Helmets will not be worn under steel helmet, but 2
    will be carried.

21. VERY   Regt.Sgt.Mjr and Lewis Gun Sgt. will each carry a Very
    PISTOLS.   Pistol and Ammunition.

22. ...Medical ...... a few rounds which can be obtained from
    7. Quartermasters and S.A.A. Store.
    8. O.C. "B"Coy.
23. 9.   "C"Coy. In BUNNY AV. in centre of B.E.F. line, up to #
    10.   "D"Coy. of advance, and then at junction of ALT TRENCH and
    11.   ....Coy. ARMY.
    12. War Diary.
24. Bombers.   "C" and "D" with Plat. HQE until capture of MONTAUBAN.

25. RUMOURS.   All ranks to be warned that the word retire is
                  absolutely forbidden and if heard can only be a trick
                  of the enemy.

26. PRISONERS.   Wounded enemy or any showing white flag to be covered
                  with the rifle until they put their hands up.

27. SIGNALS.   There is a line from Bn. to BDE.H.Q.. A Signal Station
                  will be opened at the junction of BUNNY AV. and B.E.
                  AV. by the Bn.
                  A Divisional Lamp Station will be at SUGAR COPSE S. of
                  the BRIAR, this should be visible to MONTAUBAN.
                  All ranks to be informed of position of the different
                  Signal Stations.

28.   O.C. "B"Coy. will detail 1 platoon to watch the R.flank
                  during and after the advance.

29. RUM.   On arrival at ASSEMBLY TRENCHES O.C.Coys will detail
                  parties to draw Rum from NAPIER REDOUBT YARD, for
                  consumption on "Z"Day at an hour to be stated later.

30.   O.C.Coys will report to Bn.H.Q. when their Coys are
                  present in the ASSEMBLY TRENCHES.

Issued to Orderly........pm.   ....Lieut.,
                                                           Adjutant,
Copy No.1.File.   13th.Bn.Manchester Regiment.
        2.C.O.
        3.2nd in Command.
        4.Adjutant.
        5.L.G.Officer.
        6.Medical Officer.
        7.Quartermaster.
        8. O.C. "A"Coy.
        9. " "B"Coy.
        10. " "C"Coy.
        11. " "D"Coy.
        12. War Diary.

4. FRONT LINE TRENCHES AND R. FLANK.
The 21st INFANTRY BDE. advancing at Zero, will first capture the enemy's 1st. line and 2nd. line trenches, from the point where the road running North to MONTAUBAN cuts the W. end of the GLATZ REDOUBT to point A.3.c.8/6 on the road running from TALUS BOISE to the W. end of MONTAUBAN. The 89th INFANTRY BDE. will hold the line from the right of the 21st. BRIGADE to the E. end of DUBLIN TRENCH.

18th.(Service)BATTALION.MANCHESTER REGIMENT.

SECRET.   Operation Order No.16.

Ref:- AMIENS Sheet 17 and ALBERT Combined Sheet.

1.   The 18th Bn.Manchester Regt. will move tomorrow to ETINEHEM
             CAMP.

2. ROUTE.   BREILLY - AILY-SUR-SOMME thence by train to MERICOURT and by
             march via BRAY-CORBIE Rd, BOIS-DES-TAILLES to ETINEHEM Camp.
             Starting Point VILLAGE GREEN.

3. ORDER   C,B,D,A. head of column to be past starting point at 7.10am.,
   OF   Battalion to entrain at 9.0.am., train leaves at 10.0am.
   MARCH.   Haversack Ration to be carried.

                                              ....Lieut.,
                                                   Adjutant.,
Issued by Orderly at   pm.   18th.Bn.Manchester Regt.
Copy No.1. File.
        2. "A"Coy.
        3. "B"Coy.
        4. "C"Coy.
        5. "D"Coy.
        6. Transport Officer.
        7. Quartermaster.
        8. Lewis Gun Officer.
        9. Medical Officer.
       10. Regt Sgt-Major.
       11. War Diary.

Memorandum on the organisation
of specialists.

To O Coys

Owing to the progressive increase in the number of specialists it will be necessary, until every man can be trained in what are now special duties, to provide an organisation which will enable them to be utilised to the greatest advantage without interfering with the discipline and interior economy of the company with the present very satisfactory platoon system.

The specialist duties at present confined to a comparatively small number of men are Machine gunnery, Signalling, Sniping, wiring and engineering and to some extent bombing with one or two one-man jobs like sanitation and gas.

In order to facilitate their employment in all emergencies without having to resort to the improvised organisation of specialist parties and without destroying the unity and cohesion of platoons, the time has now arrived when a platoon of specialists can be formed in each company who will be recruited from time to time as required from the non specialist platoons.

Every specialist has been trained primarily as a rifleman and although specially organised must not be allowed to forget that he may be called on at any time to act as a rifleman

It is proposed to organise the specialist platoon on the following lines - 1 section of 1 S&B 1 Cpl or L/Cpl and 10 men Lewis gunners 1 Section of 2 NCOs & 10 men Lewis gunners 1 Section of containing a complete wiring party under a NCO. 2 or 3 snipers and the gas NCO and 1 section of 8 bombers and 1 N.C.O.

The platoon would be under the command of a specially selected officer who would require to have a general knowledge of the work of his various specialists.

The platoon would be 4th in each company and as far as possible would be kept in reserve under the control of the company commanders. It would of course be available in an emergency as a tactical unit just like any other platoon though as a rule one section would be absent manning the Lewis guns. In offensive operations it could to the same extent support the other platoons but being less involved in the fight through its less prominent position would not be so liable to suffer losses or become disorganized. It should rarely be required to take part in an assault and every endeavour should be made to keep it intact.

Bicycles 9	Ring Poles 12
Winchesters 48	Signalling Lamps 4
Bugles 8	Sandbags 7/9. 2/9. 60
Axes & Bill 16	Periscopes Vigilant 40
Horseshoes 5	Pistol Illuminating 12 4
Handcuffs Kit 8	Stretchers 16
" Pich 80	Rifle Telescopic 4
Anvils 8	Lucky Luc Sights 8
Shovels 114	Aperture Sights 8
	Bags for 10 shrapnel 8
Axes Signalling 8 (16 halves)	
Flags Signal blue 48	
" white 58	
Poles 158	
Standard electric lamps 2	
Compasses (Mag) 32	
" (Prismatic) 5	
Printers 10	
S.A.A. Rifles 88,000 for Rifle	
General 768 T.O.S.	
In Town Gun 2300 } Pr Gun = 17,000
" Reg 7000 " = 72,000

Index _____

SUBJECT.

No.	Contents.	Date.
	War Diary of 18th (S) Bn. Manchester Regt for July 1916.	

Confidential

War Diary

of

18th (Service) Battalion
The Manchester Regt.

From 1st July 1916

to 31st July 1916

Army Form C. 2118

WAR DIARY
or
INTELLIGENCE SUMMARY

(Erase heading not required.) 18th (Service) Battalion MANCHESTER REGT.

Place	Date 1916	Hour	Summary of Events and Information	Remarks and references to Appendices
MONTAUBAN	July 1st		The battalion took part in the operations which led to the capture of MONTAUBAN, acting as carrying battalion to the 90th INFANTRY BRIGADE. Total casualties 6 officers wounded [CAPT. S.E. WOOLAM, Lt H.B. HARRISON, 2nd Lt A. COOPER (his 6[wounds] 2nd Lt F.A. ESSE and 2nd Lt G.H. DOUGHTY] and 140 other ranks killed wounded and missing.	APPENDIX K1
	" 2		Battalion in TRAIN ALLEY, old German support-line, in reserve to 90th Infantry Brigade.	
HAPPY VALLEY	3		Battalion was relieved in TRAIN ALLEY. Proceeds to HAPPY VALLEY, which is about 2 miles from BRAY. On the BRAY-ALBERT road. Burying parties from all cos for clearing the battlefields	
"	4		do	Lt P.A. BLYTHE promoted Capt.
"	5		Extract from to-day's orders:- The undermentioned officer, N.C.O's and men were mentioned in SIR DOUGLAS HAIG'S despatch dated APRIL 30th 1916 for gallant and distinguished conduct in the field [Extract from arms supplement to LONDON GAZETTE of 20.6.1916 dated 21.6.1916]. LT. T.J. KELLY 10816 SERGT E.C. HILL; 10045 LANCE SERGT S.W. SHIRLEY, 10383 PTE R DONE, 10390 PTE S FORSTER.	

Sheet 22

Army Form C. 2118

WAR DIARY
or
INTELLIGENCE SUMMARY

(Erase heading not required.) 18th (Service) Battalion MANCHESTER REGT

Place	Date 1916	Hour	Summary of Events and Information	Remarks and references to Appendices
HAPPY VALLEY	July 6		Fatigue parties clearing the battlefield	
	" 8		do.	
	9		Battalion moved up to old BRITISH front line trenches N.W. of MARICOURT while in support to	
	10		the 91st BRIGADE who were attacking TRONES WOOD. This began a series	
	11		of operations in and about this wood which continued until July 11th.	
			Total casualties 11 Officers [KILLED: CAPT CHENSHALL, 2nd LT B.B.	Lee
			SALMON; WOUNDED Lt COL W.A. SMITH (died of wounds) Lt W.P. KNOWLES,	Appendices
			CAPT R. HOBKIRK, Lt M BRUNTON, Lt H.G. WATSON, 2nd Lt W. WALLWORK,	K 2
			2nd LT C.T. TURPIN, 2nd O. WILCOX, 2nd LT S. FERNYHOUGH] and 290	
			other ranks killed, wounded and missing. The battalion was	
			relieved at 5.0 A.M. on the morning of July 11th and proceeded	
			to the old BRITISH trenches at MARICOURT where a half-warm meal	
			was served by BRAY and BRAY—	
			until 3.0 P.M. The battalion then proceeded by BRAY and BRAY—	
BOIS DES CELESTINS	12		CORBIE road to BOIS DES CELESTINS. Lt COL SMITH was invalided	
			to the 8th infantry and reorganising. MAJOR POOLEY assumed command from that date.	
	13		The battalion drew SMLE other units. The 90th infantry Brigade was ordered	
			by the G.O.C. XIII Corps who thanked them for their fine work at	

Sheet 23

Army Form C. 2118

WAR DIARY
or
INTELLIGENCE SUMMARY
(Erase heading not required.) 18th (Service) Battn Manchester Regt

Place	Date 1916	Hour	Summary of Events and Information	Remarks and references to Appendices
BOIS DES CELESTINS – DAOURS	July 14		MONTAUBAN. Battalion afterwards marched to billets at DAOURS. A draft of 440 other ranks from 28 different units joined today. Lt T.J. KELLY henceforth assumed the duties of adjutant on July 9th when Lt M. BRUNTON became a casualty.	See appendix K.3.
	" 15		Reorganisation and training. 1 O.R. accidentally wounded	
DAOURS	" 16		do. 1 O.R. accidentally wounded	
	" 17		MAJOR H.B.O. WILLIAMS assumed command of the battalion with effect from the 15th instant. The regimental band was started again for Reorganisation and training.	See appendix K.4. K.5
DAOURS – BOIS DES CELESTINS	" 18		Battalion marched to BOIS DES CELESTINS	
HAPPY VALLEY	" 19		Battalion marched to HAPPY VALLEY	
	" 20		Coy training. The following officers joined today; Lt C.E. POYNTON, 2 Lt W. EVANS, 2 Lt J. HUTCHISON, and 2nd Lt L.A. HARRIES-JONES	
	" 21		Coy training	
MANSEL COPSE	" 22		Battalion moved to MANSEL COPSE, old British line near MAMETZ	
	" 23		Moved to old British trenches at GILSON STREET (MARICOURT)	
GERMAN TRENCHES	" 24		Move to BRICK LANE, German front line opposite TALUS BOISE	

WAR DIARY or INTELLIGENCE SUMMARY

Army Form C. 2118

Sheet 24

18th Service Battⁿ Manchester Reg^t

Place	Date 1916	Hour	Summary of Events and Information	Remarks and references to Appendices
OLD GERMAN FRONT LINE	July 25		Battalion awaiting orders in BRICK LANE	
	" 26		do	
			Other ranks belonging to the KINGS LIVERPOOL REG^t 2nd Lt HUTCHINSON killed. 118 with the draft in the 13th instant, were transferred to the 21st and 89th Brigades. Battalion moved back to MANSEL COPSE	
MANSEL COPSE	" 27		In MANSEL COPSE awaiting orders	
	" 28		do.	
	" 29		Attack on GUILLEMONT. Battalion moved early in day to former position. See in BRICK LANE and at 11.0 P.M. proceeded to the assembly approach K6 trenches east of TRONES WOOD. Operations continued until 3.30 A.M. on the morning of July 31st when the brigade was relieved and the battalion marched back to the CITADEL. Total casualties 14 Officers and 400 other ranks killed, wounded, and missing. Congratulatory messages received during the month from the G.O.C. XIIIth Corps and See the G.O.C. 4th Army. The G.O.C. XIIIth Corps and S	K7

Army Form C. 2118

Sheet 25

WAR DIARY
or
INTELLIGENCE SUMMARY

18th Manchester Regt.

(Erase heading not required.)

Instructions regarding War Diaries and Intelligence Summaries are contained in F. S. Regs., Part II. and the Staff Manual respectively. Title Pages will be prepared in manuscript.

Place	Date	Hour	Summary of Events and Information	Remarks and references to Appendices
			The G.O.C 30th Division are attaches	

H.B.Milheam Major
Commanding 18th (Service) Battn Manchester Regt

To:-
    D. A. G.,

        3rd. ECHELON.

Herewith Appendix K.2. and K.6. will you kindly attach same to War diary of this unit for the month of July.

7.8.1916.   ....Lieut,
                                    Acting/Adjt. for O.C.
                     18th. Bn. Manchester Regiment.

App. K1

G.O.C. 90th. INFANTRY BRIGADE.

Sir,
I have the honour to report that the Brigade having begun to advance one hour after Zero as ordered the various detachments of the battalion under my command left their assembly trenches between 1hour 15min. and 1hour 30min. after Zero.

1. I had two platoons attached to the Field Company R.E. to carry stores for them to MONTAUBON.

2. Two platoons carrying R.E. stores to keep "A" at MONTAUBON.

3. Two platoons carrying S.A.A. and bombs to MONTAUBON.

4. One platoon carrying S.A.A. between dumps within our own lines.

5. One platoon carrying ammunition for the Stokes Mortar Battery.
There were left to me two companies to form the Brigade Reserve, but half of one of these companies had to carry equipment up for the Brigade Machine Gun Coy. to MONTAUBON.

Generally speaking all the carrying parties and the Brigade Reserve moved off in rear of the other three battalions of the Brigade., but as the leading battalions halted for some time these parties closed up and in one case (No.1) arrived there before some of the party for whom they were carrying and the others practically on the heels of the assaulting troops.

All carrying parties had casualties on the way up caused by machine gun fire and shells, but showing admirable devotion to duty. every man arrived at his destination with his load -excepting casualties- and among them individuals who through no fault of their own became detached from their units on their way up. The loads were found to be very heavy especially in view of the heat and most men arrived in an exhausted condition, but all parties went back for more loads and no time was lost. Many casualties occurred in subsequent journies owing to shell fire.

As regards the Brigade Reserve one company started to advance about 500 yards in rear of the 2nd. R.S.F., but as the leading battalion halted for some time and it became difficult to distinguish different units the company passed through the units in front and went straight to a front about 600 yards south of MONTAUBON and commenced digging in. During the advance the company suffered many casualties from shells and rifle and machine guns fireon our left. The platoon on the left touching the railway, crossed over and disposed of some cunning snipers.

Our other company of the reserve together with the Brigade Machine Gun Coy. and battalion H.Q. advanced close in rear of the other company but finding the battalions in front halted, it remained for about thirty minutesin the vicinity of the enemy VALLEY SUPPORT trench. Up to and during this time there was a lot of machine gun and rifle fire from the left and a fair amount of shelling which caused some casualties. During the halt I got a machine gun and Lewis gun into position in order to bring fire to bear on the trenches on our left, but as the exact spot where the fire came from could not be located and the adjoining brigade appeared to be advancing in the trenches instead of above ground I was afraid of shooting into them and had to abandon the idea but was able to fire with effect into a party of the enemy retreating on our left

As the leading battalions advanced I moved up to my intended advanced position in ALT TRENCH but as we were heavily shelled decided to go forward tothetrench S. of MONTAUBON when I joined the two companies ofR.S.F., the other company being in rear in the ravine. The half company with me then commenced digging a new trench but shortly afterwards I was ordered by O.C. MONTAUBAN to send it to reinforce the 16th. battn. Manchester Regt. in the meantime the Brigade machine gun Coy.

G.O.C. 90th. INFANTRY BRIGADE

had advanced into MONTAUBAN and the O.C. that Coy ordered the two platoons of the reserve Coy. attached to him to assist in making emplacements and to go to MARICOURT for ammunition I was afterwards ordered by O.C. MONTAUBAN to send my remaining reserve company to reinforce the 17th. battalion Manchester Regt. in MONTAUBAN.

Later in the evening I was ordered to withdraw the reserve companies and I sent them back to the ravine. The following morning I moved my H.Q. back from S. Trench to TRAIN ALLEY.

During the morning of the 2nd. inst. nothing of note occurred but I was able to increase the reserve Coy. by the addition of some of the carrying parties.

I have the honour to be Sir,
Yours obedient

(Sd) WA Smith Lt.Col.

Our total casualties during the operations were 6 officers wounded and about 170 other ranks killed and wounded.

G.O.C. 90th. INFANTRY BRIGADE

had advanced into MONTAUBAN and the O.C. that Coy ordered the two platoons of the reserve Coy. attached to him to assist in making emplacements and to go to MARICOURT for ammunition I was afterwards ordered by O.C. MONTAUBAN to send my remaining reserve company to reinforce the 17th. battalion Manchester Regt. in MONTAUBAN.

Later in the evening I was ordered to withdraw the reserve companies and I sent them back to the ravine. The following morning I moved my HqQ. back from S. Trench to TRAIN ALLEY.

During the morning of the 2nd. inst. nothing of note occurred but I was able to increase the reserve Coy. by the addition of some of the carrying parties.

I have the honour to be Sir,
Yours obedient

Our total casualties during the operations were 6 officers wounded and about 170 other ranks killed and wounded.

Operations July 8th & 9th
TRONES WOOD
app K2

SUBJECT:- Operations. July 8th. to 11th.

app. K2
G 464

To:-
   G. O. C.,
       90th. INFANTRY BRIGADE.

Sir,

      I beg to submit the following report on the movements of the battalion under my command during the operations of July. 8th. to 11th.1916.

ASSEMBLY.
July.8th.

5.30.am.   The Battalion assembled in the Old British Front line E. of TALUS BOISE.

1.0.pm.   An order was given by G.O.C. 21st.Brigade for two Companies to go up to TRAIN ALLEY and two Companies ("A" Captain Routley & "B".Captain Wolfenden) moved there.

2.0.pm.   Companies from TRAIN ALLEY were ordered to move up to TRONES WOOD and report to O.C. 2nd.WILTS. "A"Coy. went first and reached WOOD about 3.pm. by way of CHIMNEY TRENCH and TRONES ALLEY, passing through a heavy barrage. "B"Coy also passed down CHIMNEY TRENCH and the guide lost his way and led the party to BRIQUETERIE where the O.C.Coy reported to 21st.Brigade who ordered him to stand by for orders. Meanwhile information came in from a runner that Lieut Col.W.A.Smith had become a casualty and Captain Wolfenden went back to TRAIN ALLEY to take over temporary Command of the battalion. Orders were then given to "B"Coy to push on to TRONES WOOD which they reached at 4.30.pm, reporting to the WILTS H.Q. "A"Coy had taken up a position in the S.W.edge of the WOOD and begun work on a new trench eastwards from the edge of the WOOD 29 S.a.4/4 "B"Coy sent one platoon to assist "A" and the rest of the Coy (Lieut Kelly vice Captain Wolfenden) took up a position in TRONES ALLEY,establishing bombing posts at three points where unfinished trenches led northwards.

8.0.pm.   "C"Coy.(Lieut A.A.Harrison) & "D"Coy.(Captain R.Hobkirk) arrived and reinforced "A" & "B" who had had many Casualties from shell fire and the line was lengthened in the WOOD. TRONES ALLEY was shelled heavily all night.

2.0.am.
9.7.1916.   MAJOR.P.Godlee arrived and assumed Command of the Battalion

7.0.am.   The 17th.Manchr Regt attacked the WOOD. "B"Coy followed in support, their orders being to push on to the eastern edge of the wood and help in consolidating its defences "C"Coy was organised to support "B"Coy if required. On arriving at CENTRE TRENCH considerable delay occurred as it was full of men belonging to the 17th.Manchr.Regt and was too wide to jump and the attackers were forced to descend into the trench and clamber up the other side. This part of the WOOD was being shelled at the time and owing to Casualties and men getting lost in the thick undergrowth the Company was reduced to less than 50.

8.30.am.   "B"Coy. reached a point S.30.a.4/4. Attempts had been made by the enemy to begin a small trench here and the Coy made this deeper and linked together the larger shells holes for def

Contd......

2.

Hardly had the tasks been allotted when the enemy began to shell this particular spot intensely. An Officer's patrol was sent out to get in touch with the troops on the North and South but on returning reported that there was nobody holding the eastern fringe of the WOOD and that the nearest post on the North held by the South Africans was 400 yards away.

11.0.am. The report of the patrol was sent to O.C. 16th.Manch.Rgt. and as more than half the Coy had become casualties he ordered a withdrawal to the general line which was held by the 17th. Manchr. The wounded were all brought back under heavy fire.

12.noon. Orders were received from BDE.H.Q. for 16th.Manchr.R. to relieve with three Coys of which were in the WOOD and one Coy attached to 2nd.R.S.F. in BAZEN TORN TRENCH. "A"Coy were detailed for attachment to 2nd.R.S.F., remaining under that command until they were relieved on the 11th instance and proceeded to MARICOURT. The other three Coys. then took up a position on the fringe of the WOOD from S.30.a.3/8 to S.29.d.4/8. "D"Coy on the east, "C" in the centre, and "B" on the West.

1.0.pm. The shelling, which had continued without cessation from 5.0pm. the previous day, became intense throughout this part of the WOOD and continued until the eventual withdrawal was over.

3.0.pm. The 17th.Manchr.R.began to move down to BERNAFAY WOOD. Officers of the 17th. stated that the order to withdraw came from Major Whitehead who was the Senior Officer and attempts were made to get in touch with him without success. O.C. 16th.Manchr.R. then gave orders to withdraw to the BRIQUETERIE sending out messengers to warn all three Coys. B, C & D. Lieut Kelly(vice Lieut.Brunton the Adjutant who had become a casualty) himself went out after the messengers and found that the trenches on the S.E. fringe of the WOOD had been evacuated.

4.30.pm. O.C. 16th.Manchr.R. reached BRIQUETERIE and got in touch with about 25 men who stated that the rest of the battalion had gone back to TRAIN ALLEY.

5.30.pm. O.C. 16th.Manchr.R. reached TRAIN ALLEY and collected about 38 N.C.O.'s and men and two officers, reporting to BDE.H.Q. for orders. It was found that "D"Coy was not present.

9.30.pm. Orders were given by BDE. to move up again to SUNKEN ROAD BRIQUETERIE and the battalion now approximately 80 strong moved up and reported to O.C. 16th.Manch.Rgt. who ordered that 16th.Manchr. should stay in CHIMNEY TRENCH and await instruction. "D"Coy (55 strong) was found on SUNKEN ROAD having gone there at 10.pm on finding that TRONES WOOD had been evacuated. This Coy, unfortunately, never received the order to withdraw because they were further SOUTH than they were expected to be and this and the fact that they were crouching low in their cover accounts for the fact that they were not found by the messengers who were sent on four occasions to look for them. Just before the withdrawal they had been reported as "nearly wiped out". After most of the troops had passed back they were reported to have all gone by and later a runner stated they were at the BRIQUETERIE. Hence the fact that they had not received the order passed unnoticed till later on. In spite of their isolated position, however, this Company held on to its position, they shot several of the enemy trying to enter the wood on their left and eventually withdrew successfully with a strength of 55 men.

4.0.am. Two Coys moved from CHIMNEY TRENCH moved up to SUNKEN ROAD to take the place of the reserve Coys of 16th.Manchrs. who had been sent forward.

Contd....

3.

Time	
7.15.am.	One Officer and 40.Other Ranks went to trench at South end of WOOD to reinforce South African Scottish. They were sent back after three hours as Captain Russell (S.A.I.) who was in charge, considered trench overmanned in case of heavy shell fire. The remainder of the battalion (50 men) was employed during the day in carrying rations and water between SUNKEN ROAD, TRAIN ALLEY and TRONES WOOD.
9.30.pm.	TRONES WOOD was attacked by 89th.BDE and then shelled by our Artillery and battalion was ordered to occupy trench on South of WOOD which had been evacuated by S.A.Infantry.
1.0.am.	O.C.16th.Manchr.Regt. ordered that "B" & "C" be relieved in trench by 17th.Manchr. and these Coys left for MARICOURT.
3.0.am.	D.Coy ordered to leave trench and take up a position 200 yards South and lie in the open until ordered to withdraw by an Officer.
4.0.am.	D.Coy. withdrawn by its Commander to SUNKEN ROAD, 89th. BDE having gone through to attack the WOOD.
5.0.am.	H.Q. and "D"Coy. moved back to MARICOURT.

The casualties sustained during the operations dealt with above were as follows:-

	Killed.	Wounded.	Missing.	Died of Wounds.	Total.
Officers.	1.	8.	1.	1.	11.
Other Ranks.	29.	170.	64.	6.	269.

I have the honour to be,

Sir,

Your obedient servant,

July.14th.1916.

(Signed) .... P. Godlee Major.,
Commanding.18th.Bn.Manchester Regt.

Appendix K2

Report by MAJOR H.B.O WILLIAMS on the Operations at TRONES WOOD July 8th – 11th, 1916. and Operation Order No 1

COPY

R 2

To:-

BRIGADE MAJOR.,
90th. INFANTRY BRIGADE.

I have the honour to report, as follows, on my experience in TRONES WOOD:-

Undoubtedly one of the most difficult problems confronting Company Commanders in the WOOD was that of keeping touch with Battalion Headquarters. There was only one method of communication, by runner, and this method always slow and unreliable was rendered almost impossible by reason of the difficulty the men experienced in finding their way through the thick brushwood and fallen trees. The enemy had clearly marked a winding path from the eastern fringe of the WOOD, probably from the strong point in MALTZ HORN TRENCH, to the CENTRE TRENCH by attaching pieces of white paper to trees with wire. This was easily distinguishable at night and would be a good method of quickly marking routes, providing the wood has not become littered with shell debris. In some cases trees had been destroyed by shells and the marking was lost.

Where there are no trenches or paths it is absolutely necessary to make some communication, because otherwise all are compelled to depend on the compass and maps and though this is possible perhaps in the case of Officers and N.C.O.s it cannot be applied to runners. Placing paper on trees or cutting pieces off the bark of trees appear the best way of quickly marking routes, but if possible Engineers or Pioneers should be brought up with axes to clear away the brushwood. The Infantry cannot be spared to do this work, for they are wanted for the duties of the garrison and for consolidating the strong points.

In taking a Company from TRONES ALLEY to the Eastern Side of the WOOD I found it almost impossible to keep touch with the men, though precautions had been taken beforehand to split the men up into small groups of 12 under Officers and Sergeants. There were few gaps in the brushwood and the direction was lost on passing through them. Men wearing packs greatly delayed the advance. I suggest that the attack should be made in groups of 5 or 6 men each under a N.C.O. or Senior soldier and closely in touch with one another. There would not then be such delay in getting along and such crowding at gaps.

I think the number of stretcher bearers should be increased in Wood fighting and if one man, following the advance, was detailed to drop papers as in a paper chase or lay white tapes it would greatly facilitate in showing the stretcher bearers the line of advance.

On reaching the fringe of the wood a halt should be called and scouts sent found to ascertain whether it is safe to begin consolidating a few yards inside the wood. The brushwood is usually very thin at the edge and if a working party is seen heavy shelling shelling is sure to follow. This certainly happened in TRONES WOOD where men who got lost wandered to the outskirts of the wood to get their bearings, causing the enemy to imagine that the wood was full of men.

STRONG POINTS.
Strong points in TRONES WOOD were in my opinion too far apart. Communication was not established between each and even in daylight it would have been possible for the enemy to slip in between the posts and attack each separately in force.

contd........

in consolidating Keeps care should be taken to see that there is a good field of fire. This in TRONES WOOD was exceptionally difficult. Unless it is done the enemy is likely to creep up to bombing range in the darkness and escape after throwing his bombs, under cover of the fallen trees and brushwood. A small bombing attack of this nature was successfully made in TRONES WOOD by the enemy on the night of July 8/9. Had the field of fire been cleared by removing brushwood and the attackers would certainly have been seen by the sentries.

LEWIS GUNS. Lewis Guns are not of much use in these inland Keeps in dense woods unless there is a clearing in front, but should certainly be posted to command all pathways. One gun was successfully employed in this manner.

P. Godlee

20th. July. 1916.   (d) .... Major
                         Commanding. 18th. Bn. Manchester Rgt.

Ref 80 p Oper N°
7 Bde Corps

The forward dump for Grenades and SAA is at CHIMNEY TRENCH between S.19.d 1/0 and A.4.b 4/7.

The Divl reserve dump is at NAPIER REDOUBT MARICOURT. Very pistol ammunition on the scale of 6 cartridges per pistol will be drawn from NAPIER REDOUBT immediately on arrival at Ammunition refilling point. Position of dumps to be made known to all ranks.

To:- O.C. A.B.C.& D. Coys.

One Limbered Wagon will accompany the
Battalion to-morrow and can be used for
conveying Mess Goods etc.,

7.7.16.   (sd) Miles Brunton
                                    Lieut. & Adjt.
                                18th Bn. Mchr. Regt.

To :- Lieut. B.B. Salmon.

    You will be at the junction of
GILSON STREET and SUPPORT AVENUE at
7.0.a.m. tomorrow and meet there the
Div. Bombing Officer or his representative and arrange with him for issue
of S.A.A. and Grenades to Battalion.

7.7.16.
                                            Lieut&
                                           Adjutant
                                  18th. Bn. Mchr. Regt.

To :- O.C. " " Company.

Reference Operation Order No.17.

Para3/

The part of this para referring to Ammunition and Grenades is cancelled.

These will be issued on arrival in the trenches.

7.7.16.   Brunton   Lieut. &
Adjutant.
18th.Bn. Nehr. Regt.

SECRET. Copy No......

18th.Bn.MANCHESTER REGIMENT OPERATION ORDER No.17.
By
LIEUT.COLONEL. W. A. SMITH.

Reference:- ALBERT combined sheet and MONTAUBAN Trench Map.

5th.July.1916.

1. The Battalion will move up to-morrow to the old BRITISH front line trenches E. of the TALUS BOISE about A.9.Central and will be in position thereat 7.45.am.

2. ORDER OF MARCH. Companies will move off in the following order:- A, B, C, & D at 100 interval between Companies.

3. ROUTE. BRAY - BRONFAY Rd, BRONFAY FARM, A.20.a.0/2, A.21.a.2/9, and WEST Av; the leading Company will move off at 4.45.am. Current day's rations and following day's rations in addition to Iron Rations will be carried. The M.O's cart two limbered SAA Wagons and a grenade wagon, with 36 boxes SAA and the usual supply of Grenades will march in rear of the leading Company as far as the cross roads A.21.a.2/9, where every man will fill up to 170rds SAA and bombers 7 bombs each, discs and yellow patches will be worn, four flags per Company will be carried, one in each platoon. Water bottles to be filled this evening. Very pistols and flares to be carried. Lewis Guns and handcarts will march with their Companies and be parked near OXFORD COPSE. Companies will form up in the front line trench in the following order from left to right:-
"A"Coy. with its L. on TALUS BOISE. B, C, & D.
O.C.Coys. to report their arrival in position to Battalion Headquarters.

Issued to Orderly. 8.15.pm.

.....................Lieut.
Adjutant.
18th.Bn.Manchester Regt.

Copy No.1. File.
2. C.O.
3. 2nd.in.Command.
4. Adjutant.
5. O.C."A"Coy.
6. O.C."B"Coy.
7. O.C."C"Coy.
8. O.C."D"Coy.
9. Lewis Gun Officer.
10. Medical Officer.
11. Quartermaster.
12. Transport Officer.
13. War Diary.

Appendix K.3

Operation Order by MAJOR
P. GODLEE for march from
Bois des Celestins to Daours.

Appendix K 3

SECRET.   COPY No. 12

18th.(Service)BATTALION.MANCHESTER REGIMENT. ORDER No.18.
BY
MAJOR. P. GODLEE.

Ref:- Map AMIENS Sheet 17. 1/100,000.   13th.July.1916.

1.   The Battalion will march to Billets and Bivouac in DAOURS.

2. ORDER   The Battalion will parade at 11.15.am. on the ground in front
   OF   of the Orderly Room and will move off in the following order:-
   MARCH.   A, B, C, & D.

3. ROUTE.   SOMME Valley Road through SAILLY LAURETTE, CORBIE and LA
                NEUVILLE to destination.
                Head of Column to pass junction of CELESTINS - SOMME Valley
                Road-($\frac{1}{4}$ mile S of the last "S" in CELESTINS.) at 12noon.

4. TRANSPORT.   1st Line Transport will march in rear of "D"Company.

                                            ....Lieut.
                                                  Acting Adjutant.
                                            18th.Bn.Manchester Regt.

Issued to Orderly............am.
Copy No.1. File.
        2. O.C.
        3. Adjutant.
        4. Lewis Gun Officer.
        5. Medical Officer.
        6. Quartermaster.
        7. Transport Officer.
        8. O.C. "A"Coy.
        9. O.C. "B"Coy.
       10. O.C. "C"Coy.
       11. O.C. "D"Coy.
       12. War Diary.

SECRET. *[handwritten: Appendix ? K4]* Copy No.......

18th.(Service) Battalion, Manchester Regiment Order No.19.
by
Major H.B.O.WILLIAMS.

Reference:- Map- AMIENS sheet 17 1/100,000.

Today the battalion will march to BOIS CELESTINS.

1. ROUTE. (1) LA NEUVILLE? CORBIE? CORBIE- BRAY road to BOIS CELESTINS.
   Head of Column to be at junction of roads DAOURS- LA NEUVILLE and DAOURS- PONT NOYELLES at 1.30.p.m.

2. ORDER OF MARCH. "D", "C", "B" & "A" Coy.

3. TRANSPORT. 1st Line Transport will follow the battalion.

Kindly acknowledge.

ISSUED TO ORDERLY AT....p.m.
```
Copy No.1. File.
     2. C.O.
     3. 2nd in Command.
     4. Adjutant.
     5. O.C. "A" Coy.
     6. O.C. "B" Coy.
     7. O.C. "C" Coy.
     8. O.C. "D" Coy.
     9. L/G Officer.
    10. M.O.
    11. Q.M.
    12. T.O.
    13. War Diary
```

.................Lieut,
A/Adjutant,
18th.Bn Mchr. Regt.

Appendix K4

Operation Order No 19 by
MAJOR H.B.O. WILLIAMS,

Appendix K 5

Operation Order No 20

by MAJOR H.B.O. WILLIAMS.

SECRET.
Copy No.13.

18th.(service)Bn.MANCHESTER REGIMENT OPERATION ORDER No.20.
BY.
MAJOR. H.B.O.WILLIAMS.

19th.May.1916.

18th.Bn.Manchester Rgt. will march to-morrow to HAPPY VALLEY.

1. ROUTE. Head of Column will be at Starting Point road junction X.28.c.6/5. at 7.10.am.
Starting Point- X roads X.21.b.70.95.-BRAY-CORBIE ROAD- L.14.d.6.8.-thence by new road to L.15.b.3.9.-ALBERT ROAD to HAPPY VALLEY.

2. BILLETING PARTIES. Coys will send the same billeting parties as today to report to 2nd.Lieut.J.P.Knowles at 6.30.am.

3. TRANSPORT. First Line Transport will follow the battalion. Present arrangements for Second Line Transport is that 2 baggage wagons will be attached to the Battalion.

....................Lieut.
Acting Adjutant,
18th.Bn.Manchester Regiment.

Copy No.1. File.
2. C.O.
3. 2nd-in-Command.
4. Adjutant.
5. O.C. "A"Coy.
6. O.C. "B"Coy.
7. O.C. "C"Coy.
8. O.C. "D"Coy.
9. Medical Officer.
10. Transport Officer.
11. Quartermaster.
12. Lewis Gun Officer.
13. War Diary.

Appendix K-6

Report on Operation at GUILLEMONT on July 29-31st. by MAJOR H.B.O. WILLIAMS.

Operation Orders No 2

App K 6

Casualties.
30.7.16

18th. SERVICE BATTALION. MANCHESTER REGIMENT.

CASUALTY List No.6. Contd.

ATTACHED-OTHER RANKS.

1st. Loyal North Lancs. Rgt.	1 wounded, 1 missing.
8th. ditto.	1 missing.
9th. ditto.	1 wounded, 1 missing.
2nd. East Lancs. Rgt.	2 wounded, 2 missing.
1st. Buffs Rgt.	1 wounded.
1st. East Kent Rgt.	1 wounded, 1 missing.
2nd. Bn. Queens Rgt.	2 missing.
12th. Bn. Manchester Rgt.	5 missing.

This cancels all previous Casualty Reports.

31st. 7. 1916.

...H.B.O.Williams...Major,
Commanding. 18th. Bn. Manchester Rgt.

18th SERVICE BATTALION. MANCHESTER REGIMENT.

CASUALTIES.—List No. 1.

2nd.Lieut. J.F.Lotler.	Killed in Action.	30.7.1916.
2nl.Lieut. H.O.Clough. (16th. .Bn.Mchr.R.).	ditto.	do.
Captain. E.A.Blythe.	Wounded & Missing.	do.
Lieut. J.A.Harrison. (4th.Bn.Mchr.R).	wounded	do.
2nd.Lieut.F.C.C.Twist.	ditto. & missing	do.
Lieut. E.G.du.V.Haworth.	Missing-Believed killed.	do.
2nd.Lieut.C.N.Green.	Wounded. (ad. to Hosp.)	do.
Captain P.Wolfenden.	Missing.	do.
Captain.W.F. Routley. (14th. .Bn.Mchr.R).	Missing.	do.
Lieut. C.K.Ingram.Poynton.	Missing.	do.
2nd.Lieut.F.Kavanagh. (14th. .Bn.Mchr.R).	Missing.	do.
2nl.Lieut.J.S.Partington. (14th. .Bn.Mchr.R).	Missing.	do.
2nd.Lieut.F.P.King.	Missing.	do.
2nd.Lieut. .F.Harries-Jones.	Missing.	do.

OTHER RANKS.	18th Mchrs.	Attached (Particulars below)	TOTAL CASUALTIES.
Killed in Action.	10.	1	11
Wounded.	73.	27	100
Missing.	210.	146	356
Missing-Believed Killed.	3.		3
			470

ATTACHED-OTHER RANKS.

1st.Lancs.Fusiliers.	2 wounded, 6 missing.	
2nd. ditto.	2 wounded, 3 missing.	
13th. ditto.	1 missing.	
14th. ditto.	4 missing.	
15th. ditto.	1 wounded, 7 missing.	
16th. ditto.	1 wounded, 9 missing.	
17th. ditto.	3 missing.	
18th. ditto.	8 wounded, 79 missing.	
19th. ditto.	1 wounded, 9 missing.	
10th. ditto.	2 wounded, 6 missing.	
22nd. ditto.	1 killed, 5 wounded, 9 missing.	
23rd. ditto.	1 wounded, 2 missing.	

contd/

18th.(Service) BATTALION. MANCHESTER REGIMENT.

REPORT:- OPERATIONS July 29th.- 31st.

(K6) War Diary

To:-
G. O. C.
90th. INFANTRY BRIGADE.

From:-
Officer Commanding,
18th.(s).Bn. Manchester Regiment.

Sir,

Move into position.
29.7.1916.
11.0.pm.

I have the honour to report as follows on the operations of July 29th - 31st.
The battalion left BRICK LANE, the old German front line, and proceeded to the position allotted to them in the assembly trenches east of TRONES WOOD, moving north of TRAIN ALLEY and the BRIQUETERIE, skirting the southern edge of BERNAFAY WOOD and thence striking north-east to the track marked through TRONES WOOD. Great difficulty was experienced in this movement as a considerable amount of shelling was taking place. The enemy was using heavy shrapnel, tear shells and large quantities of gas shells, which were so overpowering that I gave the order to put on gas helmets. With very few exceptions these gave absolute protection, but it was extremely difficult to see and make headway.

30.7.1916.
3.30.am.

I reached the western fringe of TRONES WOOD at 2.0.am. on the morning of July.30th. and halted for a quarter of an hour to allow the battalion to close up as there was naturally a great deal of straggling. Moved forward about 2.15.am. along the rough track which has been marked out with white tapes. It was necessary to proceed in single file as the path was littered with fallen trees, brushwood, and dead bodies. The last Company had passed through the wood at 3.15.am. I deployed the battalion and placed them in the assembly trenches, establishing touch with the 2nd.R.S.F. on my right. It was impossible, as ordered, to report to Brigade that the battalion was in position as I [knew] on reaching my Headquarters that I was not in telephonic communication, but a runner was sent to the Advanced R.C. Station in MALTZ HORN TRENCH and O... and ...... was also notified.

Attack on GUILLEMONT.

At 4.45.a.m.(zero) the battalion moved forward from the assembly trenches. The order of attack was as follows:-

"A" & "C" Coys. in two lines of platoons.

"D" & "B" Coys. forming the third and fourth lines respectively, each in one line of platoons.

"C" Coy,(Captain Blythe) almost immediately cleared the trench west of the village with their nettoyeur platoon, capturing about 100 prisoners, and then moved direct on to the quarry where the company commander was wounded but still carried on. Very heavy machine gun fire was opened on then, and a large quantity of bombs were thrown; the enemy also making use of smoke bombs. The action here became practically hand to hand fighting. "A" Coy (Captain Routley) on the right were requested to come to the support of "C" and Captain Routley accordingly moved his company to the north and endeavoured to give assistance. While this operation was in progress an order was passed along from the right to retire. No one, however, appears to know the source from which this order came and only a small proportion of these companies (about 50 men in all) actually withdrew to the trench in A... DE TRMP ROAD immediately in front of my Headquarters.

7.45.a.m.

About 7.45.a.m. two companies of 17th.Mchrs. were ordered up in support and the men from "A" & "C" Coys who had fallen back again moved up with them. An attempt was then made to re-establish ourselves in the quarry, but owing to the fog, which was still thick, direction must have been lost. The supports also came under very heavy fire from rifles and machine guns and were enfiladed from the north. The heavy artillery barrage between MALTZ HORN TRENCH and GUILLEMONT which the

3.

enemy had put up about 5.45.am. caused many casualties. So far as I can ascertain an order appears to have been given about 9.0.am. by an Officer to retire, which order the men attempted to obey, suffering very heavily in doing so. Only a very few men, about 8 or 10, in number, succeeded in reaching my Headquarters after dusk.

Part of the third line of "D"Coy under 2nd.Lt.Twist appear to have lost direction and arrived north of the quarry where they encountered strong wire, with gaps at intervals, commanded by machine guns. This led to many casualties.

From the outset of the operations my left flank was in the air. I received urgent messages for reinforcements from the Officer Commanding my support line ("B"Coy. Captain Wolfenden) at 5.55.am. and 7.0.am. in which he stated that he had no troops at all on his left. This message was forwarded at once to Brigade and O.C. 2nd.R.S.F.

3.0.pm. Later in the day orders were given that a counter-attack was expected on the MALTZ HORN TRENCH and the trench east of TRONES WOOD. O.C. 2nd.R.S.F. ordered me to occupy and hold on to ARROW HEAD COPSE at all costs, which I did, using runners and signallers from my Headquarters for the garrison and later placing a machine gun of the Machine Gun Coy in position in the Copse. The garrison was reinforced at 1.0.am. on the morning of the 31st. by a platoon of the 18th.H.L.I. and subsequently relieved at 3.30.am.

I have the honour to be,

Sir,

Your obedient servant,

4.8.1917.

.... Major,
Commanding.18th.Bn.Manchester Regiment.

D. Operation Order No
    BY MAJOR H.B.O. WILLIAMS
    Commanding   MURIEL.

REFERENCE.   LONGUEVAL Sheet 57 C.S.W.3

1/ BRANCH will attack GUILLEMONT in conjunction with ROOT on the night on the 30th instant. The French are attacking on the right of ROOT. Zero hour to be communicated later. GUILLEMONT STATION will be previously attacked by HEART from the direction of WATERLOT FARM. One brigade of HEART will be in support

2/ OBJECTIVE. The objective of the battalion will be the Centre of GUILLEMONT with the left resting on the South of the railway at point S 24 c ½ and their right in prolongation of the line taken up by ADA.

3/ BATTALION H.Q. At the beginning of operations battalion H.Q. will be at

SHEET 2

S 30 a 6/4.

ASSEMBLY. The battalion will be in position at 2.30.A.M. in the trenches immediately east of TRONES WOOD. The route to be followed will be notified verbally to officers commanding Companies.

ORDER OF ATTACK. First and second lines of attack :- "A" and "C" Coys. in two lines of platoons.
Third line :- "D" Coy. in one line of platoons.
Fourth line :- "B" Coy. in one line of platoons.

MACHINE GUNS & MORTARS. Machine Guns and trench Mortars will form up in the assembly trenches with "B". Coy.

CONSOLIDATION. After the capture of the village the line to be consolidated by the battalion will be from point T 19, exclusive, to the road T 19 d 3/5, about 50 yards

SHEET 3

from the house east of the village, inclusive.
The consolidation in the first place will consist of a line of small trenches to hold from 8 to 10 men each. When circumstances permit these trenches will be connected up and back to the village by occasional communication trenches.
In addition, the battalion will be responsible for two strong points, one immediately east of the village "G" at T 19 d 3/5, and the other "K" at T 19 c 0/3.

CARRYING PARTIES. One platoon of the 23rd Manchester Regt. will be employed in carrying wire & material.

DUMPS. The position of dumps for ammunition, bombs and engineers stores will be notified later.

29.7.16.

OPERATION ORDER No.2.
18th.Bn.Manchr, Regt.   29th.July. 1916.

1.   The battalion will today proceed to the trenches vacated on the 26th inst. Companies will move off in the following order C;A;D & B. by half platoons keeping 200 yards distance between half platoons.

2.   Distance must be maintained and great care taken to avoid observation from the East.

3.   Companies will arrange to have their dixies carried as the cookers will not be taken. Cooks will accompany the battalion.

4.   Breakfast 5.45.a.m. The leading half platoons of "C"Coy. must pass the starting point, Junction of CAFFREY WOOD and PERONNE Road by 7.15.a.m.

5.   All spare bombs must be issued before starting.

Issued to "A"Coy. at 1.20.a.m.   (Sd) T.J.Kelly Lieut,
         "B" "   A/Adjutant,
         "C" "   18th.Bn.Mchr.Regt.
         "D" "

OPERATION ORDER No.2.
   18th.Bn.Manchr. Regt.   29th.July. 1916.

1.   The battalion will today proceed to the trenches vacated on
the 26th inst. Companies will move off in the following order C;A;D & B
by half platoons keeping 200 yards distance between half platoons.

2.   Distance must be maintained and great care taken to avoid
observation from the East.

3.   Companies will arrange to have their dixies carried as the
cookers will not be taken. Cooks will accompany the battalion.

4.   Breakfast 5.45.a.m. The leading half platoons of "C"Coy.
must pass the starting point, Junction of CAFFREY WOOD and PERONNE
Road by 7.15.a.m.

5.   All spare bombs must be issued before starting.

Issued to "A"Coy. at 1.20.a.m.   (Sd) T.J.Kelly Lieut,
         "B" "   A/Adjutant,
         "C" "   18th.Bn.Mchr.Regt.
         "D" "

KT

Congratulatory messages on
operations in the Battle of
THE SOMME.

TO:-
Officer Commanding,
18th Bn. Manchester Regt.

30th Division wire as follows:-

"Please issue strict orders that the congratulatory messages issued with orders to-day are not to be communicated outside the Division AAA Acknowledge."

For information and necessary action, please.

Arthur Taylor
CAPTAIN,
STAFF CAPTAIN,
90TH INFANTRY BRIGADE.

18.7.16.

CONGRATULATORY MESSAGES.

Message from Lieut. General W.N.CONGREVE, V.C., C.B., M.V.O., Commanding XIII Corps; dated 1st July 1916.

To 30th Division:

    Please convey to all ranks my intense appreciation of their splendid fighting which has attained all asked of them and resulted in heavy losses to the enemy, nearly 1000 prisoners having already passed through the cage.

                                                Gen. CONGREVE.

Message from The Rt. Hon. E.G.V. Earl of DERBY, K.G., G.C.V.O., C.B.; dated 2nd July 1916.

To XIII Corps:

    Convey to 30th Division my best congratulations on their splendid work. Lancashire will indeed be proud of them.

                                                DERBY.

Message from General SIR H.S. RAWLINSON, Bart, K.C.B., C.V.O., Commanding Fourth Army; dated 2nd July 1916.

To XIII Corps:

    Please convey to all ranks 30th Division my congratulations on their capture and defence of MONTAUBAN. They have done excellent work and will be attacking again before long.

                                                RAWLINSON.

Message received by Fourth Army from General Headquarters:

To Fourth Army: 7th July 1916.

    The Commander-in-Chief wishes the following wire from His Majesty The King circulated to all ranks:
    "Please convey to the Army under your command my sincere congratulations on the results achieved in the recent fighting. I am proud of my troops none could have fought more bravely".

                                                GEORGE R.I.

Message from the General Officer Commander-in-Chief of the British Armies in FRANCE; dated 11th July 1916.

To Fourth Army:

    Commander-in-Chief desires his warm congratulations conveyed to XIII Corps for their good work, and especially to 30th Division for gallant defence of TRONES WOOD yesterday and last night by 90th Brigade against such heavy counter-attacks. XIII Corps have not only captured all its objectives, including many strong and important positions, but has held all points gained firmly against all hostile efforts to retake them. This is a record to be proud of. Such performances lead to certain and complete victory.

Extract from report by Fourth Army Liaison Officer with the French:

"General NOURRISSON, G.O.C. 39th Division, 20th Corps, who took HARDECOURT, expressed to General FAYOLLE his admiration of the British Troops his neighbours, whose bravery and discipline under heavy and continuous fire was beyond praise: "Leur attitude au feu etait remarquable"."

Advanced G.H.Q. wire to XIII Corps dated 15th July 1916:

General BALFOURIER Commanding 20th French Corps has expressed through a British Liaison Officer his admiration for the magnificent fighting qualities displayed during recent operations by our 13 Corps on his left and his desire to find himself fighting alongside this Corps during subsequent operations aaa Will you please convey this information to the 13 Corps aaa Message ends.

APPENDIX "A".

LOAD FOR CARRYING PARTIES.

1. 2 platoons "B" Coy. Carrying party to KEEP "A".
   - Wire. 30 coils.
   - Stakes. 200.
   - S.A.A. 10000 rds.
   - Mauls. 2.
   - Gloves, hedging. 16 pairs.
   - Wirecutters No.3. 22.
   - Crowbars. 2.
   - Axes. 6.

2. 2 platoons "A" Coy. Carrying S.A.A. Grenades from Bde. Forward Dump in DUKE St. to KEEP "A".
   - S.A.A. 15 boxes.
   - Grenades No.5. 600 x.
   - Rifle Grenades 5 boxes.
   - x. Grenades carried in canvas bucket at 20 grenades per man. These loads may be slightly modified to suit circumstances.

APPENDIX "B".

AMMUNITION & TOOLS.

1. Carrying parties.   S.A.A.   170 rds. per man.
                       Bombs No.5.   2.   "   "
                       Sandbags.   4.   "   "

2. Runners &   S.A.A.   170 rds. "   " only.
   Signallers.

3. Lewis Gunners.   S.A.A.   170 rds. "   "
                       Picks.   1.   " 4 men.
                       Shovels.   1.   "   "
                       Sandbags.   4.   " man.

4. Remainder of   S.A.A.   170 rds. "   "
   Battalion.   Bombs No.5.   2.(Bombers 10).per man.
   (i.e. Bde Reserve). Pick or Shovel.1.   per man.
                       Sandbags.   4.   "

5. Every man will carry in pack following articles:-

    Ground Sheet.,
    Cardigan jacket.,
    Iron Rations.
    Current day's rations.
    Rations for following day.

XXX(90)

17th Manchester
Vol. 4
30d Div

APPENDIX "C"

Articles to be drawn from the DUMP at NIEHEIM CAMP on "Y" day.

```
Sandbags.                          750 per Coy.
Picks,      ( C & D Coys )          50  "   "
Shovels     ( C & D Coys )          1.   "   "
Wirecutters No.5                     8  "   "
     "      "                        3  & per H.Q.Coy.
     "      Long                     6 per Coy.
     "      "                        3   per H.Q.Coy.
     "      Decimal                 25 per Coy.
Wire Breakers                       25  "   "
S.A.A.                           8,000 rds. per Coy.(H.Q.Coy. must
                                              draw with their Coy.)
Grenades.                          700.
```

The Battalion Bombing officer will detail a Bombing Sergt. to supervise the issue of these stores.
The Bombing Sergt will supervise the supply of Bombs throughout the operation.

18.th Manchester Rgt

30 Vol IV

90th Brigade.
30th Division.

1/18th BATTALION

MANCHESTER REGIMENT

AUGUST 1 9 1 6

Sheet 26

Army Form C. 2118

WAR DIARY
or
INTELLIGENCE SUMMARY
(Erase heading not required.)

18th S. Bn. The Manchester Regt.

Instructions regarding War Diaries and Intelligence Summaries are contained in F. S. Regs., Part II. and the Staff Manual respectively. Title Pages will be prepared in manuscript.

Place	Date	Hour	Summary of Events and Information	Remarks and references to Appendices
MANSEL COPSE	Aug 1		Batt resting after "GUILLEMONT".	
	2		Batt marched to DERNANCOURT and entrained for AIRAINES.	
AIRAINES	3		Resting	
	4	12 noon	Entrained at LONGPRE marched thence to BERGUETTE marched thence to BUSNES. Draft of 48 O.R's reported for duty from Base.	
BUSNES	5		Training. Draft of 26 O.R's joined.	
	6		"	
	7		"	
	8		"	
	9		The Army Commander 1st Army inspected the 90th Bde at 3.0 pm.	
	10	5.30 am	Batt marched to new Billets at LE HAMEL + ESSARS	for details See Appendix I.
LE HAMEL + ESSARS	11		Training	
	12		" Draft of 30 R's joined for duty from Base	
	13		"	
	14		" Lt. Adjt. M. BRUNTON rejoined Batt from Base	
	15		" Capt. W. PENN-GASKELL joined " " and assumed command of D Coy	
	16		"	
	17		"	
	18		"	
	19		" Working Parties. 2/Lts C.J. HONEYWOOD and H. DUNCAN joined the Batt from Base	
	20		"	
	21		"	
	22		"	
	23		"	
	24		"	
	25		"	
	26		" Lt T.J.KELLY promoted Capt. to date from 1/8/16 vice Capt P.A. BLYTHE (Missing)	
	27		" The G.O.C. 30th Division inspected the Billets and lines.	
	28		" Major H.B.O. WILLIAMS 3rd Dragoon Guards appointed Lt Col and assumed command of the Batt as Capt F.J. EARLES and 24 O.R's joined for duty from Base from 15/7/16.	
	29		"	
	30		Following Officers joined for duty from Base, L/H PETERS, 2/Lt R.A.WESTPHAL 2/Lts. R. RUMNEY, 2/Lt T.E. TRIMMER, 2/Lt G.RISSIK 2/Lt H.TAYLOR.	
	31		Training	

H.B.O. Williams Lt Col
Commanding 18th M'chrs

SECRET.   Copy No.....

            18th Service Battn. MANCHESTER REGIMENT. Operation Order.
                       By Major E.R.C. WILLIAMS.
                           August 10th 1916.
                           ─────────────   No.21.

Reference:- Hazebrouck Sheet 1
                           ─────────
                            100,000.

(1) The 18th Battn. Manchester Regt. will march to billets in MEARS
    on the 11th August 1916.   + LE HAMEL

(2) The 18th Battn. Manchester Regiment will follow the 2nd Royal
    Scots Fusiliers in the Brigade march; head of Brigade to pass
    starting point, 1st road junction west of the 1st "L" in
    L'HOLMER at 5.15 am. Distance of 100 yards between units on the
    march.

(3) TRANSPORT. Transport will march in the rear of the Battalion.

(4) Order of march. A, B, C and D Companies.
                                                    in mass
(5) The Battalion will fall in on the parade ground/ready to move
    off at 4.30 am.

(6) ROUTE. L'ECLEME-BUSNETTES-LILLERS BETHUNE road – CHOCQUES-LILLERS
    BETHUNE road, N ext of BETHUNE,

(7) Troops marching N of the BETHUNE-LOOCH road will march by
    companies.

                                                         Lieut.
                                                    Acting Adjutant.
                                                  18th Bn. Manchester Regt.

Copy No. 1. In file.
         2. C.O.
         3. 2nd in command.
         4. Adjutant.
         5. O.C. A. Coy.
         6. O.C. B. Coy.
         7. O.C. C. Coy.
         8. O.C. D. Coy.
         9. M.O.
        10. Transport Officer.
        11. Lewis Gun Officer.
        12. Quartermaster.
        13. War Diary.

"Secret" Vol 11

War Diary

of the

18th (Service) Battalion, The Manchester Regiment.

for the month of

September 1916.

(Volume XI.)

[signature] LIEUT. COL.
Commanding 18TH (S) Battn. Manch. R.

Army Form C. 2118

Sheet 24

WAR DIARY
or
INTELLIGENCE SUMMARY

(Erase heading not required.)

18th Service Batt'n Manchester Regt

Instructions regarding War Diaries and Intelligence Summaries are contained in F.S. Regs., Part II. and the Staff Manual respectively. Title Pages will be prepared in manuscript.

Place	Date 1916	Hour	Summary of Events and Information	Remarks and references to Appendices
LE HAMEL & ESSARS	Sept 1		Training. Extract from today's orders: "The G.O.C. 30th Division in the occasion of his recent inspection of the battalion as very pleased with the Smart and Soldierly appearance of the battalion."	See appendix #1
	2		Training	
TRENCHES	3		Battalion relieves 11th West YORKSHIRE Regt in the FESTUBERT sector "B" & "D" Coys taking the front line, "A" the support, and "C" the reserve	
	4		In the line	
	5		In the line	
	6		do One N.C.O. killed, one man wounded	
	7		do One N.C.O. killed. Capt. J. G. 2nd R.S.F. church of which W. met. One N.C.O. wounded	
LE TOURET	8		Battalion was relieved in the night of 8-9 and marches to billets at LE TOURET. Lt L.A. LION struck off strength of battalion to be sick	See 2
			One O.R. wounded. 2nd Lt N.B. GILL joins from base for duty.	
	9		Brigade Reserve	
	10		do	
	11		do CAPT. T.J. KELLY awarded the military cross.	
	12		do N°10235 L.Corp A BUTTERWORTH who already has the military medal awarded D.C.M.	
	13		20th Battalion KINGS (LIVERPOOL) REGT relieves the battalion in Brigade	See 3
HINGETTE			reserve at LE TOURET and the battalion marched to HINGETTE	
TRENCHES	14		Battalion marched back to line & relieves 2nd ROYAL SCOTS in FESTUBERT SECTOR; "A" Co. who meanwhile returned with	See 4

Army Form C. 2118

Sheet 28

WAR DIARY
or
INTELLIGENCE SUMMARY

(Erase heading not required.)

18th Service Batt n Manchester Regt

Place	Date 1916	Hour	Summary of Events and Information	Remarks and references to Appendices
TRENCHES	Sept 14		2nd R.S.F. went into reserve, "D" + "C" in support. One O.R. wounded	
– do –	15		On the line. 2nd Lt. A.F. HARRIS and 2nd Lt. J.P. KNOWLES (mouthed) to L.T.S. One O.R. killed	
HINGETTE	16		12th Batt. YORK & LANCASTER REGT & 1 coy. 13th YORK & LANCASTER REGT C 5 relieved battalion in FESTUBERT section and battalion marched back to billets at HINGETTE. One O.R. wounded	S 5
BELLERIVE	17		Battalion marches to billets at RUE BELLERIVE, GONNEHEM.	S 6
	18		Battalion marches to CHOQUES station and entrains for CANDAS (SOMME). Arrives at 6.0 A.M. at CANDAS, detraines	S 7
	19		and marches to BEAUVAL. No 9869 Pte. H.T. HOLLAND awarded the military medal.	
	20		Training	
FLESSELLES	21		Marches to FLESSELLES. Lt M. BRUNTON (adjutant) evacuated to C.C.S. CAPT. KELLY taking over his duties temporarily.	S 8
	22		Training	
	23		– do – MAJOR J.B. AIKEN was admitted to F.A. today	

Army Form C. 2118

WAR DIARY
or
INTELLIGENCE SUMMARY

(Erase heading not required.)

Sheet 29

18th Service Battn. Manchester Regt.

Place	Date. 1916	Hour	Summary of Events and Information	Remarks and references to Appendices
FLESSELLES	Sept 24		Training	
	25		— do —	
	26		— do —	
	27		— do — 2nd Lt W. PHYTHIAN and 2nd Lt J. R. BODDINGTON Joined from base for duty today	
	28		Training. 9 other ranks joined for duty from Base.	
	29		— do —	
	30		— do —	

HG Williams
Lt-Col
Commanding 18th Manchester Regt

SECRET. 19th Bn. MANCHESTER REGIMENT OPERATION ORDER No.21.
By.
LIEUT. COLONEL H.B.O. WILLIAMS.

Copy No. 1
APPENDIX. S.1.

Reference:- BETHUNE combined Sheet 1/40,000.

(1). **RELIEFS.** 19th. Manchesters will relieve the Sector now held by the 11th East Yorkshire Regt on the evening of the 3rd Sept. 1916.

(2). **ORDER OF RELIEF.** "B" Company 19th. Manchesters will relieve "C" Company 11th. East Yorks on the right Sector of the front line; "D" Coy. 19th Manchesters will relieve "D" Coy 11th East Yorks left Sector of Front line. "A" Coy. 19th Manchesters will relieve "B" Company 11th East Yorkshire Regt in RICHMOND TRENCH. "C" Coy 19th Manchesters will relieve "A" Company 11th East Yorkshire Regt in reserve Regiment trench (O.B.L.)

(3). **ORDER OF MARCH.** The Battalion will move out in the following order:- "D" Coy. followed by B, A and "C" Companies; 200 yards distance between companies as far as LE TOURET (S.13 D1/5) east of this, march will be conducted with 50 yards distance between platoons.

(4). **TIMES.** Head of "D" Company will be at junction of roads (S.13 D1/5) at 7.30.pm. "B" Coy. at same point at 7.40.pm. "A" Coy ditto 7.50. "C" Coy ditto. 8.pm. where they will be met by guides provided by the East Yorks. "D" Company will move into position via ROPE trench, and QUINQUE CROSSING. "B" Coy. by O.B.L. and PIONEER ROAD. "A" Coy. by O.B.L. and PIONEER ROAD to RICHMOND TRENCH. "C" Coy. by the trolley line straight to O.B.L.

(5) **REPORTS.** On completion of relief Officers Commanding Companies will report to the Battalion Headquarters by wire that relief is complete.

(6) **RATIONS.** All ranks will carry the unexpended portion and the following days rations on the men.

(7) **HELMETS.** "B" & "D" Coys will take over all steel helmets from "A" & "C" Coys; the latter companies should hand in at once their steel helmets to the Q.M. who will re-issue them to "B" & "D"Coys.

(8) **DISTRIBUTION OF OFFICERS.** During this tour in the trenches 2nd.Lt. Wrigner will be attached to "B" Coy and 2nd.Lieut. Riscik to "D" Coy.

(9) **SILENCE.** The necessity of carrying out reliefs as silently as possible must be impressed on all ranks.

No.1. File.   No.2. C.O.
    3. 2nd.in-command.
    4. Adjutant.
    5. O.C. "A" Coy.
    6. O.C. "B" Coy.
    7. O.C. "C" Coy.
    8. O.C. "D" Coy.
    9. M.O.   10. T.O.
   11. Q.M.   12. L.G.O.
   13. War Diary.

W. Brunton
Adjutant,   Lieut.
19th Manchester Regt.

September 8th. 1916.   OPERATION ORDER.   NO. 28.
                    By LIEUT. COL. H.B.O. WILLIAMS,
(SECRET). No.13.   Commanding 18th Battalion,
                        MANCHESTER REGIMENT.   APPENDIX.S.2.

(1) The 18th Battalion Manchester Regiment will be relieved on the Left
    Sub-Sector on the night of 8/9th September 1916, by the 2nd. Battn.
    Royal Scots Fusiliers.
    One Company of the 18th. Battalion, Manchester Regiment will remain
    attached to the 2nd. Battalion Royal Scots Fusiliers.

(2) ORDER OF RELIEF.

    (a) "A" Coy. 2nd.R.S.F. Relieve "D" Coy.18th.M/Cs. LEFT Coy of SubSector
    (b) "B" Coy.   "   "   "B" "   "   RIGHT "   "   "
    (c) "C" Coy.   "   "   "A" "   "   Support Line.
                                                      (RICHMOND TRENCH).
    (d) "D" Coy.   "   OCCUPY COVER TRENCH - FRONT LINE.

    Reference (a) 4 Guides D. Coy 18th.Manchesters will meet A.Coy.2nd.
                  R.S.Fs. at 8.15pm at 18th. Manchesters B.H.Q. and
                  proceed via ROPE TRENCH.

    Reference (b) 4 Guides B. Coy 18th.Manchesters will meet B.Coy.2nd.
                  R.S.Fs. at junction of O.B.L. & PIONEER TRENCH at 8.15pm
                  and proceed via PIONEER TRENCH.

    Reference (c) 4 Guides A. Coy 18th.Manchesters will meet C.Coy.2nd.
                  R.S.Fs. at junction of O.B.L. & PIONEER TRENCH at 8.15pm
                  and proceed via PIONEER TRENCH.

    Reference (d) Nil.

(3) Officer Commanding "B" Company will arrange that all N.C.Os and men
    of "A" Company, who are now doing duty with "B" Company, return to
    their Company by 4.pm to-day.

(4) With reference to Order No.1; "A" Company on being relieved will
    move down to the old British Line, and be in reserve to the 2nd.
    Battalion Royal Scots Fusiliers. The Company Commander will send
    down Guides to take over from "C" not later than 4.pm to-day.

(5) The Battalion on being relieved will go into Brigade Reserve at
    LE TOURET, taking over positions at present occupied by the 17th.
    Battn. Manchester Regiment. (Map Ref. X16 B/28).

(6) B,C, and D Companies on being relieved will move independently along
    the RUE DE BOIS to LE TOURET where they will be met and conducted to
    their billets.

(7) ORDER OF MARCH. Companies will move in column of Platoons at 50
    yards distance.

1. File.   9. T.O.
2. Issued by Order. 10. M.O.   ....Lieut.
3. 2nd-in-Command.   11. Q.M.   Adjutant,
4. Adjutant.   12. L.G.O.   18th. Bn. Manchester Regt.
5. O.C. "A" Coy.   13. War Diary.
6. O.C. "B" Coy.   14. O.C. 2nd. Bn. R.S.Fs.
7. O.C. "C" Coy.
8. O.C. "D" Coy.

NOTE:- Officers Commanding Companies will render a marching-out
       Parade State to the Orderly Room by 5.0.pm this evening.

Sept. 12th/16.

OPERATION ORDER NO. 23.
BY LIEUT. COL. H.B.O. WILLIAMS.
Commanding 18th (S) Battalion.,
MANCHESTER REGIMENT.

Copy No......

APPENDIX.S.3

SECRET.

Reference:- BETHUNE.
Combined Sheet 1/40000.

(1) **RELIEF.** The 20th. Battalion King's L'pool Regiment will relieve the 18th. Battalion Manchester Regt. in Brigade Reserve tomorrow the 13th instant. The latter will march to billets at HINGETTE.

(2) **ASSEMBLY.** Companies will fall in outside their Billets at 4.pm.

(3) **ORDER OF MARCH.** "B", "C" and "D" Companies; a distance of 20 yards will be maintained between Companies.

(4) **STARTING POINT.** On receipt of the order to move the head of the column will proceed to the starting point, Cross Roads (X.16.d.o/9). "A" Company on being relieved in the trenches will march independently to HINGETTE. A Guide will meet them at King's Cross Dump together with two Limber G.S. Wagons at 8.pm.

(5) **ROUTE.** RUE DE BOIS to CROSS ROADS (X.20.B.8/2). thence to Bridge over CANAL DE LA LAWE; thence to CROSS ROADS (W.13.A.o/8); thence Cross Roads (W.17.b.o/o); thence HINGETTE.

(6) **TRANSPORT.** The Transport will move independently under the orders of the Transport Officer.

(7) **LEWIS GUNNERS.** The Lewis Gunners will move with the Transport. The Transport Officer will notify the Lewis Gun Officer time at which he has to move off.

(sd) Miles Brunton. Lieut.
Adjutant,
18th. Bn. Manchester Regiment

Copy 1 C.O.
2 2nd in Command.
3 Adjutant,
4 File.
5 "C" Coy.
6 "D" Coy.
7 "A" Coy.
8 "B" Coy.
9 Q.M.
10 M.O.
11 T.O.
12 L.G.O.
13 War Diary
14 20th. Kings L'pools.

September 14th/16.　　　OPERATION ORDER NO. 34.　　　Copy No. 4.
By Lieut. Col. H.S.C. GILLAM.
16th (S) Battn. Manchester Regt.

APPENDIX. S.4.

Reference BETHUNE - Combined Sheet 1/40000.

(1) RELIEF. The 16th. Bn. Manchester Regiment will move to LE TOURET today, 14th inst. and relieve the 2nd. Royal Scots Fusiliers in the LEFT FESTUBERT Sub-sector, on the night of the 14/15th Sept.

(2) STARTING POINT. The Footbridge over Canal (W.17 Central).

(3) ASSEMBLY. The Battalion will assemble in Column of route, head of Column to be at Starting point at 2.0.pm.

(4) ORDER OF MARCH. "D", "B", and "C" Coys. proceed by the Canal, to LE TOURET: to the trenches D "C" and "B" Companies with a distance of 200 yards between Companies as far as the Cross Roads RUE DU BOIS and RUE DE L'EPINETTE, after which march will be by platoons with 50 yards distance between platoons.

(5) DISPOSITION IN TRENCHES.　　　Front Line (Left) "D" Company.
　　　　　　　　　　　　　　　　　Front Line (Right) "C" Company.
　　　　　　　　　　　　　　　　　Support　　　　　　 "B" Company.
　　　　　　　　　　　　　　　　　Reserve (O.B.L.)　 "A" Company.

"A" Coy. 16th. Manchesters, at present attached to the 2nd. R. Scots Fusiliers will remain in the trenches.

(6) GUIDES. Guides from 2nd. R. Scots Fusiliers will meet the 16th Manchesters at 6.30.pm. at the Cross Roads RUE DU BOIS and RUE DE L'EPINETTE.

(7) MACHINE GUNS AND SIGNALLERS. The Lewis Gunners under 2nd. Lt. Roberts and the Signallers under 2nd. Lieut. Charles will move from HINGETTE at 12.nn. and proceed to Cross Roads RUE DU BOIS and RUE de L'EPINETTE, where Guides from 2nd. R. Scots Fusiliers will meet them and guide them to their posts.

(8) TRANSPORT. Will move under orders of the Transport Officer to LE TOURET where baggage will be dumped out.

(9) REPORT. On completion of relief to be reported to Orderly Room by wire, Code words meaning RELIEF COMPLETE "YES, PLEASE."

　　　　　　　　　　　　　　　　　　　　Miles Brinton
　　　　　　　　　　　　　　　　　　　　.........Lieut.
　　　　　　　　　　　　　　　　　　　　Adjutant,
　　　　　　　　　　　　　　　　　　　　16th. Bn. Manchester Regiment.

1　CO.　✓
2　2nd i/c.　✓
3　Adjutant.
4　Adm.　✓
5　A Coy.　✓
6　B Coy.　✓
7　C Coy.　✓
8　D Coy.　✓
9　T.O.
10　M.O.　✓
11　L.G.O.　✓
12　I.M.　✓
13　War Diary.
14　O.C. R.S.Fs.
15　　　✓

16th September 1916.   OPERATION ORDER NO.25.   Copy No. 12

By Lieut.Col. H.B.O. WILLIAMS,
Commdg. 18th (S) Battalion.,
SECRET.   MANCHESTER REGT. APPENDIX 55

1. The 12th. Bn. Yorks & Lancs, plus 1 Company 13th. Yorks & Lancs. will relieve the 18th Bn. Manchester Regiment in the LEFT FESTUBERT Section commencing 6.pm on the 16th instant.

2. ORDER OF RELIEF. The Signallers, Snipers and Observers of the 12th. Y.&L. will relieve those of the 18th Manchesters during the day. Guides for these to be at KINGS CROSS at 4.pm., under the arrangements of the Specialist Officers concerned. The Lewis Gun Teams will be relieved with the Battalion, less two men per team.
"C" Coy 12th Yorks and Lancs relieves "C" Coy: 18th M/G Right Front Line
"D" Coy   do.   do.   do.   do. "D" Coy: do.   Left Front Line.
"A" Coy   do.   do.   do.   do. "B" Coy: do. RICHMOND TRENCH.
"B" Coy 13th do.   do.   do.   do. "A" Coy: do. O.B.L.

3. GUIDES. will be provided as follows:-
    "D" Coy: 3 Guides - one for each island.
             2 do.   for Cover trench.
    "C" Coy: 3 do. - one for each island.
             2 do.   for cover trench.
    "B" Coy: 4 do. - one per platoon.
    "A" Coy: 4 do. - one per platoon.
    Headquarters:-   - one guide for Bn. H.Qs.
Guides to report to Orderly Room at 6.0.pm, and will then proceed to meet the incoming Battalion at KINGS CROSS at 7.pm. Guides conducting to COVER TRENCH and RICHMOND TRENCH should be able to point the out the Company Headquarters.

4. LEWIS GUNNERS. The Lewis Gun Officer will arrange to leave two men per Gun with the teams of the 12th Y.&.L. until daybreak of the 17th when they will rejoin the Battalion.

5. RENDEZVOUS. On completion of relief Companies will march independently to LE TOURET to the Cross Roads, (K.16.d.o.8.) at a distance of 50x between platoons, where they will prove their Companies. When this is done Companies will move off to Billets at HINGETTE conducted by Guides (provided by the Quartermaster) who will lead each company by the shortest route to the same billets as previously occupied. 50x distance at least will be maintained between companies.

6. COMPLETION OF RELIEF. To be reported by wire to Bn. Headquarters. Code words meaning "Relief Completed" - "SALT OF THE EARTH". Company Commanders should have this wire already written out, as failure to report completion of relief involves considerable delay.

7. TRANSPORT. The Quartermaster will arrange for the Motor Lorry and M.Gs Maltese Cart to be at KINGS CROSS Dump by 9.30.pm. All stores, Mess boxes and Company Baggage, Camp Kettles, Telephone Stores &c., must be put on the Motor Lorry. Companies will arrange that two men per Company, accompany the lorry and see that the baggage is unloaded at each Company Headquarters. 1 L.G.S. Wagon will meet Companies at LE TOURET. O.C. "A" & "B" Coys: will ensure that all bombs in possession are loaded on this wagon. No other transport will be provided.

8. BILLETS. Company Q.M.Ss. under the Quartermaster, will make all arrangements for billets.

.................Lieut.&.Adjt.
18th (S) Bn. Manchester Regiment.

1. C.O.   2. 2nd.i/c.
3. Adjutant.   4. File.
5. A.Coy.   6. B. Coy.
7. C. Coy.   8. D. Coy.
9. M.O.   10. T.O.
11. L.G.O.   12. Q.M.
13. War Diary.
14. C.O. 12th Y.&.L.

Sept. 17th. 1916.　　　　OPERATION ORDER NO.25.

By Lieut. Col. H.B.O. WILLIAMS.
Commanding 18th (S) Battalion,
MANCHESTER REGIMENT.

Reference BETHUNE Combined Sheet 1/40,000.

APPENDIX. S.6.

(1) The Battalion will move to new billets at BELLERIVE (V.12.Centre) on the afternoon of the 17th instant.

(2) ORDER OF MARCH. Band, "C" "D" "B" "A" Coys., and the transport.

(3) STARTING POINT. Cross roads just South East of HINGES (W.15.b.7.9).

(4) The head of the column to be at starting point 3.15.pm. 50^x distance to be maintained between companies.

(5) TRANSPORT. The transport will march in the rear of the Battalion.

(6) KITS. Company Commanders will be held strictly responsible that nothing but the authorised kits are carried.

(7) Please acknowledge.

　　　　　　　　　　　　　　　　　　　　　　　　Lieut. & Adjt
　　　　　　　　　　　　　　　　　　18th (S) Batn. Manchester Regt.

1. C.O.
2. 2nd in command.
3. Adjutant.
4. File.
5. A. Coy.
6. B. Coy.
7. C. Coy.
8. D. Coy.
9. M.O.
10. T.O.
11. L.G.O.
12. Q.M.
13. War Diary.
14. ....

ENTRAINING STATE.

18th (Service) Battalion, Manchester Regiment.

Adjutant

APPENDIX. S.7

1. Officers.............................	23.
2. Other Ranks........................	490.
3. Horses & Mules.....................	68
4. Vehicles:-	
G.S. 4 wheeled limbered,......	18
2 wheeled	12.
(Including L/G carts, 0	

Sept.1916.

..................Lieut.Col.
Commanding 18th Battn.Manchr.Regt.

18th. September 1916.   OPERATION ORDER NO.26.   Copy No...13.
By Lieut. Col. H.S.O. WILLIAMS.
Commanding 19th (S) Battalion,
MANCHESTER REGIMENT.

 File

(1) The 19th. Bn. Manchester Regiment will entrain at CHOCQUES Station at 2.02 am on the 19th instant. (Train No.14).

(2) STARTING POINT.   Cross Roads (W.13.a.7.3.)

(3) ORDER OF MARCH.   A.B.D.&.C. Companies preceded by the Band. Head of column to be at starting point at 12. midnight tonight. 20 yards distance to be maintained between companies.

(4) TRANSPORT.   Transport and horses under the Transport Officer; Lewis Guns and carts under the Lewis Gun Officer will move to CHOCQUES Station starting at 10.0.pm.

(5) LOADING PARTY.   Officers Commanding Companies will detail 1 Sergeant and 24 men to parade at 10.0.pm outside Headquarters Mess and report to the Battalion Sergeant Major; Lieut. H. Peters will be in command; 2nd. Lieut. C.J. Honewood will also accompany this party. On arrival at the Station the Officer Commanding Party will report to Lieut. Beaumont and hand over Entraining States. 2nd. Lieut. Honewood will also report to Lieut. Beaumont at 12.30.am for the purpose of taking over train accommodation for the Companies.

(6) DISCIPLINE.   Water Bottles to be filled before starting; On no account will men be allowed to take water from the tanks or pumps on the railway. On no account will men be allowed to climb on the tops of carriages.

(7) ORDERLY OFFICER.   2nd. Lieut. D. A. Westphal.

(8) TRAIN GUARD.   A Guard consisting of 1 Sergeant and 4 other ranks will be detailed by Officer Commanding "C" Company to prevent men leaving the train when halted. This Guard will report to the Orderly Officer who will march in rear of the Battalion.

(9) Please acknowledge receipt in writing.

Issued by Order at...... 4.0/m ......

.... Major.
for Lieut Col.
Commanding 19th(S) Battalion,
MANCHESTER REGIMENT.

1. C.O.
2. 2nd. in command.
3. Adjutant.
4. File.
5. A.Coy.
6. B. Coy.
7. C. Coy.
8. D. Coy.
9. O.M.
10. T.O.
11. M.O.
12. L.G.O.
13. War Diary.
14. 2nd. Lt. Westphal.
15. 2nd. Lieut. Honewood.
16. Lieut. Peters.

Sept. 20th, 1916.
(SECRET.)

OPERATION ORDER NO 27.
By Lieut. Col. H.B.G. WILLIAMS.
Commanding 18th Service Battn.
M A N C H E S T E R   R E G T.

Ref: LENS 1L. 1/100,000.   AMIENS. 1L. 1/80,000.

APPENDIX. S.8.

(1) The 18th. Bn. Manchester Regiment will march to billets at FLEURELLES on the 21.9.16. The Battn. will be in position opposite the Orderly Room facing South ready to move off to the Brigade Starting Point at 7.15.am.

(2) STARTING POINT. The Brigade Starting point is the Cross Roads half-mile N.S.E. of the "L" in BRUAYAL on the main BRUAYAL - AMIEN Road.

(3) ROUTE. BRUAYAL-TAISNAS-VILLERS BOCAGE. Units will turn westwards along the VIR ELLES Road half mile E. of VILLERS BOCAGE.
(Point 132 on AMIENS SHEET 1L.)

(4) ORDER OF MARCH. "A" "B" "C" and "D" Companies. Transport will march in rear of the Battalion.

(5) MARCH RULES. (a) A distance of 50x will be maintained between Units of the Brigade.
(b) There will be a 10 minutes halt after each hour's march commencing at 9.0.am.
(c) Units will march to attention for five minutes before and after the march.

(6) BILLETING PARTY. A Billeting party consisting of Lieut. Knowles, the Interpreter and the four Quartermaster Sergeants will report to the Town Major's Office FLEURELLES at 8.30.am on 21.9.16. This party will parade outside the Orderly Room at 7.0.am.

(7) TRANSPORT. All officers kits, Mess Boxes &c., will be dumped outside the Quartermaster's Stores at 6.0.am. One Ambulance Wagon will follow the Transport of each Battalion.

Issued by Orderly at.............
1. C.O.
2. 2nd.i/c.
3. Adjutant.
4. File.
5. O.C. A. Coy.
6. B. Coy.
7. C. Coy.
8. D. Coy.
9. M.O.
10. T.O.
11. Q.M.
12. L.G.O.
13. War Diary.
14.............................

........................Captain.
Acting Adjutant,
18th. Bn. Manchester Regiment.

Vol 12

90/30

<u>Confidential</u>

<u>War Diary</u>
of
<u>18th (Service) Battalion</u>
<u>The Manchester Regiment</u>

from
<u>October 1st. 1916</u>
to
<u>October 31st. 1916</u>

(Volume <u>XII</u>)

H B O Williams Lieut. Col.
Commanding 18th (S) Bn. Manch. R.

WAR DIARY
or
INTELLIGENCE SUMMARY

Army Form C. 2118

18th Service Battn Manchester Regt

Place	Date 1916	Hour	Summary of Events and Information	Remarks and references to Appendices
FLESSELLES	October 2		Training in field operations (Brigade scheme)	
	" 3		Battalion Training	
	" 4		Battalion Training. Transport left today for TALMAS-SUR-ANCRE. Transport moved by motor-omnibuses (provided by French Army) to BUIRE	X 1
BUIRE	" 5		Battalion joined today. Training of infection	
	" 6		March to FRICOURT CAMP (3½ mile N. of KING GEORGES HILL Just as last Coy. was entering Camp in darkness someone trod upon a bomb which was lying in the funnels and it exploded killing one man and wounding MAJOR R. GODLEE (Second-in-command) 2nd Lt H.C. CRICHTON, and 9 O.R.	X 2
FRICOURT CAMP	" 7		2nd Lt H.C. CRICHTON died of wounds. All officers & men attended his funeral at Divisional cemetery, BECORDEL. Battalion Training. Church services. Captain (Temporary Major) C.E. LEMBCKE, of Northumberland Fusiliers, attached from today as Second-in-command	
	" 8		Battalion Training	
	" 9		Battalion Training. 2nd Lt F.G. TRIMMER transferred to ammunS B Coy vice 2nd Lt EVANS.	
Trenches	" 10		March to MARLBOROUGH WOOD for rest until dusk and then on to support trenches in front of LIGNY THILLOY	X 3

Army Form C. 2118

WAR DIARY
or
INTELLIGENCE SUMMARY
(Erase heading not required.)

18th Service Battn. Manchester Regt.

Sheet 31.

Place	Date 1916	Hour	Summary of Events and Information	Remarks and references to Appendices
Trenches	Oct 10		LIGNY and LE BARQUE to relieve the 41st Division. Moves from support trench GROVE ALLEY to FACTORY TRENCH batln H.Q. being in Sugar factory in road from FLERS to LE BARQUE (Factory Corner). Captain F.J. EARLES wounded.	
	11			
	12		Battalion attacked enemy trenches S of LIGNY THILLOY and afterwards withdrew to our own front line. A full report of the operation is in Appendix X 4 attached. Casualties: CAPT W PENN GASKELL, LT H PETERS, 2nd LT TAYLOR killed; 2nd LT F.G. TRIMMER wounded and missing; 2nd LT S.J. BROWN, 2nd LT RUMNEY, 2nd LT H EVANS, wounded and 250 O.R. killed wounded and missing	X 4
	13			
	14			
	15			
	16		On the night of the 16th instant the batalion was relieved by the 21st Brigade and marched back to MARLBOROUGH WOOD in bivouac.	X 5
	17			
			Bivouac. Working parties on roads to LONGUEVAL	

Army Form C. 2118

Sheet 37

WAR DIARY
or
INTELLIGENCE SUMMARY

18th Service Batt'n Manchester Reg't

Place	Date 1916	Hour	Summary of Events and Information	Remarks and references to Appendices
MARLBOROUGH WOOD	Oct 20		Bivouac. Draft of 80 O.R. joined today	X 6
	21		—do—	
	22		March to billets in RIBEMONT	
RIBEMONT	23		Training. 2nd Lt H. SEDGWICK Jones for duty from 17th West Yorkshire Regiment & assumed command of "A" Coy (vice 2nd Lt WESTPHAL)	
	24		Training. Transport left by road; draft of 104 O.R. joined from the Battalion entrained at 3.0 P.M. at MERICOURT-RIBEMONT and travelled to DOULLENS, arriving at 7.0 A.M. on the 26th October	
	25			
	26		Rested from hours in DOULLENS and marched via LUCHEUX to SUS-ST-LEGER. Lt J. F. NARING, 2nd Lt W. FOGDEN, and 2nd Lt C. T. LOFTHOUSE joined for duty from base and were posted to "B" Coy & Draft fortnight	
SUS-ST-LEGER	27		Training	
	28		Training. 2nd Lt L. F. ELLIOT, 2nd Lt G. G. MILLER and 2nd Lt W. H. B. BURKITT joined from base for duty and were posted to "A", "B" and "C" Coys respectively. 2nd Lt J. E. M. TAYLOR joined from leave for duty and was posted to "D" Coy. "D" Coy left today for BAILLEUVAL, marching via SOMBRIN and GOUY	
	29			

Army Form C. 2118

Sheet 33

WAR DIARY
or
INTELLIGENCE SUMMARY

(Erase heading not required.) 18th (Service) Battn Manchester Regt

Place	Date	Hour	Summary of Events and Information	Remarks and references to Appendices
BELLACOURT	1916	6.30	Battalion (less "D" Coy) marches from SUS-ST-LEGER via WARLUZEL, SAULTY, LABRETT, BAILEUVAL to BELLACOURT relieving 7th NOTTS and DERBY Regt in Support to 90th Brigade, which is now holding the sector opposite BLAIREVILLE and RANSART. "D" Coy moves from hills at BAILLEUVAL to strong points early BELLACOURT and BRETTANCOURT. In support at BELLACOURT	
"	"31			

McMicham
Lt Col
Commanding 18th Manchr Regt

To: C.O.   **XI**   3.10.16.

Battalion Operation Order. X.B

I. The Battalion will proceed to billets in BUIRE tomorrow.

II. The Battalion will fall in in the RUE DE CHATEAU, facing west ready to march off at 9.20 a.m. Head of column to be opposite the CHATEAU Gate.

III Order of Companies; A.B.C.+D.

IV Men must be told off in parties of 26, with one Sergeant or Senior Corporal in each party inclusive. Companies must arrange between themselves to complete these parties up to 26. No party ~~[struck through]~~ below this number must be put into an omnibus.

3/10/16

T.J. Kelly Captain
Adjutant
18th Dm. Inchrs. Regt.

6th. October 1916. OPERATION ORDER NO. 18.   Copy No. 3
           By Lieut.Col. H.B.O. Williams,
SECRET.   Comndg. 18th. (S) Battalion,   X 2
           MANCHESTER REGIMENT.

Reference Sheet 62D N.E. 1/20,000.

1. The Battalion will march this afternoon to FRICOURT CAMP (F.8.c.)

2. ROUTE. DERNACOURT - VIVIER MILL - MEAULTE - CARCAILLOT FARM - B.M.68.21.

3. The Battalion will parade at 4.45pm ready to march off at 5.0.pm.

4. ORDER OF MARCH. A. B. C. & D. Coys: and the transport.

5. STARTING POINT. The leading Company will be at the Starting point, (D.30.a.8.5.). An interval of 100 yards will be maintained between companies and between "D" Coy and the transport. Distance of 200 yards between Units.

6. BAGGAGE. All Officer's kits, Company Boxes &c., must be at the Quartermaster's Stores at 3.0.pm.

Issued by Orderly at...1/45p...   (Sd) T.J. Kelly. Captain.
                                            Actg/Adjutant,
1. C.O.   18th. Bn. Manchester Regt.
2. 2nd.in command.
3. Adjutant.
4. File.
5. O.C. "A" Coy. 6. O.C. "B" Coy.
7. O.C. "C" Coy. 8. O.C. "D" Coy.
9. Q.M.   10. M.O.
11 L.G.O.   12. T.O.
13. War Diary.

War Diary October 1916
Appendix
X 2

6th. October 1916. OPERATION ORDER NO. 28. Copy No. 4
                    By Lieut.Col. H.B.G. WILKINS,
SECRET.   Commdg. 18th. (S) Battalion.,
                    MANCHESTER REGIMENT.

Reference Sheet 62D N.E. 1/20,000.

1. The Battalion will march this afternoon to POICOURT CAMP (F.S.c.)

2. ROUTE.   DERNCOURT - VIVIER MILL - MEAULTE - CARCAILLOT FARM -
            0.B.M.68.81.

3. The Battalion will parade at 4.45pm ready to march off at 5.0.pm.

4. ORDER OF MARCH. A. B. C. & D. Coys: and the transport.

5. STARTING POINT. The leading company will be at the starting point.
   (D.30.a.5.5.). An interval of 100 yards will be maintained between
   companies and between "D" Coy and the transport. Distance of 200
   yards between Units.

6. BAGGAGE. All officer's kits, Company Boxes &c., must be at the
   Quartermaster's Stores at 3.0.pm.

Issued by Orderly at ...1.45.p.m...   (sd) T.J. Kelly. Captain.
                                             Actg/Adjutant,
1. C.O.   18th. Bn. Manchester Regt.
2. 2nd. in command.
3. Adjutant.
4. File.
5. O.C. "A" Coy. 6. O.C. "B" Coy.
7. O.C. "C" Coy. 8. O.C. "D" Coy.
9. Q.M.   10. M.O.
11. L.G.O.   12. T.O.
13. War Diary.

SECRET.   OPERATION ORDER No. 28.   Copy No.....14..
           By LIEUT.COLONEL. H.B.O.WILLIAMS.,
              Commanding 18th Service Battalion,
                   MANCHESTER REGIMENT.

MONDAY. 9th October. 1916.

Reference Map Sheet 57.c. S.W. and 62d.N.E.

1. The battalion will march to-morrow to support trenches in 90th. Brigade Area, A.& B. will be in immediate support and C & D behind them in second support trench. Battalion Headquarters is situated at M.30b.5/5.

2. The battalion will ~~follow~~ *"fall in"* in mass on the ground in front of the Orderly Room, ready to march off at 7.30am, and will march via MAMETZ and thence by the first available track running off N.side of road through S.26. and CATERPILLAR WOOD to the rendezvous at S.21.b.

3. Order of March:- A,B,C & D Companies.

4. Battalion will march in full marching order and at the rendezvous the men going into the line will change to battle order, as detailed in Battalion Orders No.283.para 1. dated 7th.October.1916. Every man who goes into the line will, however, carry his greatcoat in the pack and must also have a jerkin.

5. TRANSPORT.- Lewis Gun Carts, tool carts, water carts, officers' mess cart and cookers will move with battalion; the rest of the transport will be brigaded under Lieut Knowles 16th.Bn.Manchester Regt. Brigade transport will pass starting point Cross Roads F.9a.Central at 8.30am.

6. LEWIS GUNS.- Two spare lewis guns will be carried in the limber provided for them.

7. Rations for 11th instant will be carried.

8. Officers' valises and all baggage will be outside Quartermaster's Stores at 7.0am, and all baggage for officers' mess cart must be loaded at 7.0am.

9. SPECIALISTS.- The battalion will go into action with 400 rifles. Ten per cent of all Specialists (Lewis Gunners, bombers, signallers, snipers and scouts) and N.C.O.s will be left behind at the rendezvous and only three officers per Company will be taken.

10. A reconnoitring party consisting of 2nd.Lieut RISSIK, one Sergeant per company and Lance-Cpl.Snelson will parade at Orderly Room at 7.0.am. in full battle order with greatcoats, carrying rations for 10th. & 11th. inst., and proceed to F.8.a.4/0. to catch motor Komnibus for cross roads S.17.a.4/2.

Reveille 5.30am. Breakfast. 6.0 Am.

Issued to Orderly at.......pm.   ....CAPTAIN,
1. Commanding Officer.   Acting-Adjutant,
2. 2nd.in.Command.   18th.Bn.MANCHESTER REGIMENT.
3. Adjutant.
4. A.Coy.
5. B.Coy.
6. C.Coy.
7. D.Coy.
8. Transport Officer.
9. Quartermaster.
10. Medical Officer.
11. Lewis Gun Officer.
12. 2nd.Lieut.Rissik.
13. File.
14. War Diary.

To O.C all Coys.
        A ¾
        B O⁄o
        C ~~C/H~~
        D ¾

With reference to Operation Orders No 28 just issued please note that the starting point will **not** be D 30 a 8/5 as advised. Instead the battalion will form up in fours in the lane opposite H.Q mess in the following order B Band A, B, C & D Coys & to ready to march off at 4.45 P.M.

H. Weir Capt
a/ Adjutant

SECRET.   OPERATION ORDER No.28.   Copy No. 7
           By LIEUT.COLONEL.H.B.O.WILLIAMS.,
              Commanding.18th.Service Battalion,
                 MANCHESTER REGIMENT.

MONDAY.9th.October.1916.

Reference.-Map Sheet 57.c.S.W. and 62.d.N.E.

1. The battalion will march to-morrow to support trenches in 90th.Brigade Area. A & B. will be in immediate support and C & D behind them in second support trench. Battalion Headquarters is situated at M.30b.5/5.

2. The battalion will "fall in" in mass on the ground in front of the Orderly Room, ready to march off at 7.30am. and will march via MAMETZ and thence by the first available track running off N.side of road through S.26. and CATERPILLAR WOOD to the rendezvous at S.21.b.

3. Order of March:- A,B,C & D Companies.

4. Battalion will march in full marching order and at the rendezvous the men going into the line will change to battle order, as detailed in Battalion Orders No.283. para 1. dated 7th.October.1916. Every man who goes into the line will, however, carry his greatcoat in the pack and must also have a jerkin.

5. TRANSPORT- Lewis Guns Carts, tool carts, water carts, officers' mess cart and cookers will move with battalion; the rest of the transport will be brigaded under LIEUT. KNOWLES.16th.Bn.Manchester Rgt. Brigade Transport will pass starting point Cross Roads F.9.a.Central at 8.30am.

6. LEWIS GUNS.-Two spare Lewis Guns will be carried in the limber provided for them.

7. Rations for 11th instant will be carried.

8. Officers' valises and all baggage will be outside Quartermaster's Stores at 7.0am. and all baggage for officers' mess cart must be loaded at 7.0am.

9. SPECIALISTS.-The battalion will go into action with 400 rifles. Ten per cent of all Specialists (Lewis Gunners,bombers,signallers,snipers and scouts) and N.C.O.s will be left behind at the rendezvous and only three officers per Company will be taken.

10. A reconnoitring party consisting of 2nd.LIEUT.RISSIK, one Sergeant per Company and Lance-Cpl.Shelson will parade at Orderly Room at 7.0am. in full battle order with greatcoats, carrying rations for 10th. & 11th. inst., and proceed to F.8.a.4/0. to catch motor omnibus for cross roads S.17.a.4/2.

11. Reveille 5.30.am. Breakfast 6.0am.

Issued to Orderly at.11.30...pm.   (Sd).T.J.Kelly. CAPTAIN,
                                              Acting-Adjutant,
                                          18th.Bn.Manchester Regiment.

1. Commanding Officer.
2. second-in-command.
3. Adjutant.
4. O.C.A.Coy.
5. O.C.B.Coy.
6. O.C.C.Coy.
7. O.C.D.Coy.
8. Transport Officer.
9. Quartermaster.
10. Medical Officer.
11. Lewis Gun Officer.
12. 2nd.LIEUT RISSIK.
13. File.
14. War Diary.

SECRET.   OPERATION ORDER No.28.   Copy No. 13
           by LIEUT.COLONEL. H.B.O.WILLIAMS..
           Commanding.18th.Service Battalion,
           MANCHESTER REGIMENT.

MONDAY.9th.October.1916.

Reference Map Sheet 57.C. S.W. and 62d.N.W.

1. The battalion will march to-morrow to support trenches in 90th.Brigade
   Area. A.& B. will be in immediate support and C & D behind them in
   second support trench. Battalion Headquarters is situated at K.30b.5/5.

2. The battalion will fall in in mass on the ground in front of the orderly
   Room, ready to march off at 7.30am. and will march via MONTEL and
   thence by the first available track running off N.side of road through
   S.26. and CATERPILLAR TOTO to the rendezvous at S.21.b.

3. Order of March:- A,B,C & D Companies.

4. Battalion will march in full marching order and at the rendezvous the
   men going into the line will change to battle order,as detailed in
   Battalion Orders No.283.para 1. dated 7th.October.1916. Every man
   who goes into the line will,however,carry his greatcoat in the pack
   and must also have a Jerkin.

5. TRANSPORT.- Lewis Gun Carts, tool carts,water carts,officers' mess cart
   and cookers will move with battalion; the rest of the transport will be
   brigaded under Lieut Knowles 16th.Bn.Manchester Regt. Brigade transport
   will pass starting point Cross Roads F.9a.Central at 8.30am.

6. LEWIS GUNS.- Two spare lewis guns will be carried in the limber
   provided for them.

7. Rations for 11th instant will be carried.

8. Officers' valises and all baggage will be outside Quartermaster's store
   at 7.0am. and all baggage for officers' mess cart must be loaded at
   7.0am.

9. SPECIALISTS.- The battalion will go into action with 400 rifles. Ten
   per cent of all specialists (Lewis Gunners,bombers,signallers,snipers
   and scouts) and N.C.O.s will be left behind at the rendezvous and
   only three officers per company will be taken.

10. A reconnoitring party consisting of 2nd.Lieut RIDDIK, one Sergeant per
    company and Lance-Cpl.Jackson will parade at Orderly Room at 7.0.am.
    in full battle order with greatcoats, carrying rations for 10th. & 11th
    inst., and proceed to F.8.c.4/9. to catch motor Omnibus for cross roads
    L.19.c.4/5.

11. Reveille 5.30am. Breakfast. 6.0am.

                                                    ....CAPTAIN,
Issued to Orderly at 11.30..pm.   Acting Adjutant,
1. Commanding Officer.   18th.Bn.MANCHESTER REGIMENT.
2. 2nd.in.Command.
3. Adjutant.
4. A.Coy.
5. B.Coy.
6. C.Coy.
7. D.Coy.
8. Transport Officer.
9. Quartermaster.
10. Medical Officer.
11. Lewis Gun Officer.
12. 2nd. Lieut.Hissik.
13. File.
14. War Diary.

P.O.5. Operation Orders.

Reference Map Sheet 57c SW
" 62D N.E.

The battalion will march tomorrow to support trenches in 90th Brigade area. A & B will be in immediate support. C & D remain in reserve support trench. believed of Batt HQ is situated at M30b 5/5

P06.

2) The Battn will fall in
mass on the ground in front
of the Orderly room
ready to march off
at 7.30 A.M. will march
via Maznetz & thence
by the first available track
running off N side of
road through S26 and
CATERPILLAR WOOD to the
rendezvous at S21 b.

POV

3. Order of march A, B, C & D
Coys.

4. Battalion will march in
full marching order &
at the rendezvous the
men going into the line
will ~~make~~ change to
battle order as detailed
in B.R.O. — — dated — —
Every man who goes into
the line will however
carry his greatcoat in the
valise & must also have a further

5. **Transport.** Lewis Gun Carts, Tool Carts, ~~Ammunition Carts~~ water Carts, & Cookers will move with Batt^n; the rest of the transport will be brigaded under Lt KNOWLES 16th Manchester Regt. Brigade transport will pass Starting point ~~at 8.30~~ Cross Roads F9a Central at 8.30 A.M.

6. **Lewis Guns.** Two spare Lewis guns will be carried in the limber provided for them.

7. **Rations** for 11th instant will be carried.

8. Officers valises & all baggage will be sent to 2nd line dump at 6 A.M.

Po.9

& all baggage for Officers
mess cart must be loaded
at 7.0 A.M.

9 Specialists The battalion
will go into action with
400 rifles. Ten per cent
of all specialists (Lewis
gunners, bombers, signallers,
snipers & scouts) & N.C.Os
will be left behind at
the rendezvous. Only
three Officers per Coy will
be taken.

P.O.10.

10. A reconnoitring party consisting of 2nd Lt RISSIK, one Sergt per Coy, & L Corpl SNELSON will parade at Orderly Room at 7.0 AM in full battle order with greatcoats & rations for 10th & 11th & proceed to F8a 4/0 to catch motor bus for Crossroads S17a 4/2

War Diary
October 1916
———
X 3

*Operation
October 12-16
1916.*

after
Operation Orders.

1. "D" Coy less Lewis gunners will report to the O.C. 2nd R.S.F. at 6.0 A.M. on the 12th instant and will form the fourth wave of that unit.

2. One Lewis gun platoon of "C" Coy will report to the O.C. 2nd R.S.F. at 6.0 A.M. and one Lewis gun platoon of "C" will report to the O.C. 17th Manchester Regt at 6.0 A.M. attaching the [illegible] Lewis gun platoon [illegible]

3. "A" & "B" & "C" Coys less two platoons and all Lewis Gunners will start at zero and push on so as to follow the assaulting lines at a distance of not less than

200 yards, holding themselves
in readiness to reinforce
as required. On reaching the final
objective the battalion will assist in

4/ All LEWIS Gunners and other
REDOUBTS will consolidate
and hold the present
front line now held by
the present C.O. see [illegible]
Manchester regt

5/ Battalion H.Q. will be
first part [illegible]
[illegible] [illegible] afterwards
moving forward.

6/ An advanced signalling
station will be found
at the present front
line which arranges
the initial stage of
the operations must be

Lieut. 2nd Lt ROBERTS
will be responsible for
transmitting these
messages to Batt.
H.Q

7. Should overcrowding
occur at the first
objective Officers commanding
Coys will put their
men into shell
holes South of the
objective.

Shell Capt.
acting adjt

12.10.16
2.30 A.M.

4) platoons in file at 50 yds distance. On reaching the present front line trench the Battalion will garrison with it by means of series of small posts & "news files", & will generally improve the whole position.

5) Batt'n H.Q. at start here (Factory corner); later in the front line trench (to be notified)

Hull Capt
acting Adjt

18.10.16

REPORT ON OPERATIONS
October 10th – 13th, 1916

1. 10.10.16 At 7.0 A.M. on the morning of
7.0 A.M.   October 10th the battalion
            left FRICOURT CAMP and
            marched via MAMETZ and
            MONTAUBAN to MARLBOROUGH
            WOOD arriving 11.0 A.M.
2. 4.45 P.M. The battalion moved off
            by platoons marching through
            LONGUEVAL to the trenches
            Owing to the congestion caused
            by units of the 41st DIVISION
            coming out and 89th BRIGADE
            going up great delay was
11.10.16   experienced and it was
2.0 A.M.   2.0 A.M. before the battalion
            arrived at GROVE ALLEY
            where they were to have
            relieved a unit of the 41st
            Division (vide Brigade Orders)
            who were not in fact
            there. We occupied these
7.0 A.M.   trenches until 7.0 A.M.,
            at which time, in accordance
            with verbal orders from
            G.O.C. Brigade, we moved

2) up to "FACTORY TRENCH, Batt͟n H.Q." being ordered to go to FACTORY CORNER. As it appeared that FACTORY TRENCH proper was too much to the West I deployed the batt͟n to cover the frontage from FACTORY CORNER to PIONEER ROAD, with orders to dig themselves in. This was done throughout the day with comparatively few casualties.

On the night of the 11th we received the following orders: "One Coy of the battalion under my command to report at dawn to O.C. 2nd R.S.F. In addition, one nettoyeur platoon to report to 2nd R.S.F. and one nettoyeur platoon to report to O.C. 17th MANCHESTER REGT at the same time.

12.10.16
2.5 PM

At zero (2.5 P.M) the battalion (less one coy and two platoons) moved from the trenches mentioned

(3) in Para 3 in small shallow columns covering approximately the two battalion frontage. They encountered a very severe barrage put up by the enemy immediately they left the trench, which in spite of severe casualties they resolutely pushed through.

5. I wish to draw special attention to bravery and determination of the company and platoon commanders who led their men through the barrage and through the heavy machine gun fire, which opened almost instantly at the zero hour. The Company Commanders of the two coys on the left ("A" 2nd Lt BROWN and B (2nd Lt TRIMMER) became casualties just before reaching the British front line, but notwithstanding this the men advanced under their platoon sergeants. On crossing the British line the machine gun fire became much more intense

4). and more heavy casualties ensued. A number of men of "A" and "B" Coys moved quickly forward and attached themselves to the 17th MANCHESTERS the supporting ~~attacking~~ troops thus becoming merged with the assaulting lines

6. At a distance of about 300 yards north of our front line they came across a German trench filled with enemy dead. The trench had been wired and was pretty deep, but it had been very heavily shelled by our artillery and presented no ~~obstacle~~ obstacles to our further advance. A hundred yards further north there was another enemy trench containing a number of dead bodies. This trench had evidently been hastily dug being only from two to four feet deep with practically no wire It had been much damaged

5/7. by our artillery fire.

The assaulting was carried another 100 yards further north and a site selected for a trench, the work of consolidation being commenced at once. The trench was dug to a depth of 5 feet in places & rough firesteps made. While this work was proceeding a party consisting of one German officer and four men came down the road leading towards our line apparently looking for their own trench. They were told to come in and surrender and the officer who spoke English seemed glad to do so. Attempts were made to establish touch with British troops on the right and left without success and two N.C.Os were sent back to get orders to the sergt of the 17th MANCHESTERS who had assumed command

6) in the absence of any officers. Lance Corpl NOON of the battalion under my command was one of these. The N.C.Os returned without ~~information~~ the required information and it was then decided to withdraw to our own front line as it was clear that the position was entirely isolated and at that time also our own artillery was shelling ~~the~~ position.

8) With reference to the two platoons of "C" Coy who formed the right of the battalion it appears that in moving through the barrage they suffered few casualties until reaching our front line when they too came under heavy machine gun fire, being enfiladed from the right. The assaulting troops in front ~~were~~ suffered severe casualties and men were attempting to dig themselves in in the shell holes

in front of our line. Judging from what could be seen of the enemy they appeared to be standing on the parapet of their trench. They were exposed almost to the waist, their dress seemed to be a dark blue uniform and they wore steel helmets. Finding it impossible to make any further progress the platoon withdrew with what was left of the first line to the original British trench.

9
During the attack this original trench was covered by the LEWIS guns under 2nd Lt ROBERTS. As the men returned to the front line the battalion was reorganised as far as possible. Lt COL WALSH 2nd R.S.F. assumed general command of his own battalion and the 18th MANCHESTER REGT. I was directed to remain at my battalion H.Q. at FACTORY CORNER where I established communication with the 90th Infantry

Brigade and the H.Q. of
Lt. Col. WALSH.

10. During the operations my signallers attempted to get in touch with the aeroplanes but the attempt had to be abandoned owing to heavy shell fire. The VENETIAN shutter being completely destroyed.

H H O Williams Lt Col
Commanding 18th Manchester R.

15.10.16

V. Report on Operations
October 10th – 13th, 1916

10.10.16
7.0 A.M. At 7.0 A.M. on the morning of October 10th the battalion left FRICOURT CAMP and marched via MAMETZ and MONTAUBAN to MARLBOROUGH WOOD arriving 11.0 A.M.

1.45 P.M. The battalion moved off by platoons marching via LONGUEVAL to the trenches. Owing to the congestion caused by units of the 41st DIVISION coming out and 89th BRIGADE going up progress was

11.10.16
2.0 A.M. exceedingly slow. It was 2.0 A.M. before the battalion arrived at GROVE ALLEY where they were to have relieved a unit of the 41st Division (vide Brigade orders) who were not in fact there. We occupied those

4.0 A.M. trenches until 4.0 A.M. at which time in accordance with verbal orders from G.O.C. Brigade we moved

2) in support
up to FACTORY TRENCH, Battn
H.Q. being ordered to go to
FACTORY CORNER. As it
appeared that FACTORY TRENCH
proper was too much to the
West, I deployed the batt'n
to cover the frontage from
FACTORY CORNER to
PIONEER ROAD, with orders to
dig themselves in. This was
done throughout the day with
comparatively few casualties.

3. On the night of the 11th
4. we received the following
orders: "One Coy of the battalion
under my command to
report at dawn to
O.C. 2nd R.S.F. In
addition, one nettoyeur
platoon to report to
2nd R.S.F and one
nettoyeur platoon to
report to O.C. 17th
MANCHESTER REGT at
the same time

12.10.16 At zero (2.5 P.M) the
2·5 P.M battalion (less one coy
and two platoons) moved
from the trenches mentioned

(3) in Para 4 in small shallow columns covering approximately the two battalions frontage. They Encountered a very severe barrage put up by the enemy immediately they left the trench, which in spite of severe casualties they resolutely pushed through.

I wish to draw special attention to bravery and determination of the company and platoon Commanders who led their men through the barrage and through the heavy machine gun fire which opened almost instantly at the zero hour. The company Commanders of the two Coys on the left (A 2nd Lt BROWN and B 2nd Lt TRIMMER) became casualties just before reaching the British front line, but notwithstanding this the men advanced under their platoon sergeants. On crossing the British line the machine gun fire became much more intense.

4) and more heavy casualties
ensued. A number of men
of "A" and "B" Coys moved
quickly forward and
attached themselves to the
1/5th MANCHESTERS the
supporting troops thus becoming
merged with the assaulting
lines.
    At a distance of about
300 yards north of this point
line they came across a
German trench filled with
enemy dead. The trench
had been wired and was
pretty deep, but it had
been very heavily shelled
by our artillery and
presented no obstacle
obstacle to our further
advance. A hundred yards
further north there was
another enemy trench
containing a number of
dead bodies. This trench
had evidently been hastily
dug being only from
two to four feet deep
with practically no wire.
It had been much damaged

by our artillery fire.

The assaulting was carried another 100 yards further north and a site selected for a trench, the work of consolidation being commenced at once. The trench was dug to a depth of 5 feet in places & rough firesteps made. While this work was proceeding a party consisting of one German officer and four men came down the road leading toward our line apparently looking for their own trench. They were told to come in and surrender and the officer who spoke English seemed glad to do so. Attempts were made to establish touch with British troops on the right and left without success and two N.C.Os were sent back to get orders to the in C/o the 17th MANCHESTERS who had assumed command

2) in the absence of any
officer. Lance Corpl NOON
of the battalion under my
command was one of these.
The N.C.Os returned without
~~any~~ the required
information and it was
then decided to withdraw
to our own front line as
it was clear that the portion
was quiet isolated and
at that time also our own
artillery was shelling the
position.

With reference to the
other portion of B Coy
who formed part of the right of
the battalion it appears
that in working through
the barrage they suffered
few casualties until
reaching the point
where they too came
under heavy machine gun
fire being enfiladed from
the right. The remaining
officers in front were ~~killed~~
seven being among men
~~wounded~~ ~~were~~ taken filing
there in in the shell holes

in front of our line. Judging from what could be seen of the enemy, they appeared to be standing on the parapets of their trenches. They were exposed almost to the waist. Theirs was seemed to be a dark blue uniform and they wore steel helmets. Finding it impossible to make any further progress the platoons withdrew with what was left of the first line to the original British trench.

During the attack this original trench was occupied by the LEWIS guns under 2nd Lt ROBERTS. As the men returned to the front line the battalion was reorganised as far as possible. Lt Col WALSH 2nd R.S.F. assumed general command of his own battalion and the 18th MANCHESTER REGT. I was directed to remain at my battalion H.Q. at FACTORY CORNER where I established communication with the 90th Infantry

Brigade and the H.Q. of
Lt Col WALSH.
During the operations ~~attempts~~ my signallers attempted to get in touch with the aeroplanes but the attempt ~~...~~ had to be abandoned owing heavy shell fire, the VENETIAN shutter being completely destroyed.

War Diary
October 1916
X6.

Y.K.Y.   Operation Orders
                       No

1. Batt^n will assemble
at dawn, tomorrow in the trenches
they have been digging
today

2. At zero hour the batt^n
will move forward and
occupy the ~~trenches~~ ~~now~~ ~~occupied~~
by the 17th Manchester and
2nd R.S.F

3. Move in following order from
right to left - C, B, A, & D
in small columns of half

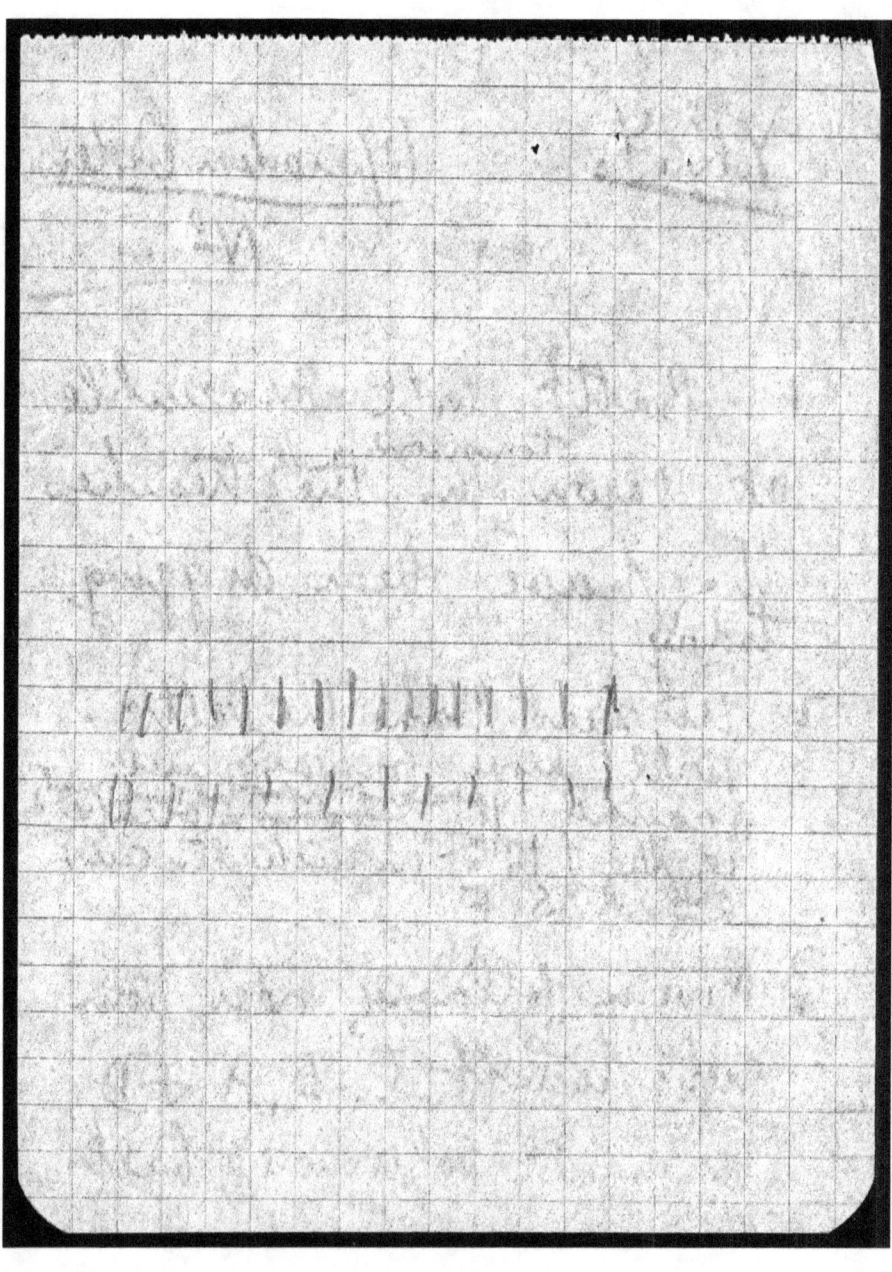

mounted, at Brigade H.Q.
tomorrow at 6.0 A.M.

T. Spell Capt
Acting Adjt
18th (S) Battn Manchester Regt

Copy 1 Commanding Officer
" 2 Second in Command.

————————

> War Diary
> October 1916
> Appendix X5

OPERATION AFTER ORDERS.

1. "D" Coy less Lewis Gunners will report to the O.C. 2nd R.S.F. at 6.0 a.m. on the 12th instant and will form the fourth wave of that Unit.

2. One nettoyeur platoon of "C" Coy will report to the O.C. 2nd R.S.F. at 6.0 a.m. and one nettoyeur platoon of "C" will report to the O.C. 17th Manchester Regiment at 6 0 a.m. After clearing the first objective these platoons rejoin the battalion.

3. "A" and "B" and "C" Coys less two platoons and all Lewis Gunners will start at zero and push on so as to follow the assaulting lines at a distance of not less than 200 yards, holding themselves in readiness to reinforce as required. On reaching the final objective this battalion will assist in consolidating on the line shewn.

4. All Lewis Gunners under 2/Lt Roberts will consolidate and hold the present front line now held by the 2nd R.S.F. and 17th Manchester Regiment.

5. Battalion H.Q. for the first part of the operation will be at FACTORY CORNER; afterwards moving forward.

6. An advanced signalling station will be formed at the present front line, to which messages in the initial stages of the operations must be sent. 2/Lt ROBERTS will be responsible for transmitting these messages to Battalion H.Q.

7. Should overcrowding occur at the first objective Officers commanding companies will put their men into shell holes south of the objective.

(Sgd) T. J. Kelly.
Acting Adjutant.

12.10.16.
2:30 a.m.

Operation Orders No 29 By 2nd
by H Col H B Williams
Commanding 18th March Regt

21st October 1916

Reference { 62 c N.W.
           { 62 d N.E.
           { 57 c S.W.

1. The battalion will march to RIBEMONT tomorrow. Order of march — A, B, C, & D Coys with 100 yards between Coys and connecting files.

2. The battalion will parade at 7.30 A.M. in mass on the ground in front of the Orderly Room ready to march off at 7.45 A.M. and move via MONTAUBAN, MAMETZ, FRICOURT, MEAULTE, VIVIER MILL, DERNACOURT, BUIRE to RIBEMONT

3. The battalion will pass the Cross

2) roads F5c 9/6 soon after 8.0 A.M. and the transport will be ready to follow in rear of the last company. Cookers with dinners preparing, will follow immediately behind the Batt'n with the Officers mess cart.
All riding horses, including one horse per coy and the horses of the Commanding Officer, Second-in-Command, Adjutant and Medical Officer will be at Batt'n H.Q. at 6.30 A.M. Horses for the cookers, water carts & officers mess cart will be at Camp at the same time; feeds to be carried.

4 Each company will detail a party of 12 men who will report to Serj't REEVES at 7.15 A.M and will assist with the LEWIS GUN carts

5. Sergt HAYTER will remain behind with two men per Coy. to hand over the camp to a batt. and details of the 8th Australian Brigade. These men will be detailed by Coys and will report to Sergt HAYTER at 7.0AM. after handing over the party will proceed to RIBEMONT

6. O.C Coys are held strictly responsible that every N.C.O and man knows the exact route to be followed and the destination of the battn

7. 2nd LT ROBERTS with the interpreter will report to the Staff Capt. at

OPERATION AFTER ORDERS.

1. "D" Coy less Lewis Gunners will report to the O.C. 2nd R.S.F. at 6.0 a.m. on the 12th instant and will form the fourth wave of that Unit.

2. One nettoyeur platoon of "C" Coy will report to the O.C. 2nd R.S.F. at 6.0 a.m. and one nettoyeur platoon of "C" will report to the O.C. 17th Manchester Regiment at 6 0 a.m. After clearing the first objective these platoons rejoin the battalion.

3. "A" and "B" and "C" Coys less two platoons and all Lewis Gunners will start at zero and push on so as to follow the assaulting lines at a distance of not less than 200 yards, holding themselves in readiness to reinforce as required. On reaching the final objective this battalion will assist in consolidating on the line shewn.

4. All Lewis Gunners under 2/Lt Roberts will consolidate and hold the present front line now held by the 2nd R.S.F. and 17th Manchester Regiment.

5. Battalion H.Q. for the first part of the operation will be at FACTORY CORNER; afterwards moving forward.

6. An advanced signalling station will be formed at the present front line, to which messages in the initial stages of the operations must be sent. 2/Lt ROBERTS will be responsible for transmitting these messages to Battalion H.Q.

7. Should overcrowding occur at the first objective Officers commanding companies will put their men into shell holes south of the objective.

(Sgd) T. J. Kelly.
Acting Adjutant.

12.10.16.
2:30 a.m.

Secret.

War Diary
of
18th (Service) Battalion
The Manchester Regiment.

From
1st November 1916.

to.
30th November 1916.

(Volume XIII)

H B O Williams Lieut.-Col.
Commanding 18th Bn. Manchester Regt.

Sheet 34

Army Form C. 2118

WAR DIARY
or
INTELLIGENCE SUMMARY

18th (Service) Batt. Manchester Regt.

Place	Date 1916	Hour	Summary of Events and Information	Remarks and references to Appendices
BELLACOURT	Nov 1		One outpost at BELLACOURT, "D" Coy in storm fronts and remainder f battalion in village in working parties.	
"	2		— do —	
"	3		Information received that 77 O.R. missing since TRONES WOOD (July 8-11) and GUILLEMONT (July 30) are officially accepted as prisoners of war.	
"	4		Bellacourt in outpost	
"	5		— do —	
"	6		Relieves 16th Manchester Regt in outpost sector D 2 and 1st BRETTENCOURT. 2nd Lt A. LUCAS proceeds for duty M.I from the Base and 2nd Lt H. DUNCAN returns from hospital.	
Trenches	7		2nd Lt W. PRYTHIAN returns from hospital in the line.	

WAR DIARY
or
INTELLIGENCE SUMMARY

Army Form C. 2118

(Erase heading not required.) 1/8 Lewis Batt Manchester Regt

Place	Date	Hour	Summary of Events and Information	Remarks and references to Appendices
Tincha	10/10		Today, Lt Col H.B.O. WILLIAMS proceeded on leave & Lieut MAJOR C.E. L. EMBCKE assumed command.	
	11		In the Trenches	
BAILLEULVAL	12		do Relieved to do by 1/6 th Lancs Fus. Regt. Battalion marched back to Divisional Reserve. Billets at BAILLEULVAL	N2
	13		Lt J.P. KNOWLES assumed command of "B" Coy vice 2/Lt N.B. GILL. Divisional Reserve Two O.R. killed today. Concert & Supper given to the Battalion today to celebrate first anniversary landing in France (November 8th 1915)	
	14		Divisional Reserve	
	15		do	
	16		do	
	17		do	
Trenches	18		Relieved 16th Manchester Regt in Dr Subsector	N 3
	19		1. O.R. died of wounds	
	20		In the trenches	
	21		do	
	22		do	
	23		do	

Army Form C. 2118

WAR DIARY
or
INTELLIGENCE SUMMARY

(Erase heading not required.) 18th Service Battn. The Manchester Regt.

Instructions regarding War Diaries and Intelligence Summaries are contained in F. S. Regs., Part II. and the Staff Manual respectively. Title Pages will be prepared in manuscript.

Sheet 36

Place	Date 1916	Hour	Summary of Events and Information	Remarks and references to Appendices
BELLACOURT	Nov 24		Battalion was relieved today marched back to Brigade	N 4
	25		Reserve at BELLACOURT	
	26		Brigade Reserve Lt Col Williams returned from leave today	
	27		do	
	28		do	
	29		do	
	30		16th Battalion marched 6 trenches today & relieves	N 5
			16th Manchester Regt in subsector D 2, opposite	
			BLAIREVILLE	

J M Williams Lt Col
Commanding 18th Manchester Regt

APPENDIX. N.1.

NOVEMBER 4th 1916.   OPERATION ORDERS NO: 30.   COPY No:......

(SECRET).   BY LIEUT-COLONEL H.B.C. WILLIAMS,
                 COMMANDING 18th (SERVICE) BATTALION,
                 MANCHESTER REGIMENT.

1. The 18th Bn. Manchester Regiment will relieve the 16th Bn.
    Manchester Regiment in the left front sector on Monday the
    6th November 1916 as follows:-

    "A" Coy 18th Mchr. relieves "D" Coy, 16th Mchr. Regt. - Right.
    "B" Coy   ditto   relieves "B" Coy,   ditto   - Centre.
    "C" Coy   ditto   relieves "C" Coy,   ditto   - Left.
    "D" Coy   ditto   relieves "A" Coy,   ditto   - In
    reserve at BRETENCOURT.

    The Officer Commanding "D" Coy will make arrangements with
    the Officer Commanding "A" Coy 16th Mchr's for the relieve.

2. The first platoon of "A" Coy will reach the entrance of
    REGINETT STREET at 9:30 am. and the remaining Platoons will
    follow at intervals of 300 yards.   Guides from the 16th
    Mchr's will be waiting.
    The leading Platoon of "C" Coy will be at the entrance to
    QUARRY STREET at 9:30 am. and the remaining platoons
    of "C" and "B" Coys will follow at intervals of 300 yards.
    One guide per Platoon from the 16th Mchrs will be waiting.

3. Two Platoons of each Company will be in the front line and
    two Platoons will be in the support line.

4. Lewis Gunners and signallers will move from BELLACOURT at
    8 o'c am. on the morning of the 6th November 1916 and proceed
    to the entrance to REGINETT STREET to meet guides of the 16th
    Mchr Regt at 8:30 am.

5. ~~Transport will move from B. Coy's ditto without cooker at~~
    ~~11 am. on the 6th Nov. 1916.~~   The Transport Officer will
    arrange to have two Limbers Officer's Mess Cart and Maltese
    Cart and horses for the Cookers and Water Carts to be at
    BELLACOURT at 7:45 am.   In accordance with 90th Brigade
    Orders No: 2. dated 3rd instant at least 500 yards to be
    maintained between Vehicles and 300 yards between Platoons. The
    transport will move from BELLACOURT to BAILLEULVAL at 11:0am.

6. Blankets will be collected and dumped in the stores near the
    Shoemakers shop at 8 am. Monday 6th November 1916 and all
    officers valises and baggage not wanted in the trenches must
    be deposited at the same place by 8:30 am.

Issued by Orderly at.......
No.1.File.   No.2.Commanding Officer.
No.3.2nd.in.Command.   (Sgd) T. J. KELLY.   CAPTAIN.
No.4.Adjutant.   Acting-Adjutant.
No.5.O.C."A"Coy.   No.11. 18th Bn. MANCHESTER REGIMENT.
No.6.O.C."B"Coy.   No.12.Lewis Gun Officer.
No.7.O.C."C"Coy.   No.13.Signalling Officer.
No.8.O.C."D"Coy.   No.14.War Diary.
No.9.Transport Officer.
No.10.Quartermaster.

APPENDIX N2

NOVEMBER 11th 1916.   OPERATION ORDERS NO: 31.   COPY NO:

(SECRET).   BY MAJOR C.E. LEMBCKE.
COMMANDING 18th (SERVICE) BATTALION,
MANCHESTER REGIMENT.
----

1. The 18th Battalion Manchester Regiment will be relieved by the 16th Battalion, Manchester Regiment and marched to Reserve billets in BAILLEULVAL on the morning of the 12th instant.

2. The relief of the Front line Coys will commence at 10:30 a.m. commencing with "C" Coy followed by "A" and "B" Coys.

   "A" Coy of the 16th Manchesters will relieve "A" Coy of the 18th Manchesters via ENGINEER STREET.

   "B" Coy of the 16th Manchesters will relieve "B" Coy of the 18th Manchesters via QUARRY STREET.

   "C" Coy of the 16th Manchesters will relieve "C" Coy of the 18th Manchesters via QUARRY STREET.

   "D" Coy of the 16th Manchesters will relieve "D" Coy of the 18th Manchesters (RESERVE).

3. The Reserve Coy of the 18th Manchesters which will be relieved earliest will proceed to billets at Bailleulval, dump their kit and will be used for work that day under R.E.

4. At least 300 yards interval will be kept between Platoons and parties. No party to be more than 25. 500 yards interval between Vehicles.

5. Everyone including Transport to halt 10 minutes each hour when out of the trenches unless within a short distance of destination.

6. Hostile aeroplanes must be remembered and guarded against by halting and getting into concealment.

7. Lewis Gun teams, Signallers, Bombers etc who will be relieved before the Coys must not block any incoming Platoons. If any meet, the outgoing parties they must stand aside.

8. All Maps, Trench Stores etc to be carefully handed over.

9. The Quartermaster will take over billets in Bailleulval as soon as the 16th Manchesters vacate them. C.Q.M.S's to proceed to-night to Bailleulval and report to the Quartermaster.

10. O's C. Coys will remove their Coys independently as each relief is completed in each Company Sector, reporting at Battln H.Q. either in person or sending another Officer on the way out.

11. Coys will occupy approximately the same billets as the 16th Manchesters occupied.

12. Trench kits (Officers) and officers mess equipment to be at entrance to ENGINEER STREET, BRETTENCOURT at 10 a.m.

13. TRANSPORT. Cookers leave BRETTENCOURT immediately after

OPERATION ORDERS, (CONTINUED).   -2-.

breakfast has been served and dixes returned from the front line Coys. The first Cooker will pass the cross roads at 8:15 a.m.

14.   Horses to be at ENGINEER STREET, BRETENCOURT, at 12:0 noon.

      (Sgd)   D.H. ROBERTS.   2nd Lieut.
                       Acting Adjutant.
      18th (s) Bn. MANCHESTER REGIMENT.

Issued by Orderly at.................

Copy No. 1. File.
"   "   2. Commanding Officer.
"   "   3. 2nd-in-Command.
"   "   4. O.C. "A" Coy.
"   "   5. O.C. "B" Coy.
"   "   6. O.C. "C" Coy.
"   "   7. O.C. "D" Coy.
"   "   8. Quartermaster.
"   "   9. Medical Officer.
"   " 10. 16th Bn. Manchester Regiment.
"   " 11. War Diary.
"   " 12.

November 17th 1916.

APPENDIX N3. 10.

COPY NO: ....

OPERATION ORDERS NO: 32.

(SECRET).

BY MAJOR C. T. LUMSDEN.,
COMMANDING 18th (SERVICE) BATTALION.,
MANCHESTER REGIMENT.

1. The 18th Bn. MANCHESTER REGIMENT will relieve the 16th Bn. MANCHESTER REGIMENT on the 19th instant in the line.

2. DISTRIBUTION OF COMPANIES:-

   FRONT LINE AND SUPPORT.

   "D" Coy. on the RIGHT.   (OSTER).
   "B" Coy. in the CENTRE.   (RAVINE).
   "C" Coy. on the LEFT.   (EPSOM).
   "A" Coy. in RESERVE. BERTRANCOURT.

3. ORDER OF MARCH:-

   LEWIS GUNNERS leave BAILLEULVAL at 7:30 am.
   SIGNALLERS   -do-   at 7:45 am.
   SNIPERS & BOMBERS   -do-   at 8: 0 am.
   "A" Coy.   -do-   at 9: 0 am.
   "C" Coy.   -do-   at 9:15 am. (via QUARRY ST.)
   "D" Coy.   -do-   at 9:30 am. (via REGINA ST.)
   "B" Coy.   -do-   at 9:45 am. (via QUARRY ST.)

4. One Gas N.C.O. per Coy and 1 N.C.O. for H.Q. will report at 16th MANCHESTER Battalion Headquarters in the trenches at 6:0 pm to-night and take over the gas arrangements. They will remain in the trenches to-night.

5. Acting R.S.M. and 1 N.C.O. per Coy will leave BAILLEULVAL at 7:30 am. and proceed to Battalion Headquarters and Company Sectors respectively for the purpose of taking over trench stores.

6. TRANSPORT.

   1st vehicle will leave BAILLEULVAL at 10:0 am. (this does not apply to Lewis Gun Handcarts).

7. No party to consist of more than 25 men - a distance of 300 yards is to be kept between each party - 500 yards between vehicles.

8. Everyone including transport will halt 10 minutes before each hour for 10 minutes when moving up.

9. Hostile aeroplanes must be guarded against by halting and getting under concealment.

(Sgd) D.H. ROBSON,   2nd Lieut.
                        Acting Adjutant.
Issued by orderly
at ... 3.0 p.m. ....   18th (S) Battalion, Manchester Regiment.

Copy No. 1.   File.
   "   " 2.   Commanding Officer.
   "   " 3.   O.C. "A" Coy.
   "   " 4.   O.C. "B" Coy.
   "   " 5.   O.C. "C" Coy.
   "   " 6.   O.C. "D" Coy.
   "   " 7.   Quartermaster.
   "   " 8.   Medical Officer.
   "   " 9.   16th Bn. Manchester Regiment.
   "   " 10.   War Diary.
   "   " 11.   Adjutant.

APPENDIX N.4

NOVEMBER 24th. 1916. OPERATION ORDERS NO. 33.   Copy No. 12

(SECRET).
BY MAJOR C.E. LYMBERY.
Commanding 18th Battalion,
MANCHESTER REGIMENT.

War Diary

1. The 18th. Bn. Manchester Regiment will be relieved by the 16th. Batn., Manchester Regiment., and will march to support billets in BELLACOURT on the morning of the 24th instant. The relief of the companies will be as follows, the first company being relieved about 9.30.am.

    1. "A" Coy: 18th. Manchesters will be relieved by "C" Coy: 16th. Manchesters and will march from the trenches to the four strong points in support.

    2. "C" Coy: 18th. Manchesters will be relieved by "D" Coy; 16th. Manchesters.

    3. "B" Coy: 18th. Manchesters will be relieved by "B" Coy: 16th. Manchesters.

    4. "D" Coy: 18th. Manchesters will be relieved by "A" Coy: 16th. Manchesters.

2. Officers commanding Companies will march out their Companies independently as the relief is completed in their sector, and report at Batn. H.Q. in person on the way out. Companies will occupy the same billets in BELLACOURT as before, except that "D" Coy: will occupy the billets formerly occupied by "A" Coy.

3. The Trench kits of Officers, Mess Baggage &c., will be at the entrance to ENGINEER STREET at 10.0.am.

4. Cookers will leave BRETENCOURT immediately after Breakfast is served and dixies returned from the front line companies. The first cooker will be at the cross roads at 8.15.am.

5. Maltese Cart and Officers Mess Cart and limbers for trench kits and baggage will be at the bottom of ENGINEER STREET at 10.0.am and each Company must detail two men as loaders.

6. 2nd. Lieut. Roberts and Sergt. Airley will proceed to Headquarters, BELLACOURT, to take over the stores &c., at 9.0.am., and Company commanders should send one Officer and C.Q.M.Sgt. to BELLACOURT to take over billets at 8.0.am.

7. List of all stores taken over in BELLACOURT will be forwarded to the Regimental Sergeant Major by 1.0.pm.

8. The usual precautions regarding distances between platoons and parties and guarding against aeroplanes will be observed.

9. The Transport Officer will arrange to have all Officer's Valises and blankets brought to BELLACOURT on the morning of the 24th, and distributed.

                                                                Captain.
                                        Acting Adjutant,
                                        18th. Bn. Manchester Regt.

Issued by orderly at...............

No.1. File.
No.2. C.O..
No.3. Adjutant.
No.4. O.C., "A" Co.
No.5. O.C., "B" Co.
No.6. O.C., "C" Co.
No.7. O.C., "D" Co.
No.8. T.O.
No.9. Q.M.
No.10. M.O.
No.11. O.C. 16th. Manchesters.
No.12. War Diary.

APPENDIX IV.5

November 29th.   BATTALION ORDER NO...   Copy No....
By Lieut. Col. H.S.O. WILKINS,
Commanding 18th. Bn.
MANCHESTER REGIMENT.

1. The 18th. Bn. Manchester Regt., will relieve the 16th. Batt'n. Manchester Regt., in the LEFT FRONT SECTOR on Thursday the 30th. November as follows:-

"C" Coy: 18th. Manchesters relieves "D" Coy: 16th. Mchrs. in EPSOM.
"D" Coy: do.   do.   "B" Coy: do.   in RAVEN.
"A" Coy: do.   do.   "A" Coy: do.   in CHALK.
"B" Coy: do.   do.   "C" Coy: do.   in reserve.

2. The first platoon of "D" Coy: will reach the entrance of WESTMINSTER BRIDGE at 5.30.pm and the remaining platoons will follow at intervals of 300 yards. The leading platoon of "C" Company will be at the entrance to the same at 5.30pm and the remaining platoons of "C" and "D" Coys: will follow at intervals of 300 yards. "B" Coy: will move into the trenches as soon as they are relieved in the strong points, moving via CLAPHAM JCN.

3. Lewis Gunners and Signallers will move from BELLACOURT at 8.0.am on the morning of the 30th. November 1916 and proceed to the trenches to take over from the 16th. Manchesters.

4. The Transport Officer will arrange to have the Limbers, Officers mess Cart, Butcher Cart, borders for the cookers and water carts at BELLACOURT at 7.45 a.m. In accordance with 90th. Infantry Bde. Orders No... 1/1 and in total, a least 80 yards to be maintained between vehicles and 200 yards between platoons. The transport will move from BELLACOURT to RIVIERVILLE at 10.0.am.

5. Blankets will be collected and dumped in the stores near the shoemakers shop at 8.0.am on Thursday the 30th. Nov: and all Officers Valises and baggage not required in the trenches, must be deposited at the same place by 9.30.am.

(Sd) P.J. Daley, Captain.
a/Adjutant;
18th. Bn. Manchester Regt.

Issued by orderly at............

No.1. C.O.
No.2. File.
No.3. Adjutant.
No.4. 2nd.-in-Command.
No.5. O.C., A.
No.6. O.C., B.
No.7. O.C., C.
No.8. O.C., D.
No.9. Q.M.
No.10. T.O.
No.11. I.O.O.
No.12. M.O.
No.13. O.C. 16th. M/C.
No.14. War Diary.

SECRET.

Vol.14

WAR DIARY.
---000---

of

18th (SERVICE) BATTALION,

THE MANCHESTER REGIMENT.

FROM...1st DECEMBER 1916.
TO.....31st DECEMBER 1916.

(VOLUME. XIV.)

Army Form C. 2118

Sheet 37

WAR DIARY
or
INTELLIGENCE SUMMARY

(Erase heading not required.) 18th (Service) Batt. Manchester Regt

Instructions regarding War Diaries and Intelligence Summaries are contained in F. S. Regs., Part II. and the Staff Manual respectively. Title Pages will be prepared in manuscript.

Place	Date 1916	Hour	Summary of Events and Information	Remarks and references to Appendices
Trenches	Dec.	1	In the line Subsector D2, opposite BLAIREVILLE	
		2	— do —	
		3	— do —	
		4	— do —	
		5	— do —	
		6	— do — Relieved to-day by 16th Manchester Regt. Battalion marched back to Divisional Reserve Billets at BASSEUX and BAILLEULVAL. Casualties during the week — 1 O.R. Killed, 8 O.Rs Wounded	D1
BAILLEULVAL & BASSEUX		7	In Divisional Reserve	
		8	— do —	
		9	— do — Capt. J.G.CUNLIFFE rejoined the Battalion from England 2nd Lieut. B.A.WESTPHAL assumed Command of "B" Coy vice Lieut. J.P. KNOWLES	
		10	Church Parade at BAILLEULVAL in the morning.	
		11	In Divisional Reserve	
		12	Relieved 16th Manchester Regt. in Subsector D2. No 10818 Sgt. E.G.HILL, 10423 Pte. A.LAW, & 103105 Cpl. J.C.LEES awarded the Military Medal.	D2
Trenches		13	In the line	
		14	— do —	
		15	— do —	
		16	— do —	
		17	— do —	
		18	— do — Relieved to-day by 16th Manchester Regt. & marched back to Brigade Reserve Casualties during the week — 2 O.Rs Wounded	D3

Army Form C. 2118

Sheet 38

Instructions regarding War Diaries and Intelligence Summaries are contained in F. S. Regs., Part II. and the Staff Manual respectively. Title Pages will be prepared in manuscript.

WAR DIARY
or
INTELLIGENCE SUMMARY

(Erase heading not required.) 18th (Service) Battn. Manchester Regt.

Place	Date	Hour	Summary of Events and Information	Remarks and references to Appendices
BELLACOURT	Dec.	19	In Brigade Reserve, "C" Coy in Strong Points; the remainder of the Battalion on Working Parties.	
		20	In Brigade Reserve.	
		21	— do —	
		22	— do — 2nd Lieut. W.M. BARRATT & 2nd Lieut. H. DAY joined the Battalion to day from 5th Bn. L.N. Lanco. Regt., & are posted to "C" & "A" Companies respectively.	
		23	In Brigade Reserve.	
Trenches		24	Relieved 16th Manchester Regt. in Subsector D2. Major C.E. LEMBCKE assumed Command of the Battalion from today vice Lt. Col. H.B.O. WILLIAMS. 2nd Lieut. J.E. SMART joined the Battalion from 5th Bn. L.N. Lanco. Regt. & is posted to "C" Coy.	
		25	In the line. 2nd Lieut. S.J.L. WYATT joined the Battalion from Base & is posted to "B" Coy.	
		26	In the line.	
		27	— do —	
		28	— do —	
		29	— do —	
		30	— do — Relieved today by 16th Manchester Regt., & marched back to Divisional Reserve billets in BAILLEULVAL & BASSEUX. Casualties during the week – 10 ORs wounded.	
BAILLEULVAL & BASSEUX		31	In Divisional Reserve.	

C.E. Lembcke Major
Commdg. 18th Battn. Manchester Regt.

1875 Wt. W593/826 1,000,000 4/15 J.B.C. & A. A.D.S.S./Forms/C. 2118.

DECEMBER 5th.1916.   OPERATION ORDERS NO.35.   COPY NO: 3.
              By Lieut.Col. M.B.O. WILLIAMS,
    (SECRET). Commanding 18th (S) Battalion,
              MANCHESTER REGT.

(1)   The 18th. Bn. Manchester Regt., will be relieved by the 16th
    Bn. Manchester Regt., and march to Reserve Billets on the 6th instant;
    "A" & "B" Coys going to BASSEUX and "C" & "D" Coys to BAILLEULVAL.
    The relief of the front line Coys will commence at 10.30.am.
    commencing with "C" Coy: followed by "A" & "D" Companies.

Right.   { Coy: of the 16th. Mchrs. will relieve "D" Coy: of the 18th.
          { Mchrs. via ENGINEER STREET.
Centre.   { Coy: of the 16th. Mchrs. will relieve "A" Coy: of the 18th.
          { Mchrs. via DARBY STREET.
Left.   { Coy: of the 16th. Mchrs. will relieve "C" Coy: of the 18th.
          { Mchrs. via HUNNY STREET.
Reserve. { Coy: of the 16th. Mchrs. will relieve "B" Coy: of the 18th.
          { Mchrs. in RESERVE.

(2)   At least 300 yards interval will be kept between platoons and
    parties. No party to be more than 25. 500 yards interval between
    vehicles.

(3)   Lewis Gun Teams, Signallers, Bombers etc., who will be relieved
    before the Companies must not block any incoming platoons. If any
    meet, the outgoing parties must stand aside.

(4)   The Regimental Q.M.S. will take over N.C. billets in
    BAILLEULVAL as soon as the 16th. Manchesters vacate them. Company
    Quartermaster Sergeants will proceed to-night to BAILLEULVAL and
    BASSEUX to take over billets for their Companies.

(5)   Officers Commanding Companies will move their Companies
    independently as each relief is completed in each Company Sector,
    reporting at Battn. H.Qs. either in person or sending another Officer
    on the way out.

(6)   Companies will occupy approximately the same billets as the
    16th. Manchesters occupied.

(7)   French Kits (Officers) and Officers Mess equipment to be at
    entrance to ENGINEER STREET, BRETENCOURT at 10.am.

(8)   TRANSPORT:- Cookers leave BRETENCOURT immediately after
    breakfast has been served and dixies returned from the front line
    Coys: The first cooker will pass the cross roads at 8.15.am.

(9)   Horses to be at ENGINEER STREET, BRETENCOURT at 12.noon.

                            (Sd) T.J. Kelly. Captain.
                                    ADJT.
                            18th. Bn. Manchester Regt.

Issued by Orderly at:-

No.1.   C.O.
No.2.   2nd.in.Command.
No.3.   Adjutant.
No.4.   O.C. A.
No.5.   O.C. B.
No.6.   O.C. C.
No.7.   O.C. D.
No.8.   Q.M.
No.9.   T.O.
No.10. L.G.O.
No.11. M.O.
No.12. C.O. 16.th. Manchesters.

11th. Dec. 1916.   OPERATION ORDERS NO.36.   Copy No. 2.
                By Lieut. Col. H.B.O. Williams,
(SECRET).   Commanding 18th (S) Battalion,
                MANCHESTER REGIMENT.

1. The 18th. Bn. Manchester Regt., will relieve the 16th. Bn. Manchester Regt. on the 12th instant in the line.

2. Distribution of Companies:-   Front Line & Support.
        "D" Coy: on the RIGHT.   (OSIER)
        "B" Coy: in the CENTRE.   (RAVINE)
        "A" Coy: on the LEFT.   (EPSOM)
        "C" Coy: in RESERVE. BRETTENCOURT & CHANCERY LANE.

3. ORDER OF MARCH.
        LEWIS GUNNERS leave BAILLEULVAL at 7.30.am.
        SIGNALLERS   -do-   at 7.45.am.
        SNIPERS   -do-   at 8.0.am.
        "C" Coy: -do-   at 8.15.am.
        "B" Coy: -do-   at 8.45.am. (via QUARRY STREET.
        "D" Coy: leave BASSEUX   at 9.15.am. (via ENGINEER ST.
        "A" Coy: -do-   at 9.45.am. (via QUARRY STREET.

4. One Gas N.C.O. per Company and 1 N.C.O. for H.Q. will report at 16th. Manchesters Battn. Headquarters in the trenches at 6.0.pm to-night and take over Gas arrangements. They will remain in the trenches tonight.

5. Acting R.S.M. and 1 N.C.O. per Company will leave BAILLEULVAL at 7.30am and proceed to Battn. H.Qs and Company Sectors respectively for the purpose of taking over trench Stores.

6.   (Over

6. TRANSPORT. 1st. Vehicle will leave BAILEULVAL at 9.30.am (this does not apply to Lewis Gun Handcarts). A limber will call at BASSEUX at 10am for Officers' trench kits.

7. No party to consist of more than 25 men - a distance of 300 yards is to be kept between each party - 500 yards between vehicles.

8. Everyone including Transport will halt 10 minutes before each hour for 10 minutes ~~before~~ when moving up.

9. Hostile aeroplanes must be guarded against by halting and getting under ~~concealment~~ cover.

(Sd) T.J. Kelly. Captain.
A/Adjutant,
18th. Bn. Manchester Regt.

Issued by Orderly at..........
No.1. File.
No.2. C.O.
No.3. Adjutant.   No.8. O.C. 16th. M/C.
No.4. O.C. A.   No.9. M.O.
No.5. O.C. B.   No.10. T.O.
No.6. O.C. C.   No.11. Q.M.
No.7. O.C. D.   No.12. R.S.M.
                   No.13. War Diary.

December 17/1915.   OPERATION ORDER NO.37.   Copy No......3...
                    By Lt.Col.N.B.G. WILLIAMS,
                    Commanding 18th. Battalion,
(SECRET).   M A N C H E S T E R   R E G T.

1. The 18th. Bn. Manchester Regiment will be relieved by the 16th. Battn. Manchester Regt. and will march to support billets in BULLACOURT on the morning of the 18th instant. The relief of the companies will be as follows, the first company being relieved about 9.30.am.

a. "A" Coy: 18th.Manchesters will be relieved by "B" Coy: 16th.Manchesters.
b. "B" Coy: ditto.   ditto.   by "C" Coy: 16th.Manchesters.
c. "D" Coy: ditto.   ditto.   by "D" Coy: 16th.Manchesters.
d. "C" Coy: ditto.   ditto.   by "A" Coy: 16th. do. and
   will march to the four strong points in support.

2. Officers Commanding Companies will march out their Companies independently as the relief is completed in their sector, and report at Battn. H.Q. in person on the way out. Companies will occupy the same billets in BULLACOURT as before, except that "A" Coy: will occupy the billets formerly occupied by "C" Company.

3. The trench kits of Officers, Mess Baggage &c., will be at the entrance to ENGINEER STREET at 10.0.am.

4. Cookers will leave ENTRENCOURT immediately after breakfast is served and dixies returned from the front line companies. The first cooker will be at the Cross roads at 8.15.am.

5. Maltese Cart and Officers Mess Cart and limbers for trench kits and baggage will be at the bottom of TRINITY STREET at 10.0.am and each Company must detail two men as loaders.

6. Lieut.KNOWLES and Corporal Fergie will proceed to Headquarters, BULLACOURT to take over the stores etc., at 9.0.am., and Company Commanders should send one Officer and the C.Q.M.Sgt. to BULLACOURT to take over billets at 8.0.am.

7. List of all stores taken over in BULLACOURT will be forwarded to the Regimental Sergeant Major by 1.0.pm.

8. The usual precautions regarding distances between platoons and parties and guarding against aeroplanes will be observed.

9. The Transport Officer will arrange to have all Officer's Valises and blankets brought to BULLACOURT on the morning of the 18th and distributed.

                        (Sd.) T.J. Kelly. Captain.
                              Acting Adjutant,
                              18th.Bn.Manchester Regt.

Issued by Orderly at...............
No.1.File.
No.2.O.C.
No.3.Adjutant.
No.4.O.C."A" Coy:
No.5.O.C."B" Coy:
No.6.O.C."C" Coy:
No.7.O.C."D" Coy:
No.8.O.C.16th.Manchesters.
No.9.T.O.
No.10.C.M.
No.11.M.O.
No.12.War Diary.

December 23rd.1916.   OPERATION ORDER No.35.   Copy.No. 13.
                                    By Lieut. Col. H. B. O. Mitchell,
WAR DIARY   Commanding 19th (Service) Battn.,
                                    MANCHESTER REGIMENT.

1. The 19th. Bn. Manchester Regt. will relieve the 16th. Bn. Manchester Regt on the 24th instant in the ___ LINE.

2. **DISTRIBUTION OF COMPANIES.**   STRONG LINE & SUPPORT.
      "B" Coy: on the RIGHT.   (ONLEY)
      "C" Coy: in the CENTRE.   (HAVING)
      "A" Coy: on the LEFT.   (EPSOM)
      "D" Coy: in RESERVE.   BRUTINECOURT AND CHERCOURT LINE.

3. **ORDER OF MARCH.**
      Lewis Gunners leave BULLECOURT at 8.0.am.
      Signallers   ditto.   at 8.40am.
      Snipers   ditto.   at 8.50am.
      "A" Coy: ditto.   at 9.40am. (via QUARRY STREET).
      "B" Coy: ditto.   at 9.15am. (via _____)
      "C" Coy: ditto.   at 9.45am. (via QUARRY STREET).
      "D" Coy: will move _____ into the trenches via QUARRY STREET as soon as they are relieved in the STRONG POINTS.

4. One Gas N.C.O. and L/N.C.O. for Headquarters will report at the 16th. Manchesters Battalion Headquarters in the trenches at 6.0.pm tonight and take over Gas arrangements. They will remain in the trenches tonight.

5. The Sdtg/S.S.M. and 2 N.C.O. per company will leave BULLECOURT at 6.0. am on the 24th and proceed to Battalion Headquarters and company sectors respectively for the purpose of taking over trench stores.

6. The Transport Officer will arrange to have two limbers, Officers' Mess Cart,(horses for the cookers and water carts at BULLECOURT at 7.45.am. Maltese Cart.) The Transport will move from BULLECOURT to BAILLEULVAL at 11.0.am.

7. No party to consist of more than 25 men. A distance of 500 yards is to be kept between each party. 500 yards between vehicles.

8. Blankets will be collected and dumped in the Stores near the Shoemaker's Shop at 8.0.am on Sunday the 24th instant, and all Officers' Valises and baggage not wanted in the trenches must be deposited at the same place by 9.30.am.

9. Hostile aeroplanes must be guarded against by halting and getting under cover.

10. The attention of Company Commander's is especially directed to Brigade Letter L.501, a copy of which was sent out this morning.

                                    (Sd) W.H. Ogden. 2nd.Lieut.
Issued by Orderly at:-   Adjutant,
                                        19th. Bn.Manchester Regt.

1. FILE.
2. C.O.
3. 2nd. in.Command.
4. O.C. A Coy.
5. O.C. B Coy.
6. O.C. C Coy.
7. O.C. D Coy.
8. O.C. 16th.Manchesters.
9. T.O.
10. Q.M.
11. M.O.
12. M.O.
13. War Diary.

O.C. All Companies.

Please note:-

Ref: Operation Order No 39 issued today,

"B" Coy: will move via ENGINEER STREET.
"A" Coy: will move via Quarry Street.

23/12/16

(Sd) W.E. Ogden 2/Lt.
Adjutant
18th Manchesters.

SECRET.

OPERATION ORDER NO 43.
By Major C.E. LEMBCKE,
Commanding 18th Battn.
MANCHESTER REGIMENT.

   COPY NO. 13.

1. The 18th. Bn. Manchester Regiment will be relieved by the 16th Battn. Battn. Manchester Regt and march to reserve billets on the 30th instant, "B" & "C" Companies going to BASSEAUX and "A" & "D" Companies to BAILLEULVAL. The relief of the front line Companies will commence at 10.30.am, "B" Coy being relieved first followed by "A" & "C" Coys.

"B" Coy: 18th. Manchesters will be relieved by "A" Coy: 16th. Manchesters
"A"   ditto.   "B"   do.
"C"   ditto.   "C"   do.
"D"   ditto.   "D"   do.

2. Officers Commanding Companies will march out their companies independently as the relief is completed in their own sector, reporting at Battalion Headquarters in person on the way out.

3. Officers trench kits, Mess Baggage &c. to be at the entrance to ENGINEER STREET at 10.0.am.

4. The Regimental Quartermaster Sergeant will take over Headquarters billets at BAILLEULVAL as soon as the 16th. Manchesters vacate them. Company Quartermaster Sergeants will proceed tonight to BAILLEULVAL and BASSEUX to take over billets for their companies.

5. TRANSPORT. Cookers will leave BRETTENCOURT immediately after breakfast has been served and dixies returned from the front line Companies. The first cooker will pass the cross roads, BELLACOURT at 8.15.am. Maltese Cart, Officers Mess Cart and limbers for trench kits and baggage will be at the entrance to Engineer Street by 10.0.am.

6. The usual precautions against hostile aircraft and regarding distance between parties and vehicles will be observed.

7. Horses to be at BRETTENCOURT at 12 noon.

                                        (SD-) W.E. Ogden. 2nd. Lieut.
                                              A/Adjutant,
Issued by orderly at:-   18th. Bn. Manchester Regt.

No. 1. C.O.
No. 2. Adjutant.
No. 3. O.C.A.Coy.
No. 4. O.C.B.Coy.
No. 5. O.C.C.Coy.
No. 6. O.C.D.Coy.
No. 7. T.O.
No. 8. Q.M.
No. 9. M.O.
No.10. L.G.O.
No.12. O.C. 16th.Manchesters.
No.13. File.
No.14. War Diary.

SECRET.

WAR DIARY.

of

18th.Service Battalion.Manchester Regiment.

from 1st.January.1917.   to   31st.January.1917.

(Volume. XV.).

...C. L. Lembcke..... Lieut.-Col.
Commanding 18th Bn. Manchester Regt.

Sheet 1A

Army Form C. 2118.

WAR DIARY
or
INTELLIGENCE SUMMARY.
(Erase heading not required.)

18th Service Battalion The Manchester Regt.

Place	Date 1917	Hour	Summary of Events and Information	Remarks and references to Appendices
BAILLEULVAL	Jan 1		New Brigade Reserve. New Year's dinner to Battalion given by Officers	
	" 2		do — Training and Working Parties.	
	" 3		do — The Battalion was inspected by the Earl of Derby Secretary of State	T 1
			for War. Congratulatory Message given and Commander attached.	
	" 4		In Brigade Reserve. Working Parties and Training.	
SUS ST LEGER	" 5		Marched to Billets in SUS ST LEGER in Corps Reserve.	T 2
	" 6		Training at SUS	
	" 7		do	
	" 8		do — 2nd Lt S.J.L. WYATT, 2nd Lt W. LINDSAY, 2nd Lt R. MAYBURY and 2nd Lt J.T. SMART joined for duty from Base. The following officers are mentioned in Despatches for Distinguished and Gallant service and Devotion to Duty :— Lt Col W.A. SMITH (Killed in action); Capt. P.A. BLYTHE (Wounded); Lt J.S. BEAUMONT; and 2nd Lt F.C.O. TWIST (Missing, believed killed) (L.G. 3.1.1917) No 9917 Lance Corpl (now Sergt) W. REEVES and 10772 Pte (now Sergt) A. HAWORTH awarded the Military Medal.	
	9-13.		Training at SUS. Lt R.S. ENGLAND joined for duty from BASE.	
	14		Brigade Parade. Distribution of ribbons by G.O.C. 30th Division and march past recipients	
	15		Training and Working Parties.	
	16		Inspection by G.O.C. 90th Infantry Brigade	
	17		Training and working parties. 2nd Lt J.H. HAGUE joined for duty today from Base. Draft of 158 O.R. also joined today.	
	18		Inspection of Battalion at ceremonial drill by G.O.C. 30th Division.	
	19-21		Training and Working parties. The following officers joined for duty viz the dates shown 2nd Lt J.S. SHANAHAN and 2nd Lt G.S. MARTIN 16.1.1917 and 2nd Lt LDADSHEAD 21.1.1917.	

L.D.A.D.S.S./Forms/C. 2118.

Sheet 2A

Instructions regarding war Diaries &
Intelligence Summaries are contained in
F.S.Regs., Part II. and the Staff Manual
respectively. Title pages will be prepared
in manuscript.

Army Form C.2118.

WAR DIARY.

18th Service Battalion The Manchester Regt.

Summary of Events and Information.

Place.	Date.	Hour.	Summary of Events and Information.	Remarks and references to Appendices.
SUS ST LEGER	Jan 28+29 1917	30	Training at SUS. Battalion attack for G.O.C. 90th Brigade	
	" 30		— do — Battalion attack before Sir E. ALLENBY, K.C.B. Commanding THIRD ARMY who expressed himself pleased with the smart turn-out of the men and the efficient manner in which attack was carried out. 1 O.R. killed and 3 O.R. wounded in rifle grenade practice during manoeuvres on Jan 28th. At 3.30 P.M. C.O. asst & 23 Officers and 540 O.R. marched to DOULLENS and billets. This party will be engaged in working parties for 110 Coy (Railway) R.E. Rest of battalion remains at SUS.	
DOULLENS & SUS	" 31		Rest day at DOULLENS and SUS.	

C. E. Lambarde Lt-Col
Commanding 18th Manchester Regt.

SECRET.   OPERATION ORDERS NO.41.   Copy No. 13.
                           By Major C.E. LEESON.,
Jany.4th.1916.   Commanding 18th. Battn.
                           THE MANCHESTER REGIMENT.

1. The 18th. Bn. Manchester Regiment will march to billets in SUS ST.LEGER
on January 5th.1917.

2. The head of column will be opposite the Quartermaster's Stores ready
to march off at 3.30.pm. An interval of 100 X will be kept between
platoons south of the DOULLENS - ARRAS ROAD.

3. The Transport will follow 100 yards in rear of ~~each unit~~ the Bn., keeping 50
yards between vehicles while south of the ARRAS - DOULLENS ROAD.

4. ROUTE. BAILLEULMONT, LARBRET, SAULTY and SOMBRIN.

5. Order of March. Band - A, B, C and D Companies.

6. March Discipline. Strict march discipline will be observed in
accordance with memo G.745 on MOVES and MARCH DISCIPLINE, issued with
these orders.

7. All Officers' kits, blankets and Mess Boxes for H.Qs and "A" & "B"
Companies must be at the Quartermaster's Stores by 1.pm. All baggage
for "C" & "D" Coys. must be deposited at "C" Coys Headquarters, BASSEUX
at 1.0.pm. One man from "C" Coy. will be detailed to stay with the
baggage at BASSEUX until the arrival of the Motor Lorry.

8. Motor Transport vehicles will be available for 200 men, this party
being composed of bad marchers and an advanced party of each company in
charge of the C.Q.M.S. The party will be under the command of 2nd.
Lieut. W.E. Ogden and will be composed as under:-
    Second Lieut. N.B. Gill.   Headquarters - 20 Other ranks.
    Second Lieut. G.G. Miller.   "A" Coy: - 45   do.
    2nd. Lieut. J.E.M. Taylor.   "B" Coy: - 45   do.
                                     "C" Coy: - 45   do.
                                     "D" Coy: - 45   do.
                                                   200.
The Motor vehicles will be drawn up on the road between LA CAUCHIE and
Cross Roads V.22.c.9/6 at 12 noon. Party parades outside the Orderly
room ready to march off at 10.0.am marching via BAILLEULMONT and LA
CAUCHIE with 200 yards distance between platoons. ~~Secsec~~
                 except "A" Coy:
9. Each Company will detail 1 N.C.O. and three men as a cleaning party.
"A" Coy will detail 1 N.C.O. and five men, who will clean up the Company,
Headquarters and transport billets. Cleaning parties assemble when
finished at Orderly Room and march under the senior N.C.O. to destination.

                                    (Sd) T.J. Kelly. Captain.
                                          A/Adjutant,
                                          18th.Bn.Manchester Regt.
Issued by Order/at..........

No.1. C.O.
No.2. 2nd.in.Command.
No.3. Adjutant.
No.4. A. Coy.
No.5. B. Coy.
No.6. C. Coy.
No.7. D. Coy.
No.8. Q.M.
No.9. T.O.
No.10. M.O.
No.11. ~~Signal Officer.~~ Asst. Adjutant.
No.12. File.
No.13. War Diary.

Volume XVI.

SECRET.

WAR DIARY.

FOR THE MONTH OF FEBRUARY 1917.

18th.(Service) Battalion, THE MANCHESTER REGIMENT.

IN THE FIELD.
28.2.17.

T. Mully Capt.
~~Lieut.Colonel.~~
Commanding 18th.(S) Battn. Manchester Regt.

Army Form C. 2118

WAR DIARY
or
INTELLIGENCE SUMMARY
(Erase heading not required.) 18th Service Battalion Manchester Regt.

Sheet 3"A"
1917

Instructions regarding War Diaries and Intelligence Summaries are contained in F.S. Regs, Part II. and the Staff Manual respectively. Title Pages will be prepared in manuscript.

Place	Date	Hour	Summary of Events and Information	Remarks and references to Appendices
DOULLENS & SUS-ST-LEGER	Feb. 1917	1-3	C.O., Adjt., 23 Officers & 540 O.Rs billetted in DOULLENS, engaged on working parties for 110th (Railway) Coy. R.E. 2nd in Command & remainder of Battalion at SUS-ST-LEGER	200 Officers and S 500 O.R.
	"	4	Headquarters Details & 1 Platoon of "B" Coy., together with the party from SUS, move to billets in HALLOY. Remainder of Battalion to staff in DOULLENS under the command of Capt. C.N. HOMEWOOD, engaged on working parties as above.	H.F
DOULLENS & HALLOY	"	5-8	Whole Battalion on working parties. Capt. T. STANSFIELD, R.A.M.C., attached to the Battalion for duty from H.Q. in Ack. VICE Capt. W.H. RUTHER. R.A.M. (to No 6 Staft Hospital)	
	"	9	Headquarters & Details at HALLOY move to BEAUREPAIRE FARM, on the ARRAS - DOULLENS RD.	
DOULLENS & BEAUREPAIRE FM	"	10-12	Battalion on working parties. Lieut. J.S. BEAUMONT appointed G.S.O. III, 14th Divn. & struck off strength of Battalion accordingly. Draft of 10 O.R.S joined Battalion on the 12th from BASE.	
	"	13-28	On working parties as above. 2nd Lieut C. LAWRENCE & 2nd Lieut A.E. KENTLEY joined the Battalion for duty on the 22nd inst. 2nd Lieut L.F. ELLIOTT proceeded to Y.30 T.M. Battery 16.2.17 & so struck off strength of Battalion accordingly. 2nd Lieut W. EVANS proceeded to England 18.2.17 for special duty, & so struck off strength from that date	

T. Hull Capt.
Commdg 18th Battn Manchester Regt.

Appendix T.

To the G.O.C.,
90th. Bde.

I congratulate you on the turnout of the 18th. Manchester Regt today.

Their appearance on parade was a credit to you, to themselves and to the Brigade.

Please convey my congratulations to them, and thank them for the trouble they took to turn out well.

(Sd). J.S.Shea,

Major-General,

Commanding.30th.Division.

Certified True Copy

1-2-1917.

H 1

SECRET. [illegible] ORDERS No.4[illegible]. Copy No.........

By [illegible]

Commanding 16th Battalion,

Manchester Regiment.

1. Headquarters details and one platoon of "B" Company will proceed today to [illegible].

2. Parade at 2.0pm. in Church Square, ready to march off under a senior officer to [illegible].

3. All officers' kits, mess luggage and blankets will be dumped in the square near the [illegible] Road (outside Y.M.C.A. Building at 1.30pm.

4. The following officers will remain in [illegible] on detachment:-

"A" Company. Captain H. Sedgwick.
Lieut. [illegible] Roberts.
2nd Lieut. [illegible]
2nd Lieut. [illegible] Martin.

"B" Company. 2nd Lieut. [illegible] Westphal.
2nd Lieut. [illegible]

"C" Company. Captain [illegible] Norwood.
2nd Lieut. [illegible] Evans.
2nd Lieut. [illegible] Merritt.
2nd Lieut. [illegible]

"D" Company. Captain [illegible]
2nd Lieut. [illegible] Taylor.
2nd Lieut. [illegible]
2nd Lieut. [illegible] Lindsey.

(Sd.) [illegible], Captain,
Acting-Adjutant,
16th Bn. Manchester Rgt.

Issued by Orderly at..........

No.1. Headquarters.
No.2. O.C. "A" Company.
No.3. O.C. "B" Company.
No.4. O.C. "C" Company.
No.5. O.C. "D" Company.
No.6. File.
No.7. War Diary.

SECRET.

WAR DIARY.

FOR THE MONTH OF MARCH 1917.

18th. (Service) Battalion - THE MANCHESTER REGIMENT.

IN THE FIELD.   C.E. Lembcke   Lt.Col.
1.4.17.   Commanding 18th (S) Battalion,
                     The Manchester Regiment.

--- Volume XVII ---

---oOoOoOo---

Sheet 4 A

Army Form C. 2118

WAR DIARY
or
INTELLIGENCE SUMMARY

(Erase heading not required.) 18th (Service) Batt The Manchester Regt

Place	Date 1917	Hour	Summary of Events and Information	Remarks and references to Appendices
DOULLENS & BEAUREPAIRE	March 1-11		On working parties with 110th Company R.E. Battalion H.Q. & one Company at BEAUREPAIRE FARM and 3 Coys on detachment at DOULLENS under command of CAPTAIN C.J. HOMEWOOD.	
POMMERA	" 12		Battalion (less 3 coys detached) moves to POMMERA	O.1.
	" 13-16		Working parties POMMERA and DOULLENS.	
	" 17		Detachment at DOULLENS rejoins the battalion	O.2.
MONCHIET	" 19		Marched to MONCHIET, where relieves 18th K. LIVERPOOL REGT	O.3.
	" 20		Refitting & reconnaissance of new line by commanding officer and O.C.'s Coys.	
In the line	" 21	1.30 P.M.	Left MONCHIET for AGNY via BEAUMETZ, BAC DU NORD, and WAILLY.	O.4.
		5.0 P.M.	Arrives in old British line in front of AGNY & attested with	
		11.0 P.M.	Left to relieve 20th KINGS (L'POOL) REGT in outpost line in front of NEUVILLE VITASSE, M.23.6.3/2 to M.30.a.3/0 (Reference FRANCE 51b. S.W. Edition 3A)	

Army Form C. 2118

Sheet 5-A

WAR DIARY
or
INTELLIGENCE SUMMARY

(Erase heading not required.) 1/8 (Service) Batt. Manchester Regt.

Place	Date	Hour	Summary of Events and Information	Remarks and references to Appendices
In the line	March 22 1917	5.0 A.M.	Relief complete. "A" Coy are on the right, "D" on the left, "B" in support and "C" in reserve.	
"	"	7.30 P.M.	A & D Coys advanced the outpost line about 500 yards the new line being M.30 central to M.24.c.0.18 thereby shortening the length of front & gaining a much improved tactical position in regard to NEUVILLE VITASSE. The advance was carried out without casualties and at 8.45 P.M. O.C. "D" telephones that line had been occupied without opposition and was being consolidated.	
"	"23	5.0 A.M.	Relief of "A" and "D" in front line by "C" & "B" platoons complete.	
		9.0 P.M.	Patrol of 2nd Lt F.A.E MINTON and 4 O.R, from NEUVILLE MILL unoccupied. It was the intention to occupy a line of trench running from N.W. to S.E. through the mill, but this could not be carried out owing to battalion on the right

Army Form C. 2118.

Sheet 6 A

WAR DIARY
or
INTELLIGENCE SUMMARY

(Erase heading not required.) 1st (Service) Batt. The Manchester Regt.

Place	Date	Hour	Summary of Events and Information	Remarks and references to Appendices
In the Field 1917	23 (contd)		declining to co-operate. Casualties 2 killed 11 wounded.	
	24		Patrol (2nd Lt WARING, 2nd Lt NYATT and 40 O.R.) reconnoitred NEUVILLE REDOUBT which was found to be held by the enemy in force. 2 O.R. wounded.	
	25	5.0 A.M.	Relief of "B" & "C" by "D" and "A" was complete. Casualties 1 O.R. wounded.	
	26	7.30 P.M.	Patrol (2nd Lt C.T. LOFTHOUSE, 2nd Lt W.D. TRUSWELL and 40 O.R.) went forward to reconnoitre NEUVILLE VITASSE which the artillery reported unoccupied. It was found that enemy held NEUVILLE REDOUBT in strength. Patrol withdrew after being heavily fired upon. Casualties 1 O.R. wounded.	
	27	5.0 A.M.	Relief of "D" and "A" by "B" & "C" complete	

Army Form C. 2118

WAR DIARY
or
INTELLIGENCE SUMMARY

(Erase heading not required.) 18th (Service) Batt. The Manchester Regt.

Place	Date	Hour	Summary of Events and Information	Remarks and references to Appendices
In the line	March 1917			
	28		Battalion H.Q. moved to Old German dugout in SCHLANGEN REDOUBT. Casualty 1 O.R. wounded. 1 O.R. wounded	
	29	12.30 A.M.	The relief of the battalion by the 18th Batth KINGS (L'POOL) REGT was complete and companies marched off independently to BASSEUX, via FICHEUX, BLAIRVILLE and BRETENCOURT. The tour of duty March 21-29 was particularly trying on account of the severe weather, snow and heavy rain, to which the men were exposed without cover of any sort. In the front line they were compelled to defend or dry rations without hot food of any kind. The shelling was not severe but the conditions of service — open warfare while the battalion holds the real-time experiences provided a	O.S.

Army Form C. 2118

WAR DIARY
or
INTELLIGENCE SUMMARY
(Erase heading not required.)

Place	Date	Hour	Summary of Events and Information	Remarks and references to Appendices
Bus[?]	March 29 1917		test of orderliness and efficiency and ability to cope with a new situation. All ranks came through the test satisfactorily and the G.O.C. 30th Division called upon the commanding officer to day to express his appreciation of the attitude shewn one by the battalion	
"	30 + 31		Resting at BASSEUX. CAPT. H SEDGWICK left for Base (instructional duties) on March 30th and 2nd LT PHYTHIAN for 30th Divisional Depot.	

C.E. Smoker Lt Col
Commanding 18th Manchester Regt

O.1.

12.3.17.
Operation
Battalion/Order
By Captain T.J. Kelly.
Commanding 18th. Battalion.
The Manchester Regiment.

No.44.

1. All working parties are cancelled from to-day and the Battalion will move into billets at POMMERA.
2. The Battalion will parade at 10.0.am. and march off under the senior officer.
3. Detachment will parade at 10.30.am and march under Captain C.J. Honeyoad to POMMERA, where guides will be detailed to meet them.
4. No Transport other than Battalion transport is available. Blankets will be carried on the men. All Officer's kits will be sent up from BOULENS on the ration limber and will be sent to the Quartermaster, B'AUMEFAIRE FARM, by 10.0.am. Cookers at BOULENS will accompany the detachment. Officers' kits and baggage at BEAUMEFAIRE must be at the Q.M. Stores at 10.0.am.
5. Lieut. D.H. Roberts with four N.C.Os will proceed to POMMERA at 8.0.am and find the billets allotted, and apportion them to Companies. Guides will be sent to meet the Battalion and the Detachment.
6. O.C. Detachment will leave 2nd. Lieut. Shanahan and a party of 2x other ranks in BOULENS to clean up all billets. This party will follow when their works is completed and when the Officer has fulfilled the orders laid down for the Town.

(Sd) P.X. Ogden. 2nd. Lieut.
A/Adjutant,
18th. Bn.Manchester Regt.

No.1. File.
No.2. C.O.
No.3. Adjutant.
No.4. O.C.A.
No.5. O.C.B. (andNo.13)
No.6. O.C.C.
No.7. O.C.D.
No.8. T.O.
No.9. Q.M.
No.10. M.O.
No.11. Lieut.Roberts.
No.13. War Diary.

To: Captain C.J. Homewood.

The Detachment at DOULLENS will join the Battalion at POMMERA at 8.0.pm tonight. The G.S. Wagons and the Regimental transport are available for blankets, but perhaps you will be able to arrange lorries as you did on Monday. If the transport available is not adequate, the men will have to carry their blankets.

Please instruct 2nd.Lieut.Shanahan to carry out all the regulations laid down by the Town Major and see that every billet is clean, leaving a small party behind to clean up, if necessary.

17.5.17.

A/Adjutant, Captain.
18th.Bn.Manchester Regt.

13.3.17.
Operation Orders. No. M.46
By Lieut. Col. G.W. LAMBERT.
Commanding 19th. Bn. Manchester Regt.

1. The Battalion will march to MONCHIET tomorrow and relieve the 18th. Battalion, King's Liverpool Regiment.

2. An advance party consisting of 2nd.Lt.J.J. Shanahan, 2nd.Lt. G.T. Lofthouse, 1 Sergeant, 1 Corporal and 8 O.Rs from "A" Coy: will proceed direct to new billets at 8.0.am. "A" Company Lewis Gun Limber will accompany this party.

3. The Battalion will parade in the GRENAS Road – facing MONS – ready to march off, at 10.30.am. Head of column to be opposite the Quarter-master's stores.

4. Order of March:– Band. A.B.C.& D. Companies.

5. Transport will accompany the Battalion. Dinners will be served on the march, at the halt of 1 hour in the vicinity of Lebret.

6. All officers' valises and baggage will be at the Quartermaster's stores by 8.30.am. Blankets rolled in bundles of 10 will be at the stores at the same time. No reserve ammunition, bombs or any Battalion tools will be carried. These will be left behind and handed over to the relieving Battalion.

7. Lieut. Roberts – 1 Sergeant – and 9 Other Ranks from "B" Coy will be left behind to hand over billets to the relieving Battalion.

8. This party will march to new billets in the evening, using the main ARRAS Road behind Lebret.

9. DRESS:– LIGHT MARCHING ORDER.

10. Coy Commanders will themselves personally inspect all billets before

(Sd) R.J. Kelly. Captain. & Acting Lieut:Col.
&/Adjutant,
19th. Bn. Manchester Regt.

11.3.17.   Operation order no. 49.   Copy No...

By Lt. Col. C. A. LEMBCK,
Commanding 16th. Bn. Manchester Regt.

Ref: 51.b. 1/20,000.

1. The Battalion will move to-day to ABBY marching via LE BAC DU NORD - BAILLY - ABBY. Guides from the 17th. K.R.R. will meet the Battalion at A.W.S. - B/9.
2. Order of march: H.Q., A, B, C, and D Coys. A distance of 100 yards will be maintained between companies and 25 yards between platoons.
3. The Battalion will parade, ready to march off, in main street at 1.30.pm. Head of column to opposite Battalion H..
4. Only trench kit will be carried. Blankets will be taken to Quartermaster's stores at once and all officer's valises must be at the stores by 11.30 am.

(sd) T. E. Ogden. Cpl. Lt.
Adjutant,
16th. Bn. Manchester Regt.

28.3.17.　　　　　Operation Order. No. 48.　　　　　No. 1.
　　　　　　　　By Lieut. Col. C. E. LUMBCKE.
　　　　　　　　Commanding:-
　　　　　　　　　18th Battn. Manchester Regt.
----

1. The 18th. Bn. Manchester Regt. will be relieved in the Outpost Line by the 18th. Battalion King's Liverpool Regt during the night 28/29th. March, and will march to billets in BASSEUX via M.27.c.7/10 - FICHEUX - BLAIREVILLE - BRETENCOURT - BELLACOURT.

2. The relief of the front line companies will commence about 8.30.pm. Coys: will move off by platoons as soon as their relief is complete, Coy: Commanders reporting personally at Battn. H.Qs. on their way down.

3. 50 yds. distance will be maintained between platoons as far as BRETENCOURT where platoons will be closed up and Coys march at not less than 200 yards distance.

4. A hot meal will be served on the road between FICHEUX and BLAIREVILLE to each platoon as it arrives.

5. Lewis Gun Limbers and Maltese Cart will be drawn up west of the Rly. Embankment in M.27.c. by 10.pm. Coy: Commanders horses will await them there at the same time. hour.

6. Acknowledge.

　　　　　　　　　　　　　　　　(sd) W. E. Ogden. 2nd. Lt.
　　　　　　　　　　　　　　　　　　　　　　　　Adjutant.
　　　　　　　　　　　　　　　　　18th Bn. Manchester Regt.

No. 1. File.　2. CoO.
　　3. Adjt.　4. "A" Co;
　　5. "B" Coy: 6. "C" Coy:
　　7. "D" Coy: 8. War Diary.

SECRET.

WAR DIARY.

FOR THE MONTH OF APRIL 1917.

18th (Service) Battalion - THE MANCHESTER REGIMENT.

(Volume 18).

IN THE FIELD.
30.4.17.

..........C.G.Lembcke......Lieut.Col.
Commanding 18th (S) Battalion,
THE MANCHESTER REGIMENT.

Army Form C. 2118

Sheet 9 C

WAR DIARY
or
INTELLIGENCE SUMMARY
(Erase heading not required.)

18th (Service) Bn. Manchester Regt.

Instructions regarding War Diaries and Intelligence Summaries are contained in F.S. Regs., Part II. and the Staff Manual respectively. Title Pages will be prepared in manuscript.

Place	Date 1917	Hour	Summary of Events and Information	Remarks and references to Appendices
BASSEUX	Dec.	1/2	In rest billets.	
		3	Battalion relieved 2nd Royal Scots Fusiliers in Brigade Reserve in the MADELEINE REDOUBT, N.E. of MERCATEL. "A" & "D" Companies proceeding in advance to BOISLEUX-AU-MONT, under Capt. RISSIK.	C 1
BOISLEUX-AU-MONT		4	Remainder of the Battalion moved to BOISLEUX-AU-MONT.	
	5/7		In Brigade Reserve, & engaged on working & carrying parties.	
		8	Battalion moved to trenches in M.32.c & d. East of FICHEUX. Companies being in position by 1.0 am. Bn. H.Q. established at M.32.c.5/1.	
Area S. of MERCATEL		9	Orders received at 2.0 p.m. for Battalion to move to area M.35.c. South of MERCATEL, & occupy old outpost line — M.30 central to M.36.d.9/9. Movement completed by 8 p.m. "B" & "D" Coys. lying in old outpost line, "C" in Road M.30.c to M.36.a, "A" on Sunken Rd. running through M.35 a to a. "A" & "C" Companies sent to reinforce 19th Manchester Regt. in the line, "A" Coy. 1 platoon of "C" taking up a position along the road — N.20.c.6/2 to N.26 central, "C" Coy. (less 1 platoon) along the road — N.25.c.5/6 to N.26 c.0/8. Other Companies remain in same positions as before.	
		10	Orders received at 10 am for Battalion to move forward to the HINDENBURG LINE, in the vicinity of PANTHER LANE. Movement completed by 4.30 p.m.) Bn. H.Q. being established at N.27.a.7/7. 3 Companies disposed in PANTHER LANE, BUFF LANE, NEUVILLE VITASSE TRENCH, THE COT, and HENINEL fire-? support trenches. Orders received at 9 p.m. from 89th Infantry Brigade (under whose orders the Battalion then were) to cross the COJEUL RIVER, & bomb down the HINDENBURG LINE to the South-East. Instructions issued to "A" & "C" Companies to push forward forthwith across the river.	
HINDENBURG SYSTEM S.W. of HENINEL		11		

Army Form C. 2118

Sheet 10 C

Instructions regarding War Diaries and Intelligence Summaries are contained in F.S. Regs., Part II. and the Staff Manual respectively. Title Pages will be prepared in manuscript.

WAR DIARY
or
INTELLIGENCE SUMMARY

(Erase heading not required.) 18th (Service) Batt. Manchester Regt.

Place	Date	Hour	Summary of Events and Information	Remarks and references to Appendices
	Apl. 12		Operation completely successful. HINDENBURG LINE cleared as far as hill in 75 a. & numbers of the enemy either killed and put to flight. 10 Prisoners, 1 Trench Gun, 2 Machine Guns, 9 Aerial Torpedo Throwers captured, in addition to a large number of rifles, ammunition & grenades. Our own casualties — 6 O.Rs. Killed, 27 O.Rs. Wounded. Battalion relieved at 6 p.m. by 20th Royal Fusiliers & marched to billets in BASSEUX.	
			A full account of the operations carried out by the Battalion during the period Apl. 9/12 is contained in the report submitted to the 90th Inf. Bde., dated 14th April 1917, a copy of which is attached hereto. The report by 90th Inf. Bde. on the work of the Battalion is also appended.	C 2
				C 3
			The following message of congratulation was received from the Divisional Commander :—	
			"Please convey to all ranks of the Battalion my very hearty thanks & admiration for the magnificent conduct they displayed during the recent operations, & the splendid manner in which they attacked & routed the enemy, thereby rendering substantial assistance to another Division."	
			The following telegram was sent to 30th Division from 21st Division, with reference to the bombing operations carried out by the Battalion across the front of the latter Division :—	
			"Very many thanks for your valuable assistance this morning. Hope that the day is not distant when we can show our gratitude."	

Army Form C. 2118

WAR DIARY
or
INTELLIGENCE SUMMARY
(Erase heading not required.)

Sheet No. 11 C.   18th (Service) Battn. Manchester Regt.

Place	Date	Hour	Summary of Events and Information	Remarks and references to Appendices
BIENVILLERS AU-BOIS	April	13	Battalion moved to BIENVILLERS-AU-BOIS	
	14/17		In rest billets	
	18		Battalion relieved 3rd London Regt in trenches North West of NEUVILLE VITASSE. M 18.9.23	C4
NEUVILLE VITASSE area	19		Battalion moved up to relieve 1/14th London Scottish in Brigade Reserve in area South East of NEUVILLE VITASSE. Bn. HQ established at N.21.c.3/9. 2nd Lt. W.D.TRUSWELL & 1 O.R. Wounded	C5
	20/21		In Brigade Reserve. Battalion left at 11 p.m. to take up assembly	
	22		— do — positions for Reserve Battalion in attack on the 23rd April. Movement completed by 3 a.m. "A" & "B" Companies in position from N.34 d.4/9 to N.34 d.4/5, "C" & "D" Companies from N.34 d.95/35 to N.34 d.95/70. Bn. HQ at N.28 d.7/7.	
Trenches S.E. of HENINEL	23		"C" Coy was sent forward at 9.30 a.m. to reinforce 16th Manchester Regt. (who were supporting the attack of the 2nd Royal Scots Fusiliers & 4th Manchester Regt.) followed at 11 a.m. by "A"&"D" Companies. The remainder of the Battalion then moved up & reoccupied the old British front line, Bn. HQ being established at N.29 d.4/5. Orders received at 3 p.m. for re-establishment of the original front line, the Battalion accordingly taking over from N.29 d.8/6 to N.35 b.2/4 with all four companies in conjunction with 19th Manchester Regt. Orders were received at 4.40 p.m. at 6 p.m. the advance was to begin, "C" Company being on the left. "D" on the right, supported by "B" & "A" respectively. The objective was gained by about 8 p.m., but owing to all the Officers being become casualties & strong attacks of superior enemy forces, our men were forced to withdraw to the original line, which was held until midnight	

Army Form C. 2118

Sheet 12C.

WAR DIARY
or
INTELLIGENCE SUMMARY
(Erase heading not required.)

Instructions regarding War Diaries and Intelligence Summaries are contained in F.S. Regs., Part II. and the Staff Manual respectively. Title Pages will be prepared in manuscript.

Place	Date	Hour	Summary of Events and Information	Remarks and references to Appendices
NEUVILLE VITASSE AREA	Apr 23		+ then handed over to 2nd Wiltshire Regt. Battalion left for trenches South East of NEUVILLE VITASSE previously occupied during the period 20/22nd April, which were reached by 8 p.m.	
	24		A full account of the operations of the 23/24th to given in the report to 90th Inf. Bde. dated 26th Apr. 1917, copy of which is appended. The casualties were 15 Officers & 339 O.Rs. - Killed, Wounded & Missing. Killed - 2/Lt. H. DUNCAN. Wounded - Capt. C. RISSIK, 2/Lt. F. WATSON, 2/Lt. J.F. WARING, 2/Lt. S.M. SHIRLEY, 2/Lt. C. LAWRENCE, 2/Lt. J.E.M. TAYLOR. Died of Wounds - 2/Lt. G.S. MARTIN. Missing - 2/Lt. R. MAYBURY, 2/Lt. B.A. WESTPHAL, 2/Lt. N.B. GILL, 2/Lt. S.D. ASHEAD, 2/Lt. J.H. HAGUE, 2/Lt. F.A. EMINTON. Wounded & Missing - 2/Lt. S.J.L. WYATT.	C6
Trenches S.E. of NEUVILLE VITASSE	25/26		Resting.	
	27		Battalion marched to ARRAS, entraining at 11 p.m. for ST. POL.	C7
	28		Battalion arrived at ST. POL at 9.0 a.m. & marched to tilloch in CROISETTE.	
CROISETTE	29/30		Training, reorganising & refitting.	

2.5.17

C.E. Lennock Lieut.-Col.
Commanding 18th Bn. Manchester Regt.

3.4.17.   Operation Order No. 48.
               By Lieut.Col.C.E.L-MBCK-,
               Commanding 18th. Battalion,
SECRET.   The Manchester Regiment.
Reference sheet 51.B.S.W.) 1/20.000.
               51.C.S.E)

1. The 18th.Bn.Manchester Regiment will relieve the Battalion in Brigade Reserve, during the night 3rd/4th April.

2. Parade in column of route on the BASSEUX - BAILLEULVAL Road, ready to march off at 7.0.pm. Head of column to be opposite the Orderly Room - facing N.W. Order of March:- "B" Coy: - "C" Coy:

3. ROUTE:- BELLACOURT - BRETENCOURT - BLAIRVILLE - FICHEUX.

4. Movement West of the old British front line will be by companies at 200 yards distance.

5. Blankets will be rolled in bundles of 10 and deposited at the Q.M. Stores by 12. Noon. Officers' kits will be there at the same hour.

6. Company Commanders will report personally at Bn. H.Q. on completion of their relief.

7. Cookers and watercart will accompany the Battalion.

8. Acknowledge.

                                   ....Ogden...... 2nd.Lieut.
                                   A/Adjutant,
                                   18th.Bn.Manchester Regt.

1. File.
2. C.O.
3. Adjt.
4,5,6 & 7. Companies.
8. T.O.
9. M.O.
10. Q.M.
11. War Diary.
12.   do.
13. 2nd.in.Command.

C2

To:-
    HEADQUARTERS,
        90TH. INFANTRY BRIGADE.

           I submit herewith a report on operations carried
out by the Battalion under my command during the period
April 9th. to 12th.

April 9th. At 2.0pm. orders were received for the battalion to move
forward by Companies from the trenches east of FICHEUX,
M32.c & d. along the infantry track to the area M35c, South
of MERCATEL. By 8pm. the Companies were disposed as follows:-
"B" & "D" in the old outpost line M30 Central to M36d9/9,
"C" in the road M30c to M36a, and "A" on the Sunken Road
running through M35a & c. Orders to reinforce the 19th.Bn.
MANCHESTER REGIMENT were received at 9pm, and "A" & "C" Companies
were despatched to do so.

April 10th. The relief was complete at 2.0am. "A"Company and 1 platoon of
"C" took up a line along the road N20c6/2 to N26 Central,
"C"Company (less 1 platoon) occupied the road,N25b5/6. to
N26c0/8, the others remaining in the same position. Twelve
hours later,2pm,preparations were made to attack HENINEL in
conjunction with the 16th.Bn.MANCHESTER REGIMENT, information
having been received that the enemy had abandoned his post,
but at 3pm this order was cancelled and the situation
remained unchanged throughout the rest of the day.

April 11th. Two platoons of "A"Company were ordered at 9am. to proceed to
the triangle where Nagpur Trench crosses the Hindenburg Line
and join a Company of the 16th.Bn.Manchester Regt who were to
bomb their way along the Hindenburg Line. It was found,
however, that the situation was not what had been supposed
on the previous day and at 10.am preparations were made for
battalion to move forward to the Hindenburg Line in the vicinity
of Panther lane. The battalion then came under orders of the
89th.Brigade. By 4.30pm the manoeuvre was complete. Headquarters
was established at N27a7/7 and Companies disposed in Panther
lane, Buff lane, Neuville Vitasse Trench, The bot, HENINEL
TRENCH and HENINEL SUPPORT, the right flank sentry
group being in position in N 28. C. just N.E. of
the ST MARTIN-SUR-COJEUL — HENINEL ROAD.
    A minor bombing operation was under-
taken by two platoons of "D" Coy under 2nd Lieut
W.D. TRUSWELL and 2nd Lieut W. LINDSAY. There
object was to bomb along an unmarked trench
which ran approximately from N. 28. A. 0/6. to
N28.b. 20/95. and thence if possible to NEPAL
TRENCH. The party moved off at 5.15.p.m. and
made progress until reaching a point
close upon the road at N28.b. 20/95.
They found a block about half way between
the road and HENINEL SUPPORT (N28.a.6/7)
but carried it after throwing a few bombs.
The road was apparently strongly held and
as the operation hampered by a driving
snow storm and the darkness, the Company

April 11th (continued).
Commander decided to withdraw, considering that the gain would not have out-weighed the possible loss of life.

Acting on the suggestion of the G.O.C. 90th Infy. Bde. I issued orders at 8.30.pm. for Companies to be ready to move off at dawn and bomb down the HINDENBURG LINE. At 9.p.m. the G.O.C. 89th Infy Bde ordered that this attack should be carried out at once and instructions were given accordingly. A preliminary reconnaissance shewed that the Operation was likely to be a difficult one, for apart from any severe fighting that might have to be undertaken the trenches were in a very bad state as a result of the snow and the men themselves had suffered greatly through the cold and wet.

April 12th.

The actual operation was carried out by "A" and "C" Companies re-inforced later by "D" Company. "A" Company's task was to work their way down the Support Line whilst "C" moved along the Fire Trench. Before starting 2nd/Lieut. G. S. MARTIN who was in command of "A" Company crossed the river with 2nd Lieut. S. M. SHIRLEY. and one man to endeavour to find out how strong the enemy were on the other side. They were fired at with rifles, but succeeded in crossing and discovered a sentry group of four Germans at the

April 12th (Continued).

trench junction N34.a.8/8., returning without mishap. 2nd Lieut. N.B.GILL. and a Sergeant who attempted to make a similar reconnaissance further north to find a crossing for "C" Coy. were held up by wire, but after sending back for wire-cutters they were able to make a crossing.

Owing to this delay "A" Company were away first, and their bombing section led by 2nd Lieut. S.M.SHIRLEY. crossed the river, under a barrage provided by rifle grenadiers and Lewis gunners, about 3.0.a.m. on the 12th inst., and advancing across the open, got into the front line HENIFIEL TRENCH. at a point N28.c.8/1. On nearing the sentry group the officer, who was on the parapet, called upon the enemy to surrender, but as they hesitated he emptied his revolver into them and then threw a bomb. One man ran away and the others were killed. About a hundred yards further down the trench the party saw a number of the enemy emerging from a dug-out and again threw bombs. The enemy who had been re-inforced by others in the trench gave way slowly, replying to our bombs and rifle grenades with small aerial torpedos and bombs, but they were gradually forced back. On reaching N34.a.9/5. the officer who was leading found that his supply of grenades and bombs was very low and, forming a block at the trench junction,

April 12th (Continued).

he sent back for further supplies and also for re-inforcements. As his men were waiting here a party of the enemy, about 30 in number were seen coming toward the post from the direction of HENINEL SUPPORT. The Lewis Gun section who, under command of 2nd/Lieut: C. LAWRENCE, had followed the bombing party were brought into action and fired at once, inflicting several casualties and wholly breaking up the counter-attack. Those of the enemy who were not hit at once fled and disappeared into HENINEL SUPPORT TRENCH again.

Meanwhile "C" Coy. had been overcoming difficult obstacles in the vicinity of the river. They had to cut the wire not only in the river but in the marshy banks as well and they did not cross until "A" Coy. were hotly engaged. 2nd Lieut. B. A. WESTPHAL, who was in command, judged by the firing and bomb explosions that "A" Coy. had got into the firing instead of the Support Line, so he deemed it advisable to push down the support line and establish touch with them by means of one of the communication trenches. Finding also that he was being heavily sniped from the direction of HENINEL he sent a platoon under 2nd/Lieut. J. E. SMART to deal with this danger. The last named officer made a wide detour and dislodged several snipers who were enfilading HENINEL SUPPORT from the

April. 2nd (Continued).

road through N.28.d. He then turned half right and got back into HENINEL SUPPORT Trench at about N.34.b.5.4 where he rejoined his company. 2nd Lieut. B.A. WESTPHAL met with strenuous opposition at first, but made progress gradually, the enemy weakening as the flanking platoon came forward from the north.

Taking one platoon across the open to the fire trench the Commander of "C" Company established touch with "A" Company and was able to give him bombs and rifle grenades. Re-inforcements of 2 platoons of "D" Coy. for "A" and 2 platoons of the same Coy. for "C" also arrived bringing with them fresh supplies, and the two Coy. Commanders decided to proceed with the attack simultaneously. It was broad day light before every-thing had been arranged to continue the operation.

The enemy followed his former tactics, using aerial torpedos and rifle grenades and then returning down the trench, and at first progress was slow. The opposition appeared to grow weaker as we neared the ridge, and just before we gained our objective it was observed that the enemy was evacuating his trenches further south and making off to the North through N.35.C & B. The target offered was such as rarely occurs in this war and the Lewis Guns of "C" Coy. in HENINEL SUPPORT trench

April 12th (Continued)

were promptly brought to bear. The guns were placed on the parapet and took the fleeing enemy in rear and enfilade causing as far as could be judged over a hundred casualties.

There is little to add about the actual operation which was now practically over for we had reached the objective. Posts were at once established at T.5.a.7.8. and along the communication trench to T.5.a.1.5. About 10.0.p.m. an Officer's patrol searched HENINEL and reported it clear of the enemy and a little later the advanced scouts of the Queen Victoria Rifles (56th Division) established touch with our left flank and a battn. of the 21st Division came forward into HENINEL SUPPORT, making communication with right.

Altogether over 1,400 yards of trench were captured by bombing and very heavy casualties were inflicted on the enemy. It was impossible to carry the line further forward, for though the enemy were so obviously disorganised our own men were extremely fatigued and the work of consolidating and holding what had been taken and clearing out dug-outs stretched their physical powers to the extreme limit. It must be admitted that the enemy was

April 12th (Continued).

taken entirely by surprise, though he put up a good fight at the start. Many Germans were in dug-outs having a meal of hot coffee and when the fighting was done, our men were able to regale themselves with hot drinks, Lager beer, eggs, and tinned meat. In one dug-out alone 50 loaves were found.

Though the HINDENBURG LINE, both firing and support trenches, was found unfurnished for defence — no fire-steps having been made and Machine Gun emplacements only half constructed — there were many deep dug-outs in the support and communication trenches. These were connected up by a continuous passage parallel with the front line, which fact enabled many of the enemy to escape. Prisoners stated that this passage was over 400 yards in length. In two dug-outs there were lying twelve wounded men of the 21st Division who had been captured the previous day. They had been bandaged and given food and drink by their captors.

Our own haul of prisoners was 10, but one was accidentally killed by a bomb thrown by mistake. Four others were wounded and sent straight to the Dressing Station. Many more prisoners would have been taken if our men had been fresh enough

April 5th (Continued).

to gather the full fruits of their victory. Owing to the thick mud many rifles became choked with earth and it was impossible to bring them to bear on the enemy as they ran back across the open. The booty included:-

1. Trench Gun
9. Throwers for aerial torpedoes
2. Machine Guns (carried away several hours after the attack by men of another division).

besides a great number of rifles, ammunition and hand grenades. The latter were freely used by us when our own bombs grew scarce.

It is impossible to give an accurate estimate of the casualties inflicted on the enemy. Certainly over a hundred were killed in the open and between COJEUL River and N.31.a.8/5. there were 30 bodies in the fire trench alone, most of whom so far as could be judged perished in our attack. The support trench was even more thickly strewn with dead Germans. Our casualties were 6 killed and 27 wounded.

During the attack an officer of "A" Coy (2nd Lieut. Bentley) who was going to inspect his sentry group by the COJEUL River came across a party of 16 Germans marching toward HENINEL TRENCH on the road through N.28.d. He had only his servant with him, but the enemy had no

April 12th. (continued).

-rifles. They were apparently making their way forward with further supplies of bombs, and on seeing him they immediately broke up and scattered. Two were killed by revolver or Rifle bullets and four others ran into the arms of another platoon of "A" Company and were captured. The rest unfortuneately escaped.

14/4/1917.

C. E. Lembcke Lieut.-Col.
Commanding 18th Bn. Manchester Regt.

War Diary

C 3

18th. Battalion, Manchester Regt.

On 11th. April an attack delivered by troops of the 21st. Division and the 89th. Brigade was held up by a stubborn Boche resistance, and bombing parties of 35th. Division troops and a Company of the 16th. Bn. Mchr. Regt. were attacking the enemy's flank in the HINDENBURG LINE.

The 18th. Battalion, Manchester Regt. were ordered to pass through these troops and carry on the work, and if possible clean the HINDENBURG SYSTEM right across the 21st. Division front to the top of the hill in x.5.a.

Under the personal supervision of the C.O. they did the job so thoroughly that before daylight on 12th. over 1000 yards of the HINDENBURG LINE was cleared, several prisoners captured, many of the enemy put out of action, and a German trench gun taken.

The Lewis Gunners of this Battalion had the good fortune to get on to retreating Germans later in the day and over 100 casualties are reported to have been inflicted.

-o-o-o-o-

C4

SECRET.   OPERATION ORDERS, 49.   Copy No......
                    By Lieut. Col. G. E. LEMBCKE,
18.4.17.   Commanding 18th Battalion,
                    THE MANCHESTER REGIMENT.

1.   The Battalion will move to the MERCATEL area to-day.

2.   Parade in column of route ready to march off at 11.45am on the main road facing N. Head of column to be opposite H.Qs Mess. Order of march - Band, A, B, C and D Companies.

3.   As far as possible, packs will be carried on limbers. Only the great-coat is to be put in the pack; all other effects will be tied up in sandbags, and deposited at the Quartermasters Stores by 11.0.am. Officers valises will also be there at the same hour.

4.   Cookers will accompany the Battalion. Dinner will be served at 1.50.pm; tea at 5.50.pm.

5.   The Quartermaster's Stores and details will remain not move with the Battalion, but will remain in their present billets until further orders.

                                    (Sd) W.E. Ogden. 2nd. Lieut.
                                            A/Adjutant,
                                        18th.Bn.Manchester Regt.

1. C.O.   2. 2nd. in/c.
3. Adjt. 4. File.
5, 6, 7 & 8 Companies.
9. Q.M. 10. T.O. 11. M.O.
12/13. War Diary.

SECRET.   OPERATION ORDERS. No. 50.   Copy No......
By Lieut. Col. C.E. LEMBCKE,
Commanding 18th Battalion,
THE MANCHESTER REGIMENT.

1. The Battalion will be prepared to move at once to relieve the 1/14th London Scottish in reserve, and will hold NEPAL TRENCH.

2. Order of march:- "A" "B" "C" & "D" Companies. Companies will take up their position in the Line in that order. "A" on the right.

3. The Battalion will move down the BEAURAINS - NEUVILLE VITASSE Road at ¼ hour intervals between Companies, the leading Company notifying the next Company when it is ready to move off.

4. Guides will meet companies at the cross roads in N.20.b. From this point the Companies will move in artillery formation. Guides will be at Cross roads at 2.30.pm.

5. One Officer per Company and 1 N.C.O. per platoon will remain with the relieving company till noon of the 20th instant. Officers Commanding Companies must arrange about rationig these men with the Officers Commanding the Companies they relieve.

6. Headquarters Company will move ¼ hour after "D" Company.
   Cookers and watercarts will accompany the Battalion. Packs will be worn.

7. S.O.S. Signal - Two Red Lights.

8. Completion of relief willbe reported personally by Officers Commanding Companies to Battalion Headquarters, situated at N.21.c.3/9.

                                (Sd) W.E. Ogden. 2nd. Lieut.
                                     A/Adjutant,
                                     18th.Bn.Manchester Regt.
19.4.17.

C6

To: Headquarters,
    90th. Infantry Brigade.

I submit herewith report on operations April 22/24.

Leaving the trenches South East of NEUVILLE VITASSE at 11.0.pm on April 22nd. the Battalion reached the assembly positions in the vicinity of HENINEL at 3.0.am on April 23rd being in reserve to the 90th. Infantry Brigade. "C" & "D" Companies were in position from N.28.d.95/35 to N.34.b.95/70 and "A" & "B" in N.34.b.4.9. to N.34.b.4/5.

At 9.30.am an order was received to reinforce the 16th.Bn. Manchester Regiment with one company, and "C" Coy were sent forward. The Battalion (less "C" Coy:) then moved to the old British front line, headquarters being established at N.29.d.4/5. "A" & "B" were ordered to reinforce at 11.0.am and advanced to join the 16th. Bn. Manchester Regt. These companies thus came under the orders of the O.C. 16th.Bn. Manchester Regt and remained so until at 3.0.pm an order was issued (B.M.180) for re-establishing the old front line. Therefore the other three Battalions of the Brigade withdrew and the 16th.Bn. Manchester Regiment took over the line from N.29.d.3/6 to N.35.b.2/4. During these operations there were very few casualties, though the three Companies who had been attached to the 16th. Bn. Manchester Regt. had borne an active share in the attack.

The order to attack the Blue Line in conjunction with the 19th. Bn. Manchester Regiment was received at 4.40.pm, and though, from the disposition of the Battalion at that time it was not easy to get into fighting formation the necessary manoeuvres were carried out speedily and at 6.0.pm (Zero) the advance towards the distant objective was begun. The formation followed was that laid down in Brigade

Brigade Orders, viz, four waves each of two lines on a four platoon frontage. "D" Coy: were on the right supported by "A", who being on the extreme right of our line had to execute a half right wheel to get into position, and "C" Coy: on the left supported by "B" Company.

The leading wave kept fairly close to the barrage as they advanced and had hardly left our line when enemy machine guns opened from the front and both flanks. Despite casualties the advance continued unchecked until the right company reached the bank at N.36.b.2/4 and the left were forward of the pature ground. At this point the whole line was temporarily held up, not only on account of the heavy machine gun fire, but also because there had been several Officer casualties and some little re-organisation was necessary. Nevertheless it was found possible to push forward very soon, though by this time the suporting companies had become merged into the firing line, and moving on steadily the line now battalion, led by 2nd.Lt. Watson and 2nd. Lt. Lawrence (the only officers remaining) reached the objective about 8.0.pm.

Almost immediately afterwards both Officers were wounded and the Companies battalion, by this time reduced to less than 100 strong, was left in the charge of Junior N.C.Os. The trench itself was not then clear of the enemy and sharp hand-to-hand fights took place in which several of the Germans were killed. For 20 minutes our men were left undisturbed, but then the enemy launched a counter attack, first opening fire from the front and right flank with rifle grenades. Under such a barrage strong bombing parties advanced towards the trench and though our men put up a good fight, using all their Mills bombs and rifle grenades with good effect they were finally overwhelmed by weight of numbers and forced to withdraw. As they came back the enemy followed, showing great daring in bringing his machine guns

guns forward. About 53 men of all Companies reached our old front line between 9.30.pm and midnight and with these and details of the 17th. Bn. Manchester Regiment and various Battalions of the Kings (Liverpool) Regiment, this line was made secure. The night defence of the line was then handed over to the 2nd. Battalion, Wiltshire Regiment.

Though every Company Officer who went forward became a casualty, a few succeeded in getting back to our lines and from interviews with them and conversations with the men who returned, I am convinced that the objective was taken. Many of our dead lie in close proximity to the blue line and the wounded and other survivors, interviewed separately, are able to supply without prompting, an exact description of the cable trench which marks the objective. If any Officers had survived to organise the defence of the position and supports had arrived in time, probably the gain would have been held. Unfortunately the Battalion in support suffered in the advance and lost direction and consequently were unable to give any assistance.

The casualties throghout the operations were 15 Officers and 339 O.R. killed, wounded and missing.

............................Lieut.Col.
Commanding 18th.Battalion,
MANCHESTER REGIMENT.

26.4.17.

SECRET.

OPERATION ORDERS.
No. 5/.
By Lieut. Col. C. E. LEMBCKE,
Commanding 18th (S) Battalion,
THE MANCHESTER REGIMENT.

No...... 6

26th. APRIL. 1917.

1. The Battalion will move to billets in the CROISETTE & WIGNACOURT tomorrow the 27th. instant., entraining at ARRAS at 4.10.pm.

2. Parade, ready to march off, at 12 noon, on NEUVILLE VITASSE ROAD, head of column to be at the cross roads N. of Battalion Headquarters facing north.

3. Order of march:- A, B, C, and D, Coys:

4. Dress:- Marching order. Great-coats and leather jerkins will not be worn.

5. All H.Q. and 2 Company horses will be on the NEUVILLE VITASSE - BEAURAINS ROAD., just outside NEUVILLE VITASSE at 12.15.pm. Band will meet the Battalion at the same hour and place. Horses to carry a days feed.

6. All first line transport, including cookers, water carts, mess cart, maltese cart and Officers horses (except as detailed in paras 5 and 7) will leave AGNY at 2.0.pm for GOUY - WANQUENTIN area, where they will rest for the night.

7. The Transport Officer will arrange for three limbers to be at Cross roads, just north of Battalion H.Q. by 11.0.am. These will be packed with Officers' kits and Company Camp kettles which must be on the road by 10.45am. These limbers will accompany the Battalion as far as ARRAS, after which they will rejoin the remainder of the First Line transport at the GOUY - WANQUENTIN area.

8. Company Commanders will ensure that the men's boots are removed, socks changed if possible, and feet rubbed before moving off.

            (Sd) W.E. Ogden. 2nd. Lieut.
               A/Adjutant,
              18th.Bn.MANCHESTER REGIMENT.

Copies issued by Orderly at:-

Copy: No.1. C.O.
     2. O.C., "A" & "B".
     3. O.C., "C" & "D".
     4. T.O. & Q.M.
     5. FILE.
     6. WAR DIARY.
     7. ---do-----.

SECRET.

WAR DIARY.

FOR THE

MONTH OF MAY 1917.

18th. (Service) Battalion, THE MANCHESTER REGIMENT.

(Volume XIX)

IN THE FIELD.　　　　　　　　　　　　　　　*C.E Limbatt* Lieut.Col.
31.5.17.　　　　　　　　　　　　　　　Commanding 18th (S) Battalion,
　　　　　　　　　　　　　　　　　　　THE MANCHESTER REGIMENT.

Army Form C. 2118

WAR DIARY
or
INTELLIGENCE SUMMARY
(Erase heading not required.) 18th (Service) Battn. Manchester Regiment

Instructions regarding War Diaries and Intelligence Summaries are contained in F. S. Regs., Part II. and the Staff Manual respectively. Title Pages will be prepared in manuscript.

Place	Date 1917	Hour	Summary of Events and Information	Remarks and references to Appendices
CROISETTE	Sep 1/2		Reorganising & refitting. Lieut. J.F. LEWIS and draft of 148 O.R.s joined the Battalion for duty from the Base.	X 1
LE QUESNOY	3		Battalion moved to billets at LE QUESNOY	
	4		Training. Battalion Memorial Service in the evening.	
	5		—Do— 2/Lt. O. WILCOX attached to the Battalion for duty from 30th Divl Depot.	
	6		Church Parade in the morning	
	7		Tactical Operations on Brigade Manoeuvre Area. Major J.K. AITKEN & Capt. J.M. GREER joined the Battalion today from the Base	
	8/9		Training	
	10		—Do— Brigade Operations on Manoeuvre Area	
	11		—Do— Lieut. J.O. McELROY & Lieut. N. KOHNSTAMM joined for duty today from the Base	
	12		Inspection of 90th Infantry Brigade by Corps Commander in the morning, followed by March Past.	
	13		Church Parade in the morning	
	14		Training. 2/Lt. J.E. LOVE joined the Battalion today from the Base	
	15		Training in the morning. Combined Sports & Gymkhana in the afternoon, organised in conjunction with 2nd Bn Royal Scots Fusiliers.	
	16/9		Training. 2/Lt. E. HOLLAND joined the Battalion for duty from the Base	

Army Form C. 2118

WAR DIARY
or
INTELLIGENCE SUMMARY

(Erase heading not required.) 18th (Service) Battn. Manchester Regiment

Place	Date	Hour	Summary of Events and Information	Remarks and references to Appendices
	1917			
	May 20		30th Division moved to HAZEBROUCK area. The Battalion marching from LE QUESNOY to CROISETTE	×2
	21		From CROISETTE to PRESSY-LES-PERNES	×3
	22		From PRESSY-LES-PERNES to AUCHY-AU-BOIS	×4
	23		Resting 2/Lt. H. WHINCUP joined the Battalion to duty from the Base	
	24		From AUCHY-AU-BOIS to ISBERGUES	×5
	25		From ISBERGUES to camp N of HAZEBROUCK	×6
HAZEBROUCK area	26		Training	
	27		Church Parade in the morning. Lieut. H.G. WATSON reported the Battalion from ENGLAND to day. The following N.C.O.'s & men were mentioned in Sir Douglas Haig's despatch dated 9th April 1917 for gallant & distinguished conduct in the field :- 9921 Sergt. H.V. RAVENSCROFT 10838 Sergt. O. SEDGWICK (since killed), 10119 Corpl. A.S. FERGIE 10526 Pte. P.J. KENNEDY	
	28/30		Training 2/Lt. T.W. COWAN joined the Battalion for duty	
	31		Battalion moved to billets Ex LUMBRES, travelling by train to ST. OMER & hence by bus.	×7

W. E. Lembcke Lieut.-Col.
Commanding 18th Bn. Manchester Regt.

X 1

OPERATION ORDER NO.52.
By Lieut.Colonel. C. E. LEMBCKE,
Commanding 18th. (S) Battalion,
THE MANCHESTER REGIMENT.

SECRET.

Copy No......

2.8.17.

1. The Battalion will move to billets in LE QUESNOY tomorrow.

2. Parade in column of route on the WIGHACOURT ROAD facing S.E., at 9.20.am, ready to march off at 9.30.am. Head of column to be opposite the Orderly Room.

3. ORDER OF MARCH:- Band, Headquarters, "C", "B", "A" and "D" Coys:

4. TRANSPORT and train wagons will march with the Battalion. Blankets will be rolled in bundles of 10 and deposited at the Quartermasters Stores at 8.30.am. Officer's valises will be there at the same time.

5. 1 N.C.O. will be detailed from "C" Coy: and 1 man from A, B, and D Companies to act as guard over the blankets.

6. A billeting party consisting of the Quartermaster, the four Coy: Quartermaster Sergeants, Corporal Clynn, and one N.C.O. from the Transport will proceed in advance at 8.0.am.

7. Dinners will be served on the march at 12.30.pm. Greatcoats and leather jerkins will not be worn.

............................2nd.Lieut.
A/Adjutant,
13th.Bn.Manchester Regt.

1. C.O.   2. 2nd.in.Command.
3. Adjt.   4. File.
5 to 8. Companies.
9. T.O.   10. M.O.
11.Q.M.   12.13. War Diary.

SECRET.

X 2

OPERATION ORDERS NO.55.
By Lieut.Col. G.E. LARDEN,
Commanding 12th (S) Battalion,
THE MANCHESTER REGIMENT.

Copy No....

19/5/17

1. The Battalion will march to billets in CROISETTE tomorrow.

2. Parade in column of route at 8.0.am, ready to move off at 8.15am; Head of the column to be at the Cross Roads N.E. of the village.

3. Order of march: Band, H.Qs., "D", "A", "B", "C" Companies.

4. Route: WARLINCOURT - HOUVELIN - OSLAGNY - PHILLEVICH - LIGNEUX - CROISETTE.

5. An advance party consisting of Lieut.& Quartermaster T.C. Pierce, the four Company Quartermaster Sergeants, Corporal Glynn, one N.C.O. to be detailed by the Transport Officer and 1 other representative from each Company will leave WARLINCOURT at 7.30.am.

6. Blankets will be rolled in bundles of 10 and deposited at the Quartermaster's Stores by 8.0.am. Officers' kits will be there (not later than 7.0.am.

7. The strictest attention must be paid to march discipline en route. Any man given permission to fall out on the line of march will be collected by the Provost Sergeant and marched in rear of the column.

Issued by Orderly at.....

1. C.O.
2. 2nd.in.Command.
3. File.
4.5.6.7. Coy:Commanders.
8. T.O.
9. Q.M.
10.M.O.
11. Adjutant.
12/13. War Diary.

..................2nd.Lieut.
A/Adjutant,
12th.Bn. MANCHESTER REGIMENT.

SECRET.   X 3

OPERATION ORDERS NO. 54.
By Lieut.Col. G. E. LAMBCKE,
Commanding 18th Battalion,
THE MANCHESTER REGIMENT.

21/5/17

1. The Battalion will march to billets at PRESSY-LEZ-PERNES and FAUX tomorrow.
2. Parade in column of route - facing N.W. - ready to move off at 9.15am. Head of column to be opposite the Orderly Room.
3. Order of march: Band, H.Qs. "A", "B", "C" and "D" Companies.
4. Route:- ST. POL - WAVRANS - HESTRUS - TANGRY - PRESSY-LEZ-PERNES.
5. An advance party, as already detailed, under Lieut. & Quartermaster T.G. Pierce will leave for PRESSY at 7.0.am.
6. Blankets to be at the Quartermaster's Stores by 6.30.am. Officers' valises by 8.0.am.
7. The Orderly Officer will march in rear of the Battalion to collect stragglers.
8. Officers Commanding Companies will report in writing when their Companies have arrived in billets.

Note: Company Commanders will ensure that march discipline, which the Commanding Officer noticed was rather lax to-day, is tightened up.

                                                            2nd.Lieut.
                                            A/Adjutant,
Issued by Orderly at....   18th. Bn. Manchester Regt.

No.1. C.O.
   2. 2nd.in.Command.
   3. Adjutant.
   4. File.
   5.6.7.8. Coys:
   9. Q.M.
  10. T.O.
  11. M.O.
  12 and 13. War Diary.

Copy No. 12.

OPERATION ORDERS NO.56.

By Lieut. Colonel. C.J. LEDGARD,
Commanding 18th (Service) Battn.,
THE MANCHESTER REGIMENT.

1. The Battalion will march to billets at LEBUCQUIERE tomorrow.

2. Parade in column of route - ready to march off - at 9.35.am. Head of column to be opposite the Orderly Room, facing N.E.

3. Order of March: Band, Headquarters, "C", "D", "A" and "B" Coys:

4. Route:- Mt. HILAIRE -- HAM-EN-ARTOIS - BROQUETS - INBEQUES.

5. Advance Party under Captain H.G.S. Bower will leave for LEBUCQUES at 7.0.am.

6. Blankets to be at the Quartermaster's Stores by 6.30.am. Officers' valises by 8.15.am.

7. The Orderly Officer will march in rear of the Battalion and bring along any stragglers. Strict march discipline will be enforced.

/signed/
2nd. Lieut.,
Adjutant,
18th.Bn. Manchester Regt.

1. C.O.
2. 2nd. in-Command
3. Adjutant.
4. File.
5.6.7.8. Coys.
9. T.O.
10. Q.M.
11. M.O.
12/13. War Diary.

24.5.17

X6

OPERATION ORDERS No. 57.
By Lieut. Colonel. G. E. LEMBKE,
Commanding 18th (S) Battalion,
THE MANCHESTER REGIMENT.

1. The Battalion will march to Camp N. of HAZEBROUCK tomorrow.

2. Parade in column of route, ready to march off at 7.30.am. Head of column to be opposite the Boys' School, facing S.E.

3. Order of March: Band: Headquarters, D, A, B and C Companies.

4. ROUTE:- ST. VENANT - HAVERSKERQUE - STEENBECQUE Station - MORBECQUE - HAZEBROUCK.

5. Blankets to be at the Quartermaster's Stores by 6.30.am: Officers' valises by the same hour.

6. A halt will be made for dinners on the road North of MORBECQUE.

7. Strict march discipline will be maintained: and orders regarding stragglers &c., adhered to in every respect.

                                                    E Ogden   2nd. Lieut.
1. C.O.   A/Adjutant,
2. 2nd.in.Command.   18th. Bn. Manchester Regiment.
3. Adjutant.
4. File.
5.6.7.8. Coys.
9. Q.M.
10. T.O.
11. M.O.
12.13. War Diary.

X 7

Copy No. 13

OPERATION ORDER No. 52.

By LIEUT.COLONEL C. E. LAMBERT.,
Commanding, 19th. SERVICE BATTALION,
THE MANCHESTER REGIMENT.

Reference:- Map BAPAUOME. 1/100,000.

1. The Battalion (less Transport) will move to billets at LHEULUE, tomorrow 31st May, entraining at CARNOY at 11.a.m.

2. Movement will be by train as far as St.OMER; thence by bus.

3. Parade in column of route - facing S.E.- ready to march off at 10.a.m, tail of the column to be at the Camp Gates.

4. Order of March:- Band, Headquarters, A, B, C, & D Companies.

5. Blankets to be at the Quartermaster's Stores by 7.a.m; Officers' kits not later than 8.a.m.

6. The Transport will move by road, billetting for the night 31st.May/1st June at LONGUENESSE, and rejoin the Battalion at LHEULUE on the 1st June.

30th.May.1917.

2nd.Lieut,
A/Adjutant,
19th.Bn.MANCHESTER REGIMENT.

Copy 1. Commanding Officer.
2. 2nd.in.Command.
3. Adjutant.
4. File.
5. "A"Coy.
6. "B"Coy.
7. "C"Coy.
8. "D"Coy.
9. Quartermaster.
10. Transport Officer.
11. Medical Officer.
12.& 13. War Diary.

SECRET.

WAR - DIARY.

for the

MONTH OF JUNE 1917.

18th. SERVICE BATTALION - THE MANCHESTER REGIMENT.

(Volume XX.)

IN THE FIELD.   *C.E Lembcke*   Lieut.Colonel.
                                 Commanding 18th (S) Battalion,
30.6.17.   THE MANCHESTER REGIMENT.

Seif /14 A

Army Form C. 2118

WAR DIARY
or
INTELLIGENCE SUMMARY
(Erase heading not required.)

18th (Service) Batt. Manchester Regt.

Instructions regarding War Diaries and Intelligence Summaries are contained in F. S. Regs., Part II. and the Staff Manual respectively. Title Pages will be prepared in manuscript.

Place	Date 1917	Hour	Summary of Events and Information	Remarks and references to Appendices
LUMBRES	June 1/2		Training. Draft of 83 O.R.s joined the Battalion from the Base.	
	3		Church Parade in the morning.	
	4/5		Training.	
	6		Battalion moved by bus to area N. of POPERINGHE, and billetted in the vicinity of HIPSHOEK. The following Officers were struck off the strength of the Battalion with effect from to-day :— 2/Lt. G.G. MILLER (transferred to 3rd Field Survey Company, R.E.) 2/Lt. H. DAY (to U.K. sick)	A1
HIPSHOEK	7/8		Training. 2/Lt. J.E. CROSS, 2/Lt. E.U. GRIFFITH & 26 O.R.s joined the Battalion for duty from the Base.	
	9		Battalion marched to TORONTO CAMP (BRANDHOEK Area). The following N.C.O.s awarded D.C.M. for gallant & distinguished conduct in the field (Birthday Honours List) :— 43658 L/Sgt. A.C. DEAN, 9952 L/Cpl. C. WOODWARD.	A2
TORONTO CAMP	10		Church Parade in the morning. "A" Company, under the command of Major T.J. KELLY, proceeded to CAVALRY BARRACKS, YPRES, in the evening, not rejoining the Battalion until the 14th inst. During this time they were engaged on nightly working parties.	
	11/13		Training, & supplying working parties in the forward area. 2/Lt. H.J.S. REYNOLDS joined the Battalion for duty from the Base.	
	14		Battalion left TORONTO CAMP at 8.45 p.m. to relieve 17th Manchester Regt. in the Left HOOGE Sector, moving by companies along the Infantry Track as far as ZILLEBEKE, & thence by VINCE STREET to their allotted positions. "A" Company moved into position under orders issued direct to them by Brigade Headquarters.	A3
	15		By 2.0 a.m. the relief was complete, & Companies disposed as follows:—	

1875 Wt. W593/826 1,000,000 4/15 J.B.C. & A. A.D.S.S./Forms/C. 2118.

Army Form C. 2118

Sheet 15.A

Instructions regarding War Diaries and Intelligence Summaries are contained in F.S. Regs., Part II. and the Staff Manual respectively. Title Pages will be prepared in manuscript.

WAR DIARY
or
INTELLIGENCE SUMMARY
(Erase heading not required.)

18th (Service) Batt. Manchester Regt

Place	Date 1917	Hour	Summary of Events and Information	Remarks and references to Appendices
Trenches	June 16		"A" Coy. FRONT LINE, "C" Coy. MAPLE TRENCH, "B" Coy. WELLINGTON CRESCENT, "D" Coy. RITZ ST. Battalion Headquarters situated in MAPLE TRENCH (I.24.a.2/6) An inter-Company relief was carried out during the night 16/17th. "B" Coy relieving "A" in the front line, "D" Coy. relieving "B" in WELLINGTON CRESCENT, "A" Coy going back to reserve in RITZ ST. The same night a patrol of 1 Officer & 10 O.Rs. under 2/Lt. J.E.SMART. reconnoitred No Mans Land with a view to the construction of a forward trench running from I.2.a.6/3.	
	17/19		Work was commenced on this trench the following night, but progress was slow owing to the difficult nature of the ground, & thick undergrowth. By the third night, however, a considerable portion had been dug, to a depth varying from 2 to 4 feet.	
	20		About 4 a.m. on the morning of the 20th, a hostile patrol of 1 N.C.O. & 11 men attempted to enter our forward line. Rapid fire was opened by the garrison, after which the Officer in Command, Capt. J.G.CUNLIFFE led a party of men over the parapet & succeeded in capturing 4 prisoners (2 unwounded), including the N.C.O in charge of the patrol. The prisoners were identified as belonging to the 463rd R.I.R.	
	21		The relief of the Battalion by the 2nd Wiltshire Regt. commenced about 10.30 p.m. & on completion, the Battalion marched by Companies to MICMAC CAMP, the last company arriving by 6 a.m.	
	22		At 7.30 p.m. the Battalion left the Camp & marched to RENINGHELST, entraining at 10 a.m. for WATTEN, & marching from thence to billets at NORDAUSQUES. The casualties for the period 13/22nd June	

Army Form C. 2118

Sheet 16 A

WAR DIARY
or
INTELLIGENCE SUMMARY

(Erase heading not required.) 1/8 (1st line) Batt. Manchester Regt

Instructions regarding War Diaries and Intelligence Summaries are contained in F.S. Regs., Part II. and the Staff Manual respectively. Title Pages will be prepared in manuscript.

Place	Date	Hour	Summary of Events and Information	Remarks and references to Appendices
NORDAUSQUES	June		were :- Officers. Wounded. 2/Lt. J.E. SHANAHAN Other Ranks. - Killed 6. Wounded 22. Died of Gas poisoning 3. The following Officers joined the Battalion for duty on the dates shown :- 2/Lt. H. SIMMONDS - 16.6.17, 2/Lt. R.F. EGERTON, 2/Lt. HINXDEN, 2/Lt. W.E. HARDING, 2/Lt. A.V. DYSON - 17.6.17	
	23		Resting.	
	24		Church Parade in the morning.	
	25		Training.	
	26		-Do- Attack Practice in the morning, in conjunction with 16th Manchester Regt. The names of the following Servant Officers were brought to notice for gallant & distinguished conduct in the field on 20th June :- 10209 C.S.M. G. RYAN, 47656 Pte. S. GUNTERNICK, 28752 Pte. N. BROOKS.	
	27		Training.	
	28		Battalion moved to MICMAC CAMP by train from NATTEN to ABEELE thence by march route, via RENINGHELST & OUDERDOM. Drafts of 81 O.Rs & 60 O.Rs joined the Battalion for duty today.	A4
	29		Battalion moved to DICKEBUSCH HUTS by Companies commencing at 9 a.m. The following N.C.O's & men were awarded the Military Medal for gallantry in the field :- 9946 L/Cpl. W.F. WEBB, 47656 Pte. S. GUNTERNICK, 28752 Pte. N. BROOKS. 2 Companies engaged on working party during the night 29/30th.	A5
DICKEBUSCH Area	30		Working parties as yesterday. Capt. S.E. WOOLLAM struck off the strength at the Battalion with effect from 9.5.17. Names of the following men brought to notice for gallant & distinguished conduct :- C.S.R. Ipbecke Lieut. Col. Commdg. 1/8 (1st) Bn. Manchester Regt 47909 Pte. J. COWLEY.	

1875   Wt. W593/836 1,000,000 4/15   J.B.C. & A.   A.D.S.S. (Forms) C.2118.

OPERATION ORDER NO. 59.
By Lieut. Colonel. G.B. DUBERY,
Commanding 10th (S) Battalion,
THE MANCHESTER REGIMENT.
Ref. Meaulte 1/40,000 MAP.

1. The Battalion (less Transport) will move to the POPERINGHE area tomorrow the 6th instant, by Bus.

2. Parade in close column of Companies on the Square facing Headquarters Mess at 8.0.a.m.

3. Dress: Full marching order. Steel helmets to be worn except whilst actually in the Busses, when soft caps may be worn.

4. Officers' Kits to be at the Quartermaster's Stores not later than 7.30.a.m.

5. Special care must be taken that all Billets are left in a clean and sanitary condition. The Orderly Officer will report to the Adjutant at 8.15.a.m. that he has inspected Billets and found them in a satisfactory condition.

                                         J.E.Ogden
                                    Capt. and 2nd. Lieut.
                                         A/Adjutant,
                                    10th.Bn. MANCHESTER REGT.

1. C.O.
2. Maj.in.Command.
3. Adjutant.
4. File.
5. O.C.
6. I.O.
7. O.C. Companies.
11. War Diary.

5/6/17.

June 8th, 1917.   Battalion OPERATION ORDERS No.60.
                   By Lieut.Colonel. C.E. LAMBCKE,
                   Commanding 18th (S) Battalion,
                   THE MANCHESTER REGIMENT.
Ref. Map Sheets 27 and 28 - 1/40,000.

1. The Battalion (less Transport) will march to TORONTO CAMP tomorrow the 9th inst. and relieve the 20th King's Liverpool Regt.

2. Parade in column of route on the ST.JAN - TEN - BIELEN Road ready to move off at 1.30.pm. Head of column to be 500 yards N.E. of Cross Roads at t.1.c.9/0 facing N.E.

3. Order of march: Band, H.Qs. "D" "A" "B" "C" Companies.

4. Movement as far as POPERINGHE will be by Companies at 300 yards distance; thence by platoons at 100 yards distance.

5. Precautions will be taken against hostile aircraft by halting on the side of the road and if possible getting under cover.

6. The Transport will move to VLAMERTINGHE starting at 1.0.pm. Officers' Kits to be at the Q.M. Stores by 12 noon.

7. Acknowledge.

                                              ....[signed] E.Ogden........2nd.Lieut.
1.C.O. 2.2nd.i/c.   /Adjutant,
3. Adjt. 4. File.   18th. Bn. Manchester Regt..
5.6.7.8. Coys.
9.T.O. 10.Q.M.
11.M.O. 12.I.O. War Diary.

Issued by Orderly at..........

SECRET.
Battalion Operation Orders No.61.
By Lieut. Colonel. C.E. LEMBCKE.,
Commanding 18th (Service) Battalion,
THE MANCHESTER REGIMENT.

Ref. Sheet 28 N.W. 1/20000 (& ZILLEBEKE 1/10,000).

1. The 18th.Bn. Manchester Regt. will relieve the 17th. Bn. Manchester Regiment, in the Left HOOGE Sector during the night 14/15th June 1917.

2. The disposition of Companies in the line will be as follows:-
   "A" Company -   Front Line.
   "C" Company - (with Coy: H.Q.)   MAPLE TRENCH.
   "B" Company - ("   "   ")   WELLINGTON CRESCENT.
   "D" Company - (with "   ")   RITZ STREET.

3. Battalion H.Qs. will be situated in MAPLE TRENCH (I.24.a.1/6).

4. Movement will be by Platoons at 200 yards distance, in the order:-
"C", "B", "D" Companies, the first platoon of "C" Company moving off at 8.45.pm. Companies will proceed by Infantry Track as far as ZILLEBEKE and thence by VINCE STREET to their allotted positions.
   "A" Company will move in accordance with orders issued direct to them by Brigade Headquarters.

4a. The Acting R.S.M. and four Company Sergeant Majors, Gas N.C.Os (1 per Company and Battn. H.Q.) and Signalling Sergeant with a proportion of Signallers, will leave at 2.0.pm this afternoon and proceed to the Line to take over from the 17th.Bn. Manchester Regt.

5. Lewis Gun Limbers will be taken up as far as possible, and then unloaded and sent back to the Transport Lines in G.24.c. In order to facilitate unloading, each limber will move with its own Company.

6. The Maltese Cart will follow with Battalion H.Q. Cookers and Water-Carts proceed direct to Transport Lines, after teas have been served. Officers Mess Cart will call at H.Q. Mess to convey all Cooking utensils etc., not required in the trenches, to the Transport Lines.

7. Officers' valises to be at the Orderly Room by 7.0.pm

8. Care must be taken to ensure that the Camp is left in a clean and sanitary condition; Officers Commanding Companies are held responsible that all huts, tents, etc., vacated by them, are left perfectly clean.

9. Completion of reliefs to be wired to Bn. H.Q. - using SECOND ARMY TRENCH CODE.

10. Acknowledge.

                                                     2nd.Lieut.
                                            A/Adjutant.
                                            18th.Bn. Manchester Regt.

14th. June. 1917.
Issued by Orderly at _____ pm.
1.C.O.   2.2nd.in.Command.
3.Adjt.   4.File.
5.6.7.8. Coys.
9.T.O.   10.Q.M.
11.M.O.   12.17th.Bn.M/C.Rgt.
13.14. War Diary.

OPERATION ORDERS No. 62

27th June.1917. By Lieut. Colonel. C.E. LEMBCKE,
Commanding 18th (S) Battalion,
THE LANCASHIRE REGIMENT.

Ref: HAZEBROUCK 1/100,000 -Sheets 27 and 28 - 1/80,000.

1. The Battalion will move to MICMAC CAMP tomorrow the 28th instant, entraining at BAYEUX at 10.0.am.
2. Movement will be by train as far as ARNEKE; thence by march route via RUBROUCK and CUHEM to the Camp.
3. Parade in Column of Route on the main CALAIS Rd., ready to march off at 7.30.am; head of the column to be at the junction of TOURNEHEM and main CALAIS Roads (just E. of the final 'U' in NORDAUSQUES) facing S.E.
4. Order of march:- Band, H.Q., A, B, C and D. Coys.
5. The Orderly Officer will march in rear of the battalion to collect stragglers. It is essential that, should any men fall out on the way to the Station, they are brought along with the least possible delay.
6. Company Commanders will ensure that all men in their Companies are warned of the necessity of observing strict Train Discipline, any breach of which will be severely dealt with.
7. No baggage of any kind will be taken on the train. Lewis Guns will be handed in to the Q.M. Stores by 6.30.am and conveyed by lorry to the Camp. Officers' valises will not be taken forward but will be deposited at the Quartermaster's Stores before the Battalion moves off. "Trench Kits" and Company Mess Boxes &c., to be taken to the forward area must be at the Q.M. Stores not later than 7.0.am; it is most important that Mess Boxes should be as light as possible.
8. All billets must be left clean. The Orderly Officer will report to the Adjutant before the Battn. moves off that they have been inspected and found in a clean and sanitary condition.
9. Acknowledge.

1. C.O. 2. 2nd.in.C. 3. Adjt. 4. File.

H.E.Ogden
2nd.Lieut.

A5

OPERATION ORDER   No 63.

Sheet 28 N.W.   1/40,000.

1. The Battn. will march to Camp at H.20.d.9. tomorrow the 29th inst.

2. Movement will be by Companies, 'A' Coy. leaving MICMAC CAMP at 9.0. am and the remainder at intervals of 5 minutes in the following order — B. C. D. H.Q.

3. Route :- Road Junction H.31.b.1/4. thence by road running through H.31.b.; H.25.A. H.26.a.; H.20.c. and d.

4. The Transport will follow in rear of H.Q. Coy. at an interval of 10 minutes.

5. The usual precautions must be taken to guard against hostile aircraft, by halting, getting on the side of the road under cover if possible.

6. Acknowledge.

Issued by orderly at 10.15 pm
1. File. 2. O.C. A. Coy
3. O.C. B Coy 4. O.C. C Coy
5. C.O.   6. T.O.
7. War diary
28.6.1917.

H.E Ogden
2nd Lt
A/Adjt
18th Bn. Mchr. Regt.

CONFIDENTIAL.

WAR DIARY.

for the

MONTH of JULY 1917.

18th. (Service) Battalion - THE MANCHESTER REGIMENT.

(VOLUME XXI)

In the Field.
31.7.17.

C.E. Lembcke Lieut.Colonel.
Commanding 18th (S) Battalion,
THE MANCHESTER REGIMENT.

Sheet No. 17 G

Army Form C. 2118.

WAR DIARY
or
INTELLIGENCE SUMMARY.
(Erase heading not required.) 18th (Service) Batt. Manchester Regiment

Place	Date	Hour	Summary of Events and Information	Remarks and references to Appendices
	1917			
DICKEBUSCH HUTS	July 1/3		Battalion engaged on working & carrying parties in the forward area. Capt. C.J.HOMEWOOD rejoined the Battalion from Senior Officers Course, England, & is taken on the strength of the Battalion accordingly. 2/Lt. J. WALSH joined the Battalion for duty from the Base	
	4/5		Battalion engaged with remainder of the Brigade on digging assembly trenches. (A copy of runs from 30th Divn. to 90th Bde. congratulating them on the work done, is attached.) Capt. R. MOBKIRK and 2/Lt. J.E.BODDINGTON struck off the establishment of the Battalion. Casualties for the period July 1st-5th :- Killed - 1 O.R. Wounded 7 O.Rs	G 1
	6		Battalion proceeded to RENINGHELST by march route & thence by train to WATTEN, where detrained marched to billets at RUMINGHEM, arriving about 10 p.m.	G 2
	7		Left RUMINGHEM at 9.30 a.m. & marched to billets at LOUCHES, arriving at 2 p.m. Capt. J.G CUNLIFFE awarded the Military Cross, and 10207 C.S.M. G. RYAN the D.C.M. for gallantry in action	

Sheet 18 G

WAR DIARY
or
INTELLIGENCE SUMMARY.

(Erase heading not required.) 18th (Service) Batt. Manchester Regiment

Army Form C. 2118.

Place	Date	Hour	Summary of Events and Information	Remarks and references to Appendices
	1917			
LOUCHES	July 8		Church Parade in the morning. Lieut. M. BRUNTON rejoined the Battalion from U.K., today.	
	9/14		Battalion engaged on training & carrying out Attack practices on the TOURNEHEM Picture Ground. Draft of 34 O.Rs. joined for duty from the Base, 9.7.17. 2/Lt. C.T. TURPIN struck off the establishment of the Battalion with effect from 15.4.17.	
	15		Divisional Horse Show & Band Display at NORDAUSQUES, in the afternoon.	
	16		Brigade Attack Practice on the Picture Ground.	
	17		Battalion moved by bus to camp near WIPPENHOEK, arriving at 11.30 p.m.	G 3
WIPPENHOEK Area.	18/21		Training. 2/Lt. W. LINDSAY transferred to U.K., sick, & struck off the strength of the Battalion accordingly.	
	22		Battalion moved to OTTAWA CAMP (G.30.a.5/7.)	G 4
	23/24		Battalion left for CHATEAU SEGARD at 10 p.m., arriving in position by 1.30 a.m. on the morning of the 24th inst.	G 5

Sheet. 19.

Army Form C. 2118.

WAR DIARY
or
INTELLIGENCE SUMMARY

(Erase heading not required.) 18th (Service) Batt. Manchester Regt.

Place	Date	Hour	Summary of Events and Information	Remarks and references to Appendices
CHATEAU SEGARD	July 1917 24/27		Battalion engaged on working and carrying parties in the forward area.	
	26		On the 26th inst., the Battalion carried out a daylight raid on the enemy's trenches from J.24.b.9/8 to J.19.a.2/4 inflicting casualties on the enemy & obtaining information as to his dispositions. The report on this operation by OC. Infantry Brigade, is attached. The casualties sustained by us were:- 2/Lt. W. PHYTHIAN Wounded, 3 ORs. Killed, 9 ORs. Wounded.	G 6 / G 7
Line	28		At 9p.m. on the 28th inst. the Battalion left CHATEAU SEGARD, to relieve the 19th Kings Liverpool Regt. in the line, the relief being complete by 3 a.m. the following morning. During the whole of the 29th & 30th. the companies remained in the front line & outposts trenches.	G 8
	30		At 10 p.m. on the night of the 30th inst. assembled in No Mans Land in readiness for the attack next morning.	
	31		At Zero (3.50 a.m.) the Battalion advanced across SANCTUARY	

Sheet. 20 G

Army Form C. 2118.

WAR DIARY
or
INTELLIGENCE SUMMARY.

(Erase heading not required.) 18th (Service) Batt. Manchester Regt.

Place	Date	Hour	Summary of Events and Information	Remarks and references to Appendices
	1917			
	July 31		WOOD, and by 5.30 a.m. had succeeded in capturing its final objective, the BLUE LINE East of STIRLING CASTLE. A detailed account of the operations July 28th to Aug 1st will be found in the attached report, submitted to 90th Infantry Brigade.	G 9
			Casualties (Officers)	
			Killed :- 2/Lt. H. MADEN, 2/Lt. H. SIMMONDS	
			Wounded :- Capt. J.G.CUNLIFFE, M.C. (Died of Wounds, 1.8.17) 2/Lt. E.HOLLAND, 2/Lt. E.V.GRIFFITH, 2/Lt. A.V.DYSON 2/Lt. T.W. COWAP.	
			Wounded slightly, at duty :- Lieut.Col. C.E.HEMBCKE, Lieut. J.O.McELROY.	
			(Other Ranks)	
			Killed :- 32	
			Wounded :- 116	
			Missing :- 79	

C. E. Lenbcke Lieut. Col.
Commdg 18th (S) Bn. Manchester Regt

G 1.

COPY OF TELEGRAM RECEIVED FROM 30TH. DIVISION HEADQUARTERS.

To:- "DRAT"

B.M.205.   5th.July.1917.

Following just received from EDITH aaa G.O.C. Division congratulates DON on their work of last night aaa It shows both good training and organization aaa Ends.

From:- "DON"
Time:- 10.35.am.

G 2.

(SECRET)   BATTALION OPERATION ORDER NO 64.
By Lieut. Colonel. C.E. LEECHE.
Commanding 19th (S) Battalion.,
THE MANCHESTER REGT.

Reference: (Sheet. 28.   1/40,000.
(HAZEBROUCK. 5a. 1/100,000.

1. The Battalion Mess Carrying Party as detailed in para 4) will move to RUMINGHEM tomorrow the 6th instant, and thence to LOUCHES on the morning of the 7th instant.

2. Movement will be by march route (via OUDEZEEM) to RENINGHELST, and thence by train to WATTEN where the Battalion will detrain and march to billets at RUMINGHEM.

3. Companies will move off tomorrow morning at a time to be notified later (between 4.0.am and 6.30.am) in the order: A, B, C, D, H.Qs. 200 yards distance to be maintained between Companies.

Arrangements will be made for breakfast to be served in the vicinity of RENINGHELST.

4. "D" Company will continue to supply the carrying party of 4 Officers and 126 O.Rs. for the 2nd. Canadian Tunnelling Company R.E. on the nights of 5/6th and 6/7th instant. This party will proceed to the LOUCHES area with and under the orders of the 90th Infantry Brigade on the morning of the 7th instant. The remainder of the Company under 2/Lt W.E.HARDING will march with the Battalion tomorrow.

5. The Transport will accompany the Battalion until breakfasts have been served after which, it will move independently in accordance with instructions already issued.

Lewis Guns, Company Mess Boxes &c., to be at the Q.M. Stores tonight.

Issued by Orderly at _6.15 p.m_.

1. C.O.
2. 2nd.in.Command.
3. Adjutant.
4. File.
5.)
6.) All
7.) Coys:
8.)
9.) T.O.
10. M.O.
11.)
12.)-War Diary.

N E Ogden
2nd.Lieut.
A/Adjutant,
19th.Bn. MANCHESTER REGT.

G.3.

July 16th. 1917.   BATTALION OPERATION ORDER NO.66.

By Lieut.Colonel. C.E. LEMBCKE,
Commanding 18th (Service) Battalion,
THE MANCHESTER REGIMENT.

Reference:- HAZEBROUCK 5a. 1/100,000.

1. The Battalion will move by bus to the WIPPENHOEK area tomorrow the 17th instant.

2. Parade in column of route ready to march off at 1.15.pm. Head of the column to be opposite Headquarters Mess facing N.E.

3. Order of march: Headquarters Coy: Band: "A", "B", "C" and "D" Coys.

4. Companies will be told off into parties of 24 each under an Officer or Senior N.C.O. and on arrival at the embussing point will be formed up on the right of the road with an interval of 5 yards between parties. Each party will occupy one bus.

5. Steel helmets must be worn except whilst actually in the busses.

6. A halt will be made at 7.0.pm in the STEENEVOORDE area for about 2 hours when the men may debus and tea be prepared. On receiving the order to re-embus, all ranks will re-occupy the busses in which they travelled previously.

7. The following baggage only is allowed to be carried on vehicles:-
   Two Camp Kettles per Bus.
   Officers' "Tea Baskets".

(All other baggage, Officers' valises, Mess stores etc., will be conveyed by lorry to the new area and must be at the Quartermaster's Stores by 8.0.am. tomorrow.)

8. Company Commanders will ensure that all billets are left scrupulously clean and will render a certificate to this effect to the Orderly Room by 1.0.pm.

9. ACKNOWLEDGE.

H E Ogden
Lieut.
A/Adjutant,
18th.Bn.Manchester Regt.

Issued by Orderly at 9.50 pm.

1. C.O.
2. 2nd.in.Command.
3. Adjutant.
4. File.
5.6.7.8. Coys.
9. M.O.
10. S.O.
11. Q.M.
12.13. War Diary.

21.7.17.   OPERATION ORDERS NO.67.   (SECRET).
By Lieut. Colonel. C. E. LEMBCKE,
Commanding 18th (S) Battalion,
THE MANCHESTER REGIMENT.

Reference: Sheets 27 and 28 - 1/40,000.

1. The Battalion will move to OTTAWA CAMP (G.30.a.5/7) tomorrow, the 22nd.instant.

2. Parade in column of route ready to march off at 6.30.am., on the road W. of the Camp. Head of the column to be opposite the Orderly Room, facing S.

3. Order of March: H.Q., Band, "C", "D", "A" and "B" Companies.

4. Route:- Cross Roads, L.35.d.15/35 - RENINGHELST - OUDERDOM.

5. 200 yards interval will be maintained between companies after passing RENINGHELST.

6. An advance party consisting of Lieut. & Qr.Mr. T.C.PIERCE and the four Company Quartermaster-Sergeants will leave present camp at 6.0.am. tomorrow and will proceed to the new area where they will take over from the 12th. Battalion. MIDDLESEX REGIMENT.

7. One Officer and 2.O.Rs. per Company will be left behind to clean up, and to hand over the Camp to the incoming Battalion. This party will rejoin the Battalion as soon as possible at OTTAWA CAMP.

8. Tea will be issued before the commencement of the march. Breakfasts will be served immediately on arrival in the new area.

9. The Transport will follow in rear of the Battalion; 300 yards distance behind the rear Company after passing RENINGHELST.

10. ACKNOWLEDGE.

........................Lieut.
A/Adjutant,
18th.Bn.Manchester Regiment.

1. C.O.
2. 2nd.in.Command.
3. Adjutant.
4. File.
5.6.7.8. Coys.
9. T.O.
10. M.O.
11. S.O.
12. Q.M.
13.14.War Diary.

-o-o-o-o-

G5.

SECRET.

OPERATION ORDERS. No.66.
By Lieut. Colonel. G. E. LAMBCKE,
Commanding 18th (Service) Battalion,
THE MANCHESTER REGIMENT.

1. The Battalion will move to the CHATEAU SEGARD area, during the night 23/24th July.

2. Movement will be by companies in the order: "A", "B", "C", "D", H.Q., – "A" Coy: moving off at 10.pm. and the remainder following at intervals of 200 yards.

3. Lewis Gun Limbers will follow ~~~~ in rear of their respective companies and must be unloaded immediately on arrival and sent back.

4. Cookers will not accompany the Battalion. Sufficient utensils for cooking must be taken for each company. One cook per company will remain with the cookers.
   One watercart will be taken.

5. The equipment, tools, rifles &c., of the 3 platoons of "B" Coy: engaged on carrying party to-night, will be deposited at the Q.M's Stores by 7.pm. and conveyed by limber to the new area. O.C., "B" Coy: will detail a party to unload these kits immediately on arrival.

6. The Band will form a carrying party to take up bombs &c. and will report to the Quartermaster at 9.30.pm for instructions.
   Dress: Fatigue dress with Box Respirators & Steel helmets.

7. Officers valises will not be taken forward, but should be deposited at the Q.M's Stores not later than 9.pm. Trench kits to be there by the same hour.

8. ACKNOWLEDGE.

            J E Ogden
              Lieut.
              A/Adjutant,
              19th.Bn.Manchester Regt.

Issued by Orderly at..6.30.pm
Copy No.1. C.O.
        2. 2nd.in.Command.
        3. Adjutant.
        4. File.
        5.6.7.8. Coys.
        9. T.O.
        10. M.O.
        11. Q.M.
        12. S.O.
        13.14. War Diary.

July 23rd, 1917. OPERATION ORDER NO. 67.
By Lieut. Colonel. C. E. LEMBCKE,
Commanding 18th Battalion,
T H E   M A N C H E S T E R   R E G T.

1. The Battalion will carry out a raid on the enemy trenches situated between points from Left to Right (North and South) I.24.b.9.8. to J.19.a.2/4, up to and inclusive of JAM SUPPORT TRENCH between the points J.19.a.50.95 and 19.a.65.50, with the object of inflicting casualties on the enemy, obtaining prisoners and capturing or destroying hostile machine guns.

2. The raid will be carried out on a date and at an hour to be notified later.

3. "D" Company will execute the raid and will be organised as follows:-

    Four Platoons of 25 O.Rs with 1 Lewis Gun.

    The Platoons will be organised as follows:-

    Nos. 14, 15 and 16 platoons:-
        10 Riflemen.
         9 Bombers.
         6 Rifle Grenadiers.
        25 O.Rs.

    and No.13 Platoon:-
         9 Riflemen.
         7 Bombers.
         6 Rifle Grenadiers.
         3 Lewis Gunners with one Gun.
        25 O.Rs.

4. The attack will be carried out in two waves and four lines. Nos. 14, 15 and 16 Platoons in the leading or assaulting wave; No.13 platoon in the 2nd. or covering wave.

    Lieut. KOHISTAMM will be in command of No. 14. Platoon.
    2nd.Lt.PHYTHIAN " " " " " No. 15. Platoon.
    2nd.Lt.HARDING   " " " " " No. 16. Platoon.

    The Covering Party or second wave will be under the personal control of the O.C., Company: Captain J.F. LEWIS.

    The leading wave will be preceded by two guides or scouts per platoon, who will have already reconnoitred, carefully, "No Man's Land" on the day prior to the raid.
    These Scouts will be responsible for the correct direction being kept by their platoons and will also lay out tapes to guide the raiders back to our Lines on completion of the raid.
    The Platoon Commanders will also reconnoitre the ground they have to cross over to reach their objectives and will have made themselves fully acquainted with all of its peculiarities. On this depends the success of the raid and of future operations.

5. The CORPS and DIVISIONAL Artillery will co-operate with a creeping barrage. The 'Jumps' of the barrage have been communicated separately to all concerned.

6. The assaulting and covering waves will leave the assembly trench five minutes before 'ZERO' and assemble in 'No Man's Land' ready to dash forward as soon as the barrage lifts from the enemy front line. No real opposition may be expected before reaching JAM SUPPORT but all ranks must be prepared for any eventuality and must press the raid successfully home at all costs as the experience and information gained will be invaluable during future operations.
    DIRECTION, which is most important will be kept by compass bearings and by means of white tapes which will be laid across "No Man's Land" by the guides of the leading wave.

(over:-

7. PROCEDURE OF THE ASSAULTING WAVE IN THE ENEMY TRENCHES.

On entering the enemy trenches the assaulting wave will break up into three parties as follows:-

No.14. Platoon on the Right.
No.15. Platoon in the Centre.
No.16. Platoon on the Left.

No.14. Platoon working up JAM ROW communication trench with a bombing party in the trench.

No.16. Platoon will move up the BEAK and JACKDAW AVENUE Communication Trench, in the same manner, and

No.15. Platoon - or Centre Platoon - will move forward with the barrage over the top to JAM SUPPORT TRENCH.

Blocks will be established at points as marked on attached map and mopping up will then be proceeded with.

8. PRISONERS.
Prisoners will be sent back at once to Battalion Headquarters. Also captured material. Prisoners will be handed over to the covering party who will be responsible for bringing them back with as small an escort as possible. An escort of 2 men for 10 prisoners should suffice. Escorts must remember that all prisoners that are made are more useful alive than dead. This must be impressed upon all ranks taking part in the raid, but if it is found necessary to kill a prisoner his body must be brought in.

9. The Raid will last 45 minutes from the time the barrage lifts from the enemy front line, until the raiders are back in "No Man's Land". the O.C. Coy: will give his signal for the withdrawl by blowing his whistle and firing 2 VERY Lights in quick succession. On the signal for the withdrawl being given, forward blocking parties will be withdrawn then the remainder of the raiders, the very greatest care being taken that any of our own men who have been either killed or wounded are brought back.

On no account must the body (if we are unfortunate enough to have a man killed) be left to the enemy. The covering wave will be responsible for watching the flanks, bringing back prisoners and covering the withdrawal and will move back to "No Man's Land" when the O.C., Company is fully satisfied that all men of ~~his~~ the assaulting waves are clear of the enemy trenches.

10. INFORMATION.
Information as to the progress of the raid will be continually sent back by O.C. Company, by means of runners, to the Battalion Headquarters, which will be situated in or close up to our own front line. Officers Commanding Companies will have four runners with them.

11. All badges/of rank will be removed from the uniform and all papers orders, maps and identity discs will be left behind by all ranks.
(except badges)

C. E. Lembcke Lieut Col.

Copy No.1.
No.2.
No.3.
No.4.
No.5.
No.6.
No.7.

30th Division."G" G/159.

REPORT ON OPERATIONS OF July 26th 1917.

Party of 2 Officers and 40 Men 18th Bn. Manchester Regt. acted as directed in Operation Order No.94.

Party was assembled on night 25/26th and reconnoitred their route, laying a tape along undergrowth in SANCTUARY WOOD for better guidance, advanced in columns through the wood at Zero and just kept up with barrage. No resistance met with & slight hostile barrage started at about Zero plus 8 and was in patches, mostly over the heads of our party, and would have done some damage to rear waves of a larger operation.

Party was lightly equipped and found ground difficult, but not seriously so for active men, choosing their paths, who just covered 100 yards in 2 minutes, and the 100 yards in 3 minutes. It would have been better if barrage had been slower with a concentration on JAM SUPPORT from the start, giving plenty of time before lifting off. For this minor operation such a barrage would have ensured the capture of a few prisoners in JAM SUPPORT.

Party reached J.19.a.25.60. easily and found trenches up to that along the line of advance filled with wire.

Barrage was not heavy enough to prevent enemy posts in JAM SUPPORT from manning their positions, and mounting a machine gun at J.19.a.40.80. Party was not really up to the barrage now and found themselves at a disadvantage. One Officer and few men pushed on towards J.19.a.5.5. The Officer and some men were wounded and they got as far as J.19.a.4.5. then withdrew bringing all casualties with them.

An Officer and another party moved on the machine gun at J.19.a.40.80., had some casualties and withdrew bringing all in.

Party in support had remained at J.19.a.25.60., and the whole party then withdrew.

It appears nearly established that the old enemy front line JACKDAW TRENCH from J.19.a.2.4. to I.24.b.90.75. is only an obstacle and not an occupied trench, and that the line of resistance is JAM SUPPORT - whether this so continues further North is not so certain, but previous reports by night parties appear to indicate that the same defences does continue on those lines.

Patrols from the Battalion who attacks that portion will reconnoitre these tomorrow night and satisfy themselves.

Map has been forwarded giving the total result of our observations and conjectures on this matter.

26th July, 1917. (Sd) J.H.LLOYD. BRIGADIER GENERAL.
COMMANDING 90TH. INFANTRY BRIGADE.

G 8

Operation Order No. 69.   6

Ref. Zillebeke 1/10.000.
Sheet 28.N.W. 1/20.000

1. The 18th Bn. Manchester Regt. will relieve the 19th King's Liverpool Regt. during the night 28/29th July.

2. Coys. will be disposed as follows:-
   "A" Coy.   { RITZ ST
              { NORMAN ST
              { NILE ST
   "B" Coy: WELLINGTON CRES.
   "C" Coy.   { STANLEY ST &
              { BARK ST
   "D" Coy   FRONT LINE.
   Bn. HQ. will be at DORMY House.

3. Coys. will move by the Infantry Track, already reconnoitred, so as to pass the starting point (IRON BRIDGE - I.26.c.4/6) at the following hours:-
   "D" Coy.   9.30. p.m.
   "C" Coy: 9.40. p.m.
   "B" Coy: 10.0. p.m.
   "A" Coy: 10.10. p.m.
   H.Q. Coy: will follow in rear of

A Coy:

4. Movement as far as Iron Bridge will be by Companies at 200 yards distance.

Guides from the 19th W.L.R. will meet each Platoon & B.H.Q.s at this point. 200 yards to be maintained between Platoons after passing the bridge.

5. Lewis Guns will be carried by the teams on the clear understanding that each man is to take a share in carrying the gun. Lewis Gun boxes will be loaded on the empty ration Limbers & taken to the Transport Lines. Mess boxes & Officers trench kits will also be taken back by the transport & should be ready by 6.30 p.m.

6. The Officers & O.R.s detailed to remain out of the action will return to the transport Lines with the ration party tonight.

7. Completion of relief to be wired to Batn. H.Q. using BAB Code.

8. Acknowledge.

J E Dyde
Lieut
& Adjt.
"Bawl"

28/2/17

G.9.

To: Headquarters,
    90th. Infantry Brigade.

I beg to submit the following report on operations
July 28th - August 1st.

On the night of the 28/29th the Battalion under my command moved up from the CHATEAU SEGARD area to the front line and was disposed as follows:-
"D" Coy: Holding the front line by isolated posts in WARRINGTON AVENUE and STANLEY STREET stretching over the whole Brigade Front.
"C" & "B" Coys: In WELLINGTON CRESCENT.
"A" Company: In unnamed trench behind RITZ STREET.
Battalion Headquarters was established at the Brigade H.Qs. in RIDGE STREET and the Regimental Aid Post in VINCE STREET.

The dispositions remained unchanged until the night of the 30th. ult. when "D" Coy: threw forward outposts into "No Man's Land" "C" Coy: went forward to STANLEY STREET and BARK STREET and "B" and "A" Companies to MAPLE TRENCH. Patrols were sent out on both nights. They crossed to the enemy front line, but neither saw the enemy nor heard sounds indicating his near presence.

On the night of the 30/31st I went forward at 9.0.pm and personally disposed the Battalion in "No Man's Land" in readiness for the attack.

"D" Company, assembled with the four platoons in line, had its right flank resting on THE GAP and its left about 150 yds. north of the German Gourock Street, and lay about 200 yards from the German Front Line. Twenty-five yards behind was "C" Coy: covering the same frontage but with the platoons in line of sections. "A" & "B" Coys: lay about 25 yards behind "C", also drawn up in line of sections, but sharing the ~~whole~~ battn frontage between them - "A" on the left and "B" on the right. I placed H.Q. Coy: 25 yards behind "A" & "B" and established my personal H.Q. in "A" Coy: in the third wave.

Five minutes before ZERO the companies gradually crept forward until the leading company was about 150 yards from the enemy front line.

Therefrom I went forward with my Adjutant and Intelligence Officer to the second wave. At Zero the Battalion advanced behind the barrage across SANCTUARY WOOD to the enemy front line. Immediately the Germans sent up a great number of flares and S.O.S Rockets and opened fire with Machine Guns, besides putting down a light barrage of mustard gas shells. Nevertheless the leading wave captured its objective with little difficulty although they came under pretty severe machine gun fire. The enemy defence system evidently consisted of small isolated posts and these were rushed and the garrisons killed or captured. After leap-frogging the front wave successfully the second wave met with considerable opposition but they continued to press home the attack and overcame it.

There was great difficulty in identifying the battered enemy trenches and many men in this second wave passed right over the objective and took part in the assault on STIRLING CASTLE. In this strong point the enemy had evidently decided to make a stand and showed no desire to surrender. One batch of 44 Germans fought very stoutly until surrounded and forced to lay down their arms. By 5.30.am. however STIRLING CASTLE was captured and the Third wave had passed on and captured the BLUE LINE, the trench traced east of this strong point which was the final objective of the Battalion.

There was then a pause in the proceedings and it was expected that the assaulting lines of the supporting battalions would pass through.
(The work

Page 2 / Contd:

The work of mopping up still continued and finally it was found that the total number of prisoners captured was 101 - 98 unwounded or with slight wounds and three seriously wounded. Two machine guns and three minenwerfers were also captured but were ~~abandoned~~ unfortunately left for removal later, being placed in a place of safety and ~~covered with leaves~~ camouflaged.

Battalion H.Q. was established in a dug-out at J.13.c.7/1, which was occupied by the enemy when taken over and yielded four prisoners (included in the total above.)

The situation at 8.0.am was as follows:-
"A" & "B" Coys: holding a line of shell holes east of STIRLING CASTLE: "C" Coy: in battered shell-holes and trenches on the line JAM RESERVE and about STIRLING CASTLE: "D" Company in craters and portions of JAM SUPPORT and shell holes close to Battalion Headquarters.

About 9.0.am units of the 89th Brigade came up and reinforced the BLUE LINE and STIRLING CASTLE. At 10.30.am. I was instructed to send a party of 1 Officer and 60 Other Ranks to Brigade H.Qs for the purpose of bringing up ammunition and acting under Brigade Orders, this party did not rejoin during operations.

Between 10.0.am and 11.0.am the enemy shell fire became severe and continued to be so until the Battalion was relieved on the 1st. instant. Heavy H.E. Shells and shrapnel were fired unceasingly in a haphazard way over the area occupied by the Battalion and over SANCTUARY WOOD. The front line Companies especially came under heavy fire. The enemy machine gunners and snipers went on unceasingly and movement up to the front line became extremely perilous.

I issued orders for the reorganisation of the Battalion for defence in case of counter-attack as follows:-
"A" Coy: on the Left and "B" Coy: on the right to hold the front line, constructing for themselves a line of strong points and keeping in touch with units on the flanks. "A" Coy: got in touch at once but "B" Coy experienced great difficulty in trying to do so.
"C" Coy: "C" Coy: was ordered, when carrying party returned, to consolidate in JAM RESERVE and
"D" Coy: to make strong points from the craters, JAM SUPPORT and JAM ROW, keeping in touch with the WILTSHIRE REGT.

Before "D" Coy: could carry out the orders it was instructed to supply a party of 100 men for clearing the battlefield, a demand that was met with difficulty.

At 4.30pm a message was received from the King's Liverpool Regiment that a counter-attack was threatening "from the wood in front" and it being presumed that this referred to INVERNESS COPSE, the only wood in front of the Battalion, a message to this effect was sent by pigeon to Brigade Headquarters all the signal wires having been cut. No counter-attack took place. About 5.30.pm a message was received from the King's Liverpool Regiment that a counter-attack was imminent from the direction of GLENCORSE WOOD. Our Artillery promptly got on to the target and the attack failed to reach our trenches.

About 8.0.pm the only surviving Officer of "A" & "B" Coys: at that time in hand action reported that he had sustained very severe casualties, his total strength being about 20 rifles, and, as at that time STIRLING CASTLE and the line east of it was strongly held by the 89th. Brigade, and owing also to the fact that the men of "C" Coy: had not returned, it was deemed advisable to to concentrate the Battalion under close control from Battalion Headquarters and form with it a Support Line in rear of the King's Liverpool Regiment. Accordingly the remains of "A" & "B" Companies were withdrawn and the Battalion redisposed as follows:-
"D" Coy: on the line of craters, JAM SUPPORT AND JAM ROW;
A combined company from "A" ~~&~~ "B" ~~~~ and "C" Coys in close support in shell-holes about 100 yards in rear on a line with Battalion Headquarters extending to the South.

This situation continued overnight until the Battalion was withdrawn from the line at 12.50pm on the 1st. The withdrawal to the CHATEAU SEGARD area was made by small parties, but throughout the enemy shell fire was uninterrupted and there were several casualties.

over:-

page 3/ Contd:

Great difficulty was experienced throughout the course of the operations in keeping up communications. The Signal wires were constantly cut by shell fire and runners proved very slow and uncertain. Messages sent through signal stations in rear failed to reach their destinations.

The casualties were severe: 9 Officers killed and wounded, and 227 Other Ranks killed, wounded and missing.

3.8.17.

Lieut. Colonel.
Commanding 18th (S) Battalion,
THE MANCHESTER REGIMENT.

CONFIDENTIAL.

WAR DIARY.

for the

MONTH OF AUGUST. 1917.

18th. (SERVICE) BATTALION. MANCHESTER REGIMENT.

(VOLUME XXII).

In the Field.
31.8.1917.

..........C. E. Lembcke.......... LIEUT COLONEL,
Commanding. 18th. Service Battalion,
THE MANCHESTER REGIMENT.

Sheet 215

Army Form C. 2118.

WAR DIARY
or
INTELLIGENCE SUMMARY.

(Erase heading not required.) 18th (S) Batt. Manchester Regiment

Place	Date	Hour	Summary of Events and Information	Remarks and references to Appendices
	1917			
Line.	Aug. 1		Holding positions East of SANCTUARY WOOD, captured during fighting of July 31st (See July "War Diary"). Relieved at 11 a.m.; & proceeded by companies to CHATEAU SEGARD, last company arriving at 6 p.m.	
	2		Battalion left CHATEAU SEGARD at 6.30 p.m.; & marched to DICKEBUSCH NEW CAMP, arriving at 8.30 p.m.	
	3		Moved by lorry to area East of STEENVOORDE, & billetted for the night. 2/Lt. T.W.GREEN, – 2/Lt. J. ARNOLD, & 19 O.Rs. joined the Battalion from the Base.	
	4		Proceeded by lorry & march route in the afternoon to camp near TERDEGHEM, arriving at 6 p.m.	
TERDEGHEM.	5		Church Parade, followed by Inspection in the morning	
	6		Resting	
	7		Battalion moved to billets at STRAZEELE.	J*
STRAZEELE.	8/9		Training. Draft of 11 O.Rs joined the Battalion for duty to day.	

Army Form C. 2118.

WAR DIARY
or
INTELLIGENCE SUMMARY.

(Erase heading not required.) 18th (S) Batt. Manchester Regiment

Sheet 22 J

Instructions regarding War Diaries and Intelligence Summaries are contained in F. S. Regs., Part II. and the Staff Manual respectively. Title pages will be prepared in manuscript.

Place	Date	Hour	Summary of Events and Information	Remarks and references to Appendices
	1917			
	Aug 10		Battalion moved to FRONTIER CAMP (East of BERTHEN)	J 2
BERTHEN	11		Training	
	12		Church Parade in the morning. 2/Lt. L.S. BURGESS & 2/Lt. F. SCHOFIELD joined the Battalion today from the Base	
	13/14		Training	
	15		Inspection of got Inf. Bde in the morning by Genl. Sir Herbert Plumer, G.C.M.G., G.C.V.O., K.C.B., A.D.C., Commanding Second Army. 2/Lt. J.B. BARKER joined the Battalion for duty	
	16/18		Training	
	19		Church Parade in the morning. Major J.K. AITKEN transferred to Fourth Army (status - P.B.) & is struck off the strength of the Battalion accordingly	
	20/21		Training	
			Following Officers, N.C.O.'s & Men received awards as shown, for gallantry in action :-	
			Military Cross	
			Lieut. W.E. OGDEN. 2/Lt. E. HOLLAND, 2/Lt. W.E. HARDING.	

Sheet 23 J.

Army Form C. 2118.

WAR DIARY
or
INTELLIGENCE SUMMARY.
(Erase heading not required.)

18th (S) Batt. Manchester Regiment

Place	Date	Hour	Summary of Events and Information	Remarks and references to Appendices
	1917		Distinguished Conduct Medal	
			37552 Pte. A. PIGGOTT	
			Military Medal	
			43658 Sgt. A.C. DEAN, 7661 L/Cpl. E. NEALE, 10951 Sgt. T. PYGOTT,	
			10390 Sgt. S. FORSTER, 43957 L/Sgt. F.G. SHUTTLEWORTH,	
			21337 Pte. W. HODGERT.	
	Aug 22		Battalion moved to PARRAIN FARM Camp, in Divisional Reserve.	J 3
PARRAIN FARM Camp	23		In Divisional Reserve. Following Officers joined for duty:-	
			2/Lt. L. ILLINGWORTH, 2/Lt. J. HOUGHTON, 2/Lt. T. PICKERING,	
			2/Lt. E. BURGIS.	
	24		Do — Draft of 11 ORs joined the Battalion from the Base.	
	25/26		Do — Companies engaged on working parties for R.E.	
	29		Battalion moved to MESSINES Area & relieved 16th Bn.	
			Manchester Regt. in Brigade Support.	J 4
MESSINES	30/31		In Brigade Support, & on working parties.	

C. P. Lembcke Lieut.-Col.
Commanding 18th Bn. Manchester Regt.

J.1.

Ref.Sheet
7.
1/40,000.

OPERATION ORDER NO....
By Lieut.Colonel. J. H. LLOYD,
Commdg. 18th (S) Battalion, The MANCHESTER REGT.

1. The Battn. will move to the MARLES Area tomorrow the 7th. instant.
2. March in column of route at 9.0.am ready to march off at 9.5.am on the road south of the camp. Head of column to be opposite "A" Coy's billet facing east.
3. Order of march: H.Q., Band, B/C, D & A Coys.
4. Route: Road Junction, P.12.c.7/7. – St.SYLVESTRE–CAPPEL – CAESTRE – ROUGE CROIX.
5. Transport will follow in rear of the Battalion.
6. Officers' valises to beat the Q.M. stores not later than 8.15am.
7. Coy: Commanders are responsible for seeing that all tents and billets occupied by their men are left in a clean and sanitary condition and will render a certificate to this effect to the Orderly Room before the Battalion moves off.
8. Adrum ledge.

Issued by Orderly at...7.30.pm

1. C.O.   2. 2nd.in Command.
3. Adjt.   4. File.
5. 6. 7.8. Coys:
9. T.O.
10. M.G.
11. Q.M.
12. S.O.
13. 14. War Diary.

(sd.)....L.........Lieut.
A/Adjutant,
18th.Bn.Manchester Regt.

AMENDMENT TO BATTALION OPERATION ORDER
d/d 9.8.17.

Under instructions received from the 90th. Brigade, the move tomorrow will now take place 1 hour later, the Battalion parading therefore at 8.0.am, ready to march off at 8.5.am.

Officers valises to be at the Q.M's Stores at 7.15am instead of 6.15am.

                                                        ....Lieut.
                                                        A/Adjutant,
9.8.17.   18th.Bn.Manchester Regt.

9.8.17.

OPERATION ORDER NO. 70
By Lieut.Colonel. C. N. LEMBCKE,
Commanding 18th (S) Battalion,
THE MANCHESTER REGIMENT.

Ref.Sheet 27.SE.

J 2

1. The Battalion will move to the area east of BERTHEN tomorrow the 10th. instant.

2. Parade in column of route on the BAILLEUL ROAD at 7.0.am, ready to march off at 7.5.am. Head of the column to be opposite the Quarter-Master's Stores - facing East.

3. Order of March: H.Q., Band, "C", "D", "A", & "B" Coys:

4. ROUTE: Road via U.24.c - X.19.c.a.d. - X.21.a. - METEREN - LES 4 FILS AYMON - SCHAEXKEN.

5. Transport will follow in rear of the Battalion.

6. Officers' Valises to be at the Q.M. Stores by 6.15.am.

7. ACKNOWLEDGE.

                                                      H E Ogden
                                       ....Lieut.
1. C.O.
2. 2nd.in.Command.   A/Adjutant,
3. Adjutant.   13th.Bn.Manchester Regt.
4. File.
5.6.7.8. Coys.
9. T.O.
10.M.O.
11.S.O.
12.Q.M.
13.14. War Diary.

Secret. OPERATION ORDERS. No. 9t
By Major T.J. Kelly, M.C.
Commanding 18th. (Service) Battn.
THE MANCHESTER REGIMENT.

1. The battalion will move to the KEMMEL area to-morrow 22nd. Aug.

2. Order of March: H.Qs., Band, "A", "B", "C" & "D" Companies. Transport will follow in rear of Battalion.

3. East of HYDE PARK CORNER M17.C. Central, movement will be by Companies at 200 yds. distance.

4. Route via WESTOUTRE M17.C.5.4. road through M17.d. M24.A.8.4. and via KEMMEL.

5. Parade ready to march off at 8-25 a.m. Head of column at WESTOUTRE ROAD, 300 yds. east of Frontier post.

6. Officers' valises to be at Q.M's. Stores by 7-30 a.m.

7. ACKNOWLEDGE.

Issued by orderly at.. 7-50 p.m.
Copy No. 1. C.O.
     2. 2nd. in Command.
     3. Adjutant.
     4. File.
     5.6.7.8. Coys.
     9. T.O.
    10. M.O.
    11. Q.M.
    12. S.O.
    13.14. War Diary.

Lieut.
A/Adjutant,
18th. Bn. Manchester Regiment.

23.8.17.

(SECRET).

BATTALION OPERATION ORDER NO 72.
By Major. T.J. KELLY, M.C.
Commanding 19th (S) Battalion,
THE MANCHESTER REGIMENT.

1. The Battalion will move to the MESSINES area tomorrow evening and relieve the 16th. Bn. MANCHESTER REGIMENT in Brigade Support.

2. Parade in full marching order, ready to march off at 6.30.pm in the following order:- "A", "B", "D", "H.Qs" and "C" Company at intervals of 200 yards between companies. East of WULVERGHEM the march will be by platoons at 100 yards interval.

3. ROUTE:- SPY FARM - WULVERGHEM. Guides will meet companies at WULVERGHEM CHURCH.

4. Camp kettles will be taken up on the transport. Lewis Gun Limbers Maltese Cart and Mess Cart will accompany the Battalion, but not the water carts.

5. Trench Kits will be taken by Officers: valises to be handed in to the Q.M's Stores by 3.0.pm.

6. Reliefs when complete will be reported to Battalion H.Qs by runner.

7. Duplicate copies of all stores etc., taken over will be rendered to Orderly Room by 12 noon on 25th inst.

8. ACKNOWLEDGE.

1. C.O.
2. Adjutant.
3. File.
4.5.6.7. Coys.
8. T.O.
9. M.O.
10.Q.O.
11.Q.M.
12.13. War Diary.
14. R.S.M.

J.O. McElroy Lieut.
A/Adjutant,
19th.Bn.Manchester Regt.

Issued by Orderly at_____ :

CONFIDENTIAL.

WAR DIARY

for the

MONTH OF SEPTEMBER.

1917.

18TH. (SERVICE BATTALION - THE MANCHESTER REGIMENT.

(VOLUME XXIII)

In the Field.   C. L. Lembcke......LIEUT.COLONEL.
30.9.17.   Commanding, 18th (SERVICE) BATTN.
                     THE MANCHESTER REGIMENT.

-o-o-o-o-

Army Form C. 2118.

Sheet 24 K

WAR DIARY
or
INTELLIGENCE SUMMARY.

(Erase heading not required.) 18th (S) Batt. Manchester Regiment

Instructions regarding War Diaries and Intelligence Summaries are contained in F. S. Regs., Part II. and the Staff Manual respectively. Title pages will be prepared in manuscript.

Place	Date	Hour	Summary of Events and Information	Remarks and references to Appendices
	1917			
MESSINES Area	Sept 1		In Brigade Support, and on working parties	
	2		Relieved by 9th Bn Kings Royal Rifles, and marched to camp	K 1
			near DRANOUTRE. Capt. C.J. HOMEWOOD booked as 2i/c in Command to 8th Bn Lincolnshire Regt., and struck off the strength of the Battalion accordingly.	
DRANOUTRE	3/8		Engaged on working parties in the forward area	
	9		Relieved the 19th Bn. Manchester Regt. in support. Battalion being disposed in the vicinity of LUMM FARM and WYTSCHAETE	K 2
	10		Moved into the line and relieved the 2nd Bn. Wilts. Regt.	
			Dispositions as follows :-	
			Front line. On the right "D" Coy. - with Coy. H.Q. - O 28 d 1/7	
			On the left "C" Coy. - do KILO FARM - O 28 d 5/1	
			In support. On the right "B" Coy. - do O 28 c 5/1	
			On the left "A" Coy. - do HOW FARM - O 27 d 1/9	
			Batt. H.Q. situated at CABIN HILL - O 27 c 92/07.	
			Relief completed by midnight.	

Sheet 25 K

Army Form C. 2118.

WAR DIARY
or
INTELLIGENCE SUMMARY.

(Erase heading not required.) 18th (S) Batt. Manchester Regiment

Place	Date	Hour	Summary of Events and Information	Remarks and references to Appendices
	1917			
In the line.	Sept 11/21		Wiring parties and patrols out each night along the whole Battalion sector, but no enemy patrols encountered. During the night 15/16th Sept., a patrol consisting of Corpl. LEACH and 4 men ("D" Coy) supported by a Lewis Gun, attempted to rush an enemy machine gun post situated at O.29.c.95/95, after subjecting it first to a severe bombardment with rifle grenades. The effort was unsuccessful owing to the marshy nature of the ground, and the thickness of the enemy wire, but the patrol was able to gain much useful information, and to establish the location of an enemy Trench Mortar, and two other hostile Machine Guns. On the night 16/17th Sept., an inter-company relief was carried out, "A" Coy. relieving "C", and "B" Coy. relieving "D", in the left and right front line sectors respectively	K 3
		22	Battalion relieved by the 19th Bn Manchester Regt., and moved	

Sheet 26K

Army Form C. 2118.

WAR DIARY
or
INTELLIGENCE SUMMARY.

(Erase heading not required.) 18th (S) Batt. Manchester Regt.

Place	Date	Hour	Summary of Events and Information	Remarks and references to Appendices
	1917		back into Brigade Reserve in CHINESE WALL (N23b) Casualties for the period Sept 11th/22nd:- 1 O.R. Killed; 23 O.R.s Wounded	K4
CHINESE WALL	Sept 23		In Brigade Reserve. Lieut. R.S. ENGLAND struck off the strength of the Battalion on proceeding to England 14.9.17 pending transfer to the Indian Army.	
	24		–Do– Draft of 13 O.R.s joined the Battalion today from the Base.	
	25		–Do– Major P. GODLEE and Capt. W.P. KNOWLES struck off the establishment with effect from 18.6.17. 2/Lieut. A.E. WAKEFIELD and 2/Lieut. L.H. BURROWS joined the Battalion for duty.	
	26/30		Battalion engaged on working parties	

C.E. Lambeth Lieut.-Col.
Commanding 18th (S) Manchester Regt.

OPERATION ORDERS NO. 95.
BY LIEUT. COLONEL C.E. LEMBCKE.
commanding 18th. (S) Battn.
THE MANCHESTER REGIMENT.

1. The 18th. Battn. THE MANCHESTER REGIMENT will be relieved by the 9th. Battn. K.R.R. on Sept. 2nd., less "C" Coy., which will be relieved by one Coy. Shropshire Light Infantry 5th. Battn., on the night Sept. 2nd./3rd.

2. O.C. "A" "B" & "D" Coys. will send one guide per platoon to be at Bde. H.Q. at 7 a.m. to-morrow 2nd. instant to guide platoons of the 9th. K.R.R. Guides, who will be specially selected, to report to Battn. H.Q's. at 6-15 a.m.

3. Five guides, one from Battn. H.Q. Coy., and one from each Coy. to be at Bde. H.Q. T.B.C.6.7. at 9-15 a.m. 2nd. inst. to take up advance parties of 5th. SHROPSHIRE L.I. to reconnoitre the area (MESSINES) held by the Battn. Guides will report to Battn. H.Q's. at 8-15 a.m.

4. "A" Coy. Lewis Gun teams and men employed on O.P. duties will be relieved to-morrow evening 2nd. inst. ad will accompany "C" Coy. to KEMMEL area. O.C. "C" Coy. will be responsible for their relief.

5. Breakfast rations only will be drawn to-night for "A" "B" and "D" Coys., full rations will be drawn by "C" Coy., "A" Coy. Lewis Gun Teams, men employed on O.P. duties, and men of the R.S.F. and 16th. MANCHESTER REGT. attached for rations to the Battn.

6. "A" "B" & "D" Coy's Lewis Gun Limbers, Officers' Mess Cart, Maltese Cart, will be at Ration Dump at 8-30 a.m. H.Q. riders same place at 9-30 a.m. "C" Coy's limber to be at same place by 9-30 p.m.

7. The relief to be completed by 10 a.m.

(Sd) J.O.McElroy. Lieut.
A/Adjutant,
18th.Bn.MANCHESTER REGT.

SECRET.
K2

OPERATION ORDERS No. 96.
By Lieut. Colonel C.E. Lemhcke.
Commanding 18th. (Service) Battalion.
THE MANCHESTER REGIMENT.

18/9/17

Ref. WYTCHAETE Ed. 6a.   1/10,000

1. The 18th. Battn. Manchester Regiment will relieve the 19th. Bn. Manchester Regt. in the support area (Right Sub Sector) during the night 10/11th. Sept. 1917.

2. Movement will be by Companies at intervals of 5 minutes, as far as LINDENHOEK cross roads, thence by platoons at 200 yards distance, to LAMP POST CORNER (O.19.c.5.6.) where guides will be met at 8-0 p.m. (one per platoon, one for Battn. H.Q., and one for M.O.)

3. Order of March :- H.Q., A. B. C. D. H.Q. Coy. to move off at 6-30 p.m.

4. Transport lines will remain at present location.

5. Coy. Lewis Gun Limbers will move in rear of their respective Companies, and on arrival will be unloaded and sent back.
   Maltese Cart, and Officers' Mess Cart will move with H.Q. Coy.

6. Trench Kits only will be taken. All Officers' Valises, Mess Kit, etc., not required in the forward area, must be handed in to the Q.M. Stores before leaving the present area.

7. Ration Limbers will move up with Companies, and on arrival will be unloaded, and sent back to the Transport Lines.

8. Move for Night 11/12th. Sept.
   The Battn. will relieve the 2nd. Battn. Wiltshire Regt. in the line during the night 11/12th. Sept.

9. Coys. will be disposed as under :-
   Front Line. On the right "D" Coy. with Coy. H.Q. at O.28.d.1.7.
               On the left "C" Coy. with Coy. H.Q. at KILO FARM O.28.b.5.1
   SUPPORT.   On the right "B" Coy. with Coy. H.Q. at O.28.c.5.1.
               On the left "A" Coy. with Coy. H.Q. at HOW FARM O.27.d.1.9.

   Battn. H.Q. at CABIN HILL O.27.c.92/07.

10. Coys. will move into the line in the order D, C, B, A, H.Q.
    Guides (1 per platoon and 1 Bn. H.Q. will be at LUMM FARM at 8-30 p.m.

11. Duplicate copies of all Trench Stores taken over will be rendered to Bn. H.Q. by 12 noon on the 12th. instant.

12. Completion of reliefs to be reported to Bn.H.Q. by the code word "BRITAIN".

13. Please acknowledge.

.....................CAPTAIN.
ADJUTANT.
18th.Bn. MANCHESTER REGIMENT.

ADDENDUM TO OPERATION ORDER NO. 96.
The Battn., whilst in the line, will devote the utmost energy into making a continuous line of wire, five yards wide, across the front of shell hole line, and a similar belt across picquet line along the whole Battn. front. This duty must be kept constantly in mind by all officers.

Issued by runner at...............
Copy No. 1. C.O.   8 Q.M.
         2. 2nd.1/c   9. T.O.
         3. Adjt.   10. M.O.
         4. O.C. "A" Coy.   11. 90th.Bde.
         5. O.C. "B" "   12. O.C. 16th. Manchesters
         6. O.C. "C" "   13. File.
         7. O.C. "D" "   14 & 15 War Diary.

(SECRET).   BATTALION OPERATION ORDERS NO.97.

By Lieut. Colonel. C. E. LEMCKE,
Commanding 18th (S) Battalion,
15.9.17.   THE MANCHESTER REGIMENT.

1. An inter-company relief will be carried out during the night 16/17th September 1917, "A" Coy relieving "C" Coy and "B" Coy relieving "D" Coy in the Left and Right front line sectors respectively.

2. The relief will take place as early as possible after dusk. Guides (1 per platoon and company H.Q.) from "C" and "D" Companies will report at the Headquarters of the relieving companies at dawn on the 16th instant and will remain with them during the day.
Guides from "A" and "B" Companies will report at the front line at dusk and will remain with "C" and "D" Companies and will remain with "C" & "D" Companies during the whole of the 17th.

3. Rations will be issued to the relieving Companies before moving off from the support positions. O.C. "A" Company will detail a party for bringing up his rations to report at Battn. H.Qs. at 7.pm. Headquarters Company will provide a carrying party for "B" Company. "C" and "D" Companies will send down for their rations as soon as they have been relieved in the front line.

4. O.C.s. "C" and "D" Companies will each detail 1 N.C.O. and 2 men per platoon to remain in the front line after the remainder of the Company have been relieved. These men will rejoin their companies at dawn on the 17th.

5. Completion of reliefs to be reported to Battn. H.Qs by runner.

6. Acknowledge.

Issued by Orderly at 7.30.pm   ....Capt.&.Adjt.

1. 90th.Infy.Bde.
2. O.C. "A" Coy:
3. O.C. "B" "
4. O.C. "C" "
5. O.C. "D" "
6. Retained.
7.   do.

20.9.17.
(SECRET)

K 4

BATTALION OPERATION ORDERS.

No.98.

By Lieut. Colonel. C.E. LEMBCKE,
Commanding XXXX (S) Battalion,
THE MANCHESTER REGIMENT.

Reference: WYTSCHAETE - Ed.6a. 1/10,000.

1. The 18th.Bn.Manchester Regiment will be relieved in the Line by the 19th. Bn. Manchester Regt. during the night 21st/22nd September and on completion of relief will move into Brigade Reserve in the CHINESE WALL AREA (N.23.b.)

2. Guides (1 per coy: and Bn.H.Q.) will report to Lieut. J.O.McELROY at Bn. H.Qs. at 9.0.am. on the 21st inst. to reconnoitre the route to be followed. They will rejoin their companies at dusk.

3. Companies will move off by platoons as soon as they have been relieved, Company Commanders reporting personally at Bn.H.Qs. on the way down.

4. Route: Track via O.26.c.8.3. - PICK HOUSE - PECKHAM and thence to N.23.b. 100 yards distance to be maintained between platoons as far as PECKHAM.

5. One Platoon of "C" Company (less Lewis Gun Team) under 2nd.Lt.T.W. GREEN will relieve a platoon of the 17th.Bn. Manchester Regt. attached to the 201st. Field Coy: R.E. at SPY FARM (N.29.c.8.6.). 2nd.Lieut. GREEN will reconnoitre the route tomorrow so as to move off independently as soon as relieved in the present sector. This platoon which must be up to 25 other ranks in strength will be rationed by the 201st. Field Coy: R.E. from the 22nd. instant inclusive.

6. O.C. "D" Company will detail 4 men to take over dumps in the new area. This party will report at Bn. H.Qs. at 7.0.am. on the morning of the 21st. inst. for further instructions. They should bring rations with them.

7. Lists of all trench stores, aeroplane photographs &c., handed over to the relieving Battalion will be forwarded to Bn. Headquarters by noon the 22nd. instant.

8. Completion of all reliefs to be wired to Battn. Headquarters using the Code Word "VICTORY".

Coy. H.Q. Limbers will be at Ration Dump at 10.15pm.

9. PLEASE ACKNOWLEDGE.

CAPT. & ADJT.

Issued by Orderly at 8.10 pm.

No.1. C.O.
No.2. Adjt.
No.3. Asst.Adjt.
No.4.5.6.7. Coys.
No.8. T.O.
No.9. M.O.
No.10.Q.M.
Copy. to 19th.Bn.Manchester Regt.
Copy. to 90th.Infy.Bde.
2 copies - War Diary.

-o-o-o-o-o-o-o-

CONFIDENTIAL.

WAR DIARY

for the

MONTH OF OCTOBER.

1917.

18TH. (SERVICE) BATTALION - THE MANCHESTER REGIMENT

(VOLUME XXIV)

In the Field
31.10.1917.

.... MAJOR
Commanding 18th. (SERVICE) BATTN.
THE MANCHESTER REGT.

--------oOo------

Sheet 27 M.

Army Form C. 2118.

WAR DIARY
or
INTELLIGENCE SUMMARY.

(Erase heading not required.) 18th (S) Batt. Manchester Regiment

Instructions regarding War Diaries and Intelligence Summaries are contained in F. S. Regs., Part II. and the Staff Manual respectively. Title pages will be prepared in manuscript.

Place	Date	Hour	Summary of Events and Information	Remarks and references to Appendices
	1917			
	Oct. 1		Battalion moved from CHINESE WALL (N 23 b) to KENMEL CHATEAU Area being billetted as follows:-	M.1.
			"A" Coy. LA POLKA FARM (02 L 95/65)	
KEMMEL CHATEAU Area.			"B" "C" & "D" Coys. BEAVER HALL (N 31 d 95/35)	
			Battalion Headquarters KEMMEL CHATEAU (N 31 d 25/55)	
			All Companies engaged on fitting parties under R.E.	
		2	2/Lt. A.H. SMITH and 2/Lt. T. POTTS joined the Battalion to-day from the Base and were posted to "C" and "D" Coys respectively.	
		3	2/Lt. J.D. PRESTON and 2/Lt. J.M. PLATT joined from duty from the Base and were posted to "A" and "B" Coys respectively.	
		4	Nothing further no above	
		5	Batt H.Q. & "A" Coy moved to camp at DAYLIGHT CORNER (N 33 a 70/65).	
DAYLIGHT CORNER	1 to 9		Coys. engaged on fitting parties until the 10th inst. Lieut. J.F. LEWIS accepted an absence (on probation) in R.F.C. and struck off the strength of the Battalion accordingly. 2/Lt. L.M. BURROWS and 2/Lt. A.E. WAKEFIELD admitted to F.A. sick	

Sheet 28 M

Army Form C. 2118.

WAR DIARY
or
INTELLIGENCE SUMMARY.
(Erase heading not required.)

18th (S) Batt. Manchester Regt.

Place	Date	Hour	Summary of Events and Information	Remarks and references to Appendices
	1917			
	Oct. 10		Battalion relieved the 2nd Bn Dubblins Regt. in support, being disposed as under:-	M 2
			"A" Coy. LANCASHIRE HOUSE (O 19 d 9/9)	
			"B" Coy. RAILWAY DUMP (O 20 c 25/20)	
			"C" Coy. LUMM FARM (O 26 d 1/7)	
			"D" Coy. "THE CATACOMBS" (O 19 b 9/11)	
			Bn. HQ. TORREKEN FARM (O 20 d 2/3)	
			2/Lieut. E.L. CARPER and 3 ORs joined the Battalion for duty from the Base.	
			Casualties 2/Lieut. F. PICKERING - Killed. 5 ORs - Wounded	
		11	Battalion relieved the 19th Bn Manchester Regt. in the front line (Right Sub-Sector). Relief was completed by 12 midnight and the Battalion disposed as follows:-	
			Front line :- On the right "D" Coy. with HQ at O 28 d 4/7	
			On the left "C" Coy. — do — O 28 b 5/1	
			Support :- On the right "B" Coy. — do — O 28 c 5/1	
			On the left "A" Coy. — do — O 27 d 1/9	

Army Form C. 2118.

WAR DIARY
or
INTELLIGENCE SUMMARY.
(Erase heading not required.)

18th (S) Batt. Manchester Regt.

Sheet 29M

Instructions regarding War Diaries and Intelligence Summaries are contained in F. S. Regs., Part II. and the Staff Manual respectively. Title pages will be prepared in manuscript.

Place	Date	Hour	Summary of Events and Information	Remarks and references to Appendices
	1917			
			Bn. HQ at DERRY HOUSE (O 27 a 3/6)	
			Major T.J.KELLY M.C. assumed temporary command of the Battalion vice Lieut Col. C.E.LEMACKS admitted to F.A. (sick)	
	Oct 12		Little work could be carried out owing to the lateness of relief. Into a thorough reconnaissance of the line on the Battalion sector was made with a view to reforming and strengthening it, during the hours in the line. Patrols were also sent along the whole front reconnecting. No Mans land and establishing touch with Battalions on the left and right flanks.	
IN THE LINE	13		In the line Work on reforming front and support line kept working parties to 2/Lieuts T.HARTLEY and 2/Lieut A.V.MICHAELIS joined the Battalion for duty to-day and posted to "A" "B" Coys. respectively. Casualties – 1 O.R. Wounded	
	14		Patrol reconnoitred craters at O 29 a 77/29 and found it	

Wt. W1422/M1160 350,000 12/16 D. D. & L. Forms/C/2118/14

Army Form C. 2118.

WAR DIARY
or
INTELLIGENCE SUMMARY.

(Erase heading not required.) 18th (S) Batt Manchester Regt.

Sheet 30 M

Place	Date	Hour	Summary of Events and Information	Remarks and references to Appendices
	1917			
			unoccupied by the enemy, and the wire in front considerably broken by our shell fire. Work carried on on front and support lines, and LANCASTER TRENCH wiring in front of front and support lines.	
			Casualties - 2 O.Rs Wounded	
IN THE LINE	Oct. 15		During the night 14th/15th an inter-company relief was carried out. "A" Coy relieving "C" and "B" Coy relieving "D", in the left and right front line sub-sectors respectively. Patrol found enemy M.G. post at O.29.a.9/4. unoccupied - also an unwired post at O.29.a.9/2. but no identification could be obtained. Work done on clearing BOG STREET, and new trench near R.gth support Coy HQ. Elaval wiring parties.	
			Casualties - 2 O.Rs Wounded.	
	"	16	Patrols out all along Battalion sector. Unoccupied trench	

Army Form C. 2118.

WAR DIARY
or
INTELLIGENCE SUMMARY.

(Erase heading not required.) 18th (S) Batt. Manchester Regt.

Sheet 31 M

Instructions regarding War Diaries and Intelligence Summaries are contained in F. S. Regs., Part II. and the Staff Manual respectively. Title pages will be prepared in manuscript.

Place	Date	Hour	Summary of Events and Information	Remarks and references to Appendices
IN THE LINE	1917		found at O.29.b.0/3, protected by belt of wire 10ft thick. Work on new support trench continued 46.0 Frame being put in and trench revetted and duckboard to length of 50 yds. Wire strengthened and improved between O.29.c.6/4 and O.29.a.60/25. Orders received that Battalion would be relieved during the night 16/17th Oct. by 17th Batt. Manchester Regt. but these were cancelled and Battalion remained in the line for a further 24 hours. Casualties – 2/Lieut F.BURGESS Killed. 2 O.Rs Wounded. 2/Lieut F.S.BURGESS relieved the Battalion from F.A today	M.3
	Oct 17		Patrols out during the night 16/17th Oct. along whole Battalion front. Working and wiring parties as usual. Battalion relieved during the night 17/18th Oct. by 2nd Bn Royal Scots Fusiliers and marched to VROEGINDER Camp – with exception of "C" Coy who remained behind at LUMM Farm	M.4

Army Form C. 2118.

WAR DIARY
or
INTELLIGENCE SUMMARY.
(Erase heading not required.) 16th (S) Batt. Manchester Regt

Sheet 32 M

Instructions regarding War Diaries and Intelligence Summaries are contained in F. S. Regs., Part II. and the Staff Manual respectively. Title pages will be prepared in manuscript.

Place	Date	Hour	Summary of Events and Information	Remarks and references to Appendices
	1917			
VROILAND- HOEK Camp	Oct. 18		under the orders of the O.C. 2nd Bn Royal Scots Fusiliers 2/Lieuts W. TURNEY and 2/Lt R.E JAMES joined the Battalion for duty and posted to "C" & "D" Coys. respectively	
	19		Resting, refitting and training. Lieut. Col. C.E LEMBCKE relinquished command of the Battalion from F.A. and assumed command of the Battalion from today	
			Battalion engaged on hutting parties as before at DAYLIGHT 2/Lieut T.W.COWAN	
-do-			CORNER. KEMMEL Village and AIRCRAFT FARM transferred to U.K. (Dundee) and struck off the strength of the Battalion accordingly	
	20/22		Hutting parties	
	23		Engaged on making rifle range in camp occupied by the Battalion	
	24/25		Work continued on range. Company parades and training	
	26		Rifle range completed. Attack practice and training. Parade and general training	

Army Form C. 2118.

WAR DIARY
or
INTELLIGENCE SUMMARY.

(Erase heading not required.) 18th (S) Batt. Manchester Regt.

Place	Date	Hour	Summary of Events and Information	Remarks and references to Appendices
VROILANDHOEK	1917 Oct. 27		Inspection and distribution of rations by Corps Commander, Sir Aylmer Hunter-Weston, K.C.B, D.S.O., in the morning. Battalion engaged on working party during the nights 27/28th Oct resting and building up parapet and parados at "Y" line at O.27.d.4/5. Major H.G.W. Theobald D.S.O (2nd Bn.) assumed command of the Battalion vice Lieut. Col. C.E. LEMBCKE (to command 30th Div Reinforcement Camp)	
	28		Training and working on camp enlargements &c	
	29		As above. Deparation in the afternoon in view of the Yukon Reck. At 5 p.m. Battalion left to relieve the 19th Manchester Regt. in the front line (Right sub sector) M.5 Relief was complete by 11.30 p.m and the Battalion disposed as follows :- Front line = "D" Coy (with 1 Platoon of "C") = H.Q. at - KILO FARM (O.28.b.5/1) Right support = "B" Coy. (H.Q. at O 28 c.5/0)	

A6945 Wt. W14422/M1160 350,000 12/16 D. D. & L. Forms/C/2118/14.

Army Form C. 2118.

WAR DIARY
or
INTELLIGENCE SUMMARY.
(Erase heading not required.)

Sheet 34 M 18th (S) Batt. Manchester Regt

Place	Date	Hour	Summary of Events and Information	Remarks and references to Appendices
	1917			
			Left Support :- "A" Coy - HQ at HOW FARM (O.27.b.1/0.)	
			Reserve :- "C" Coy (less 1 Platoon attached to "D".)	
			HQ at CABIN HILL (O.27.c.9/0.)	
			Bn HQ at DERRY HOUSE (O.27.a.3/6.)	
IN THE LINE	Oct. 30		In the line. Work on front and support line posts.	
			YORK TRENCH revetted and cleared. 80 yds of wire put	
			out in front of the front line and 140 yds in front of	
			the support line.	
			Casualties :- 1 O.R. Killed	
	31		Work continued on front and support line posts, and digging	
			alternative position to No 4 Post at O.29.a.5/5. 180 yds	
			of wire put out round Nos 1 & 2 Posts and 85 yds in	
			front of the support line. Patrol under 2/Lieut	
			H WHINCUP found enemy posts at O.29.b.3/1 and O.29.b.2/3	
			unoccupied.	
			Casualties :- 1 O.R. Killed 3 ORs Wounded	

A.C. Mulgan? Major
18th Bn Manchester Regt

30/9/17.

SECRET.

OPERATION ORDERS NO.90.
By Lieut. Colonel. C. E. LIMBORE,
Commanding 18th (S) Battalion,
THE MANCHESTER REGIMENT.

Reference: KEMMEL - Edition 3 - 1/10,000.

1. The Battalion will move to the KEMMEL CHATEAU AREA tomorrow the 1st. October 1917.

2. Companies will move off at intervals of 10 minutes in the order "B" "D" "C" "A" "H.Qs" - "B" Company moving off at 3.0.pm.

3. ROUTE: Via Track "A".

4. LEWIS GUN LIMBERS will leave present area at 2.30pm and after unloading at KEMMEL will return to pick up Officers' valises, Orderly Room boxes &c. Cookers and watercarts will move off as soon as dinners have been served. *Horses for Cookers should be here by 3.0.pm.*

5. An Advance Party consisting of 2/Lieut. ILLINGWORTH, the four Company Quartermaster Sergeants and one other representative per Company and Battalion Headquarters, will proceed tomorrow morning at 11.0.am to take over billets and will act as guides for their respective companies in the afternoon.

6. A rear party consisting of 1.N.C.O. and 2 men per company, under 2/Lieut. Burgis will remain behind to clean up and hand over to the incoming Battalion. This party will rejoin the Battalion as soon as they are relieved.

7. Company Commanders will be held responsible that all tents, shelters &c., are left in a thoroughly clean and sanitary condition and will render a certificate to this effect to the Orderly Room before moving off.

8. PLEASE ACKNOWLEDGE.

Issued by Orderly at...... 8.20 pm

..................................Capt. & Adjt.
18th. Bn. THE MANCHESTER REGIMENT.

1. C.O.
2. 2nd.in.Command.
3. Adjutant.
4. "A"
5. "B"
6. "C"
7. "D"
8. M.O.
9. T.O.
10. S.O.
11. File.
12. 13. War Diary.
Copy to 90th. INFANTRY BRIGADE.
" " 20th. KING'S L'POOL REGT.

SECRET. BATTALION OPERATION ORDERS.
By Lieut. Colonel. C. E. LEMBCKE,   No.100.
Commanding 18th. (S) Battalion,
THE MANCHESTER REGIMENT.   Oct.9th.1917.

Ref.Sheet 28.S.W. 1/20,000.

1. The 90th. Infantry Brigade will relieve the 21st. Infantry Brigade in the Right Sector on the 10/11th October and 11/12th. October 1917. Relief to be complete by 3.0.am on 12th. October.

2. The 18th.Bn. MANCHESTER REGT. will relieve the 2nd. Bn. WILTSHIRE REGT. in Support during the night 10/11th. instant.

3. Companies will move off independently so as to pass PECKHAM (N.30.a.6/8) at the following hours:-
        H.Qs. Coy: 6.0.pm.
        "A" Coy: 6.5.pm.
        "B" Coy: 6.15.pm.
        "C" Coy: 6.25.pm.
        "D" Coy: 6.35.pm.
At this point guides will be met and movement will be by platoons at not less than 100 yards distance.

4. Tracks reconnoitred to-day will be used.

5. All blankets, Officers' valises and other stores not required in the line will be dumped at present location of companies and taken back to the transport lines. Officers Commanding "A" and "B" Companies will each detail two men to remain behind at Bn. H.Qs and BEAVER HALL respectively to look after these stores until they are collected.

6. Lewis Gun limbers will move with their companies and on arrival at destinations will be unloaded and sent back. Maltese cart and one limber will report at Bn. H.Qs at 4.30pm.

7. Each Company will arrange to take up sufficient cooking utensils for its own use. These will be carried on the Lewis Gun Limbers.

8. MOVEMENT ON THE NIGHT 11/12th OCTOBER. The Battalion will relieve the 19th.Bn. MANCHESTER REGT. in the front line (Right Sub-Sector) during the night 11/12th October.

9. Companies will be disposed as under:-
        FRONT LINE.   On the Right: "D" Coy:
                        On the left: "C" Coy:
        SUPPORT: On the Right: "B" Coy:
                        On the left: "A" Coy:
Bn. H.Qs will be at DERRY HOUSE (O.27.a.3.6.)

10. Detailed orders regarding this move will be issued later.

11. All trench stores, secret maps, aeroplane photographs &c., will be taken over and a list (in duplicate) forwarded to Bn. H.Qs within 36 hours of completion of relief.

12. Completion of relief will be wired to Bn. H.Qs. by the Code word "MECCA".

13. Please acknowledge.

                                        Capt. & Adjt.
Issued by Orderly at 8.15 pm.   18th.Bn. THE MANCHESTER REGT.
1. H.Qs. 90th. Bde.
2. C.O.
3. 2nd.in.Command.
4. Adjt.
5.6.7.8. Coys.
9. T.O.
10. M.O.
11. Q.M.
12. File.   Copy to O.C., 2nd. Bn. Wilts. Regt.
13.14. War Diary.   "   O.C., 19th.Bn. MANCHESTER REGT.

M 3

OPERATION ORDERS NO. 101.
By MAJOR. T. J. KELLY, M.C.
Commanding 18th (Service) Bn.
THE MANCHESTER REGIMENT.

15.10.17.

16.

Ref. WYTSCHAETE MAP (Ed.6a). 1/10,000.

(1) The 18th.Bn. MANCHESTER REGT. will be relieved in the line by the 17th.Bn. MANCHESTER REGT. during the night 16/17th October and on relief will march to VROILANDHOEK Camp.

(2) "D" Coy: of the 17th.Manchester Regt. will relieve "B" Coy of the 18th. Mchr. Regt..

"C" Coy:	"	"	"	"	"A"	"	"
"B" Coy:	"	"	"	"	"D"	"	"
"A" Coy:	"	"	"	"	"C"	"	"

(3) Guides (1 per platoon) from the 2 front line companies and the right support company will report at Battalion Headquarters by dawn tomorrow the 16th instant, and from the left support company by 4.30.pm. Companies will move off independently as soon as they are relieved; Company Commanders reporting personally at Battn. H.Qs on the way down.

(4) All trench stores, secret maps, aeroplane photographs, and defence schemes will be handed over to the relieving Battalion ; also details of work on hand or proposed.
Gum boots will also be handed over and a receipt obtained.

(5) The Transport Officer will arrange for the maltese cart to be at CABIN HILL at 6.30.pm; Officers' Mess Cart to be at DERRY HOUSE at the same hour.
Lewis Gun Limbers will await their companies at the junction of DORSET STREET and BAY ROAD (O.26.B.8/7) at 7.30pm.

(6) Completion of relief to be wired to Bn.H.Qs by the Code Word "MUSTARD".

(7) PLEASE ACKNOWLEDGE.

Issued by Orderly at. 5.15 pm

(Sd) W.E. Ogden. Capt. &.Adjt.
18th.Bn. Manchester Regt.

1. 90th. Inf.Bde.
2. O.C., 17th.Bn.M/C Regt.
3. C.O.
4. Adjt.
5.6.7.8. Companies.
9. M.O.
10.T.O.
11.Q.M.
12. File.
13.14. War Diary.

-o-o-o-

OPERATION ORDERS - No.102.
By Major. T.J. KELLY, M.C.,
Commanding 18th. Battalion,
THE MANCHESTER REGIMENT...

16.10.17.

Ref: WYTSCHAETE Map (Ed.6a) 1/10,000.

1. The relief of the 18th.Bn. MANCHESTER REGT. in the Right Sub-Sector by the 17th.Bn. MANCHESTER REGIMENT on the night 16/17th October is cancelled.

2. The 18th.Bn. MANCHESTER REGT. will be relieved in the Line by the 2nd.Bn. ROYAL SCOTS FUSILIERS during the night 17/18th. October and on relief will move as follows:-
Bn.Headquarters, "A" "B" & "D" Coys: To VROILANDHOEK CAMP.
"C" Company: To LUMM FARM, where they will come under the orders of the Officer Commanding R.S.Fs.

3. Companies will be relieved as under:-
"A" & "B" Coys: By 1 company of the R.S.Fs with H.Qs at KILO FARM.
"C" Coy: By 1 Coy: (less 1 platoon) of the R.S.Fs.
"D" Coy: By 1 Platoon of the R.S.Fs.
and will move off independently on completion of relief, Company Commanders reporting personally at Bn.H.Qs on the way down.

4. The Regimental Aid Post will remain at CABIN HILL and will be responsible for the Right Sub-Sector and the Company at LUMM FARM.

5. Officers Commanding "B" & "D" Companies will arrange to hand over their present Headquarters to an Officer of the 2nd.R.S.Fs. obtaining a receipt for all maps, stores etc.

6. Gum Boots will be carried down by each man slung over the right shoulder and handed over to Sgt. Baron at Bn. H.Qs at DERRY HOUSE.
Officers Commanding "C" &"D" Companies will arrange to collect all surplus Gum Boots at present in possession of the front line companies tonight, and will be responsible for handing these over at Bn.H.Qs.

7. The Transport Officer will arrange to have the four Company Lewis Gun Limbers at the junction of DORSET STREET AND BAY ROAD (O.26.b.8.7.), at 7.30pm: Officers Mess Cart to be at DERRY HOUSE at the same hour.

8. Completion of relief to be wired to Bn.H.Qs by the code word "MUSTARD".

9. PLEASE ACKNOWLEDGE.

E Ogden
..................Capt. & Adjt.
18th.Bn. Manchester Regiment...

Issued by Orderly at.12.15.pm
1. 90th. Infy. Bde.
2. O.C., 2nd. R.S.Fs.
3. C.O.
4. Adjt.
5.6.7.8. Companies.
9. M.O.
10. T.O.
11. Q.M.
12. File.
13. 14. War Diary.

OPERATION ORDERS – NO. 103
BY MAJOR H. C. THEOBALD, D.S.O.
COMMANDING 18th. BATTN.
THE MANCHESTER REGIMENT.

28.10.17.

REF. SHEET 28 S.W. 1/10,000.

1. The 90th. Infantry Brigade will relieve the 21st. Infantry Brigade in the Right Brigade Sector on the nights 28/29th. inst. and 29/30th. inst., relief to be completed by 8-0 a.m. on October 30th.

2. The 18th. Bn. Manchester Regt. will relieve the 19th. Bn. Manchester Regt. in the Right Battalion Sub-sector during the night 29/30th. inst.

3. "D" Coy. 18th.Bn.Manchester Regt. will relieve "A" Coy.19th.Bn. Manchester Regt. in the front line, with Coy.H.Q. at KILO FARM (O.28.b.6/1).
"B" Coy. 18th.Bn.Manchester Regt. will relieve "C" Coy.19th.Bn. Manchester Regt. in right support, with Coy.H.Q. at O.28.c.5/1.
"A" Coy. 18th.Bn.Manchester Regt. will relieve "D" Coy. 19th.Bn. Manchester Regt in left support with Coy.H.Q. at HOW FARM (O.27.b.1/0.)
"C" Coy. 18th.Bn.Manchester Regt. will relieve "B" Coy. 19th. Bn. Manchester Regt. in reserve, with Coy. H.Q. at CABIN HILL (O.27.c.9/1.)
Battalion H.Q. will be at DERRY HOUSE (O.27.a.3/6.)

4. Companies will move off from present camp at intervals of 10 minutes, in the order, "H.Q.", "D", "B", "A", "C". Headquarters Coy. to move off at 5-0 p.m.

5. Movement east of PECKHAM will be by platoons, at not less than 100 yards distance.

6. Guides (1 per platoon & Bn.H.Q.) will be met at TORREKEN CORNER.

7. Lewis gun limbers will move with their respective companies, - in the case of "C" Coy. as far as CABIN HILL, and in the case of the other Coys., as far as the junction of DORSET STREET and BAY ROAD (O.26.b.7/8.) where they will be unloaded and sent back.

8. Rations will be taken up on the Lewis gun limbers, as far as unloading points, and thence carried up by parties specially detailed in advance by each Coy. One pack mule carrying water will accompany each limber.

9. Gum boots will be drawn by the front line Coy. only from ULSTER HOUSE (O.27.a.1/1.) and will be put on there. Ankle boots will be carried slung over the shoulder.

10. Blankets will be rolled in bundles of 10, and deposited outside the Orderly Room not later than 12 noon. Officers' valises to be at the same place by 2-0 p.m.

11. Officers' Mess Cart and Maltese Cart, will be at Bn.H.Q. at 4-30 p.m.

12. All trench stores, secret maps, aeroplane photographs, log books, defence schemes, etc.,will be taken over, and a list of these forwarded to Battn. H.Q. within 24 hours of completion of relief.

13. O.C. "A" Coy. will detail one N.C.O. and one man to take over the Brigade Dump at HOW FARM, and O.C. "B" Coy. one N.C.O. and two men to be in charge of the Gum-boot store at ULSTER HOUSE. N.C.O's. selected should be thoroughly reliable men, and will report with their parties at the Orderly Room at 8-0 a.m. to-morrow morning for instructions. Rations for the day to be carried.

14. Completion of reliefs to be wired to Battn. H.Q. by the Code Word "N I O B E".

15. Acknowledge.

H E Ogden
CAPTAIN
ADJT.
18th.Bn. MANCHESTER REGIMENT.

Issued to Orderly at ....

```
Copy No.  1 to 90th. Bde.
          2  "  19th. Manchesters.
          3  "  C.O.
          4  "  2nd. i/c
          5  "  Adjutant
 6,7,8, & 9  "  Companies.
         10  "  Q.M.
         11  "  T.O.
         12  "  S.O.
         13  "  M.O.
         14  "  R.S.M.
         15  "  War Diary.
         16  "
         17  "  File.
```

CONFIDENTIAL.

Vol 25

WAR DIARY

for the

MONTH OF NOVEMBER

1917.

18th. (SERVICE) BATTALION - THE MANCHESTER REGIMENT.

(VOLUME XXV)

In the Field.
30.11.17.

.... MAJOR.
Commdg. 18th (S) Bn. MANCHESTER REGT.

Army Form C. 2118.

WAR DIARY
or
INTELLIGENCE SUMMARY.
(Erase heading not required.) 18th (Service) Bn. Manchester Regt.

Sheet 36 a.

Place	Date	Hour	Summary of Events and Information	Remarks and references to Appendices
SAINT JEAN	Nov 8		Battalion moved by bus to YPRES, and marched from there to camp at SAINT JEAN, Bn. HQ. being at ENGLISH FARM (C.27 b 50/25)	Q.3
	9/26		Engaged on working parties in the forward area under orders of Canadian (and subsequently VIIIth) Corps Heavy Artillery. The work that the Battalion was called upon to undertake during this period proved to be of an exceedingly difficult and arduous nature, consisting as it did, in many cases of carrying up ammunition to forward battery positions on the PASSCHENDAELE RIDGE under heavy shell fire. That the high standard of work maintained throughout was fully appreciated by the Higher Command is shown by the following letter, – received from Lieut. General Sir G.W. CURRIE, Commanding Canadian Corps:-	

Army Form C. 2118.

Sheet 35.a.

WAR DIARY
or
INTELLIGENCE SUMMARY.

(Erase heading not required.) 18th (Service) Bn. Manchester Regiment

Instructions regarding War Diaries and Intelligence Summaries are contained in F. S. Regs., Part II. and the Staff Manual respectively. Title pages will be prepared in manuscript.

Place	Date	Hour	Summary of Events and Information	Remarks and references to Appendices
	1917			
	Nov. 1/3		In the line, holding right (WYTSCHAETE) Sub-sector, from the WAMBEEK on the north to the BLAUWEPOORTBEEK on the south	
	4		Relieved during the night 4/5th by 2nd Bn. R.S.F. and moved into Support. Battalion being disposed as under :-	Q 1
			"A" Coy. LANCASHIRE HOUSE (O.18.d.9/1)	
			"B" Coy. ESTAMINET CORNER (O.20.a.2/2)	
			"C" Coy. LUMM FARM (O.26.d.1/7)	
			"D" Coy. THE CATACOMBS (O.19.6.9/2)	
			Bn. HQ. at TORREKEN FARM (O.20.d.2/3)	
	5		Engaged on working parties, &c. One O.R. wounded. 2nd Lieut. W.D.TRUSWELL rejoined the Battalion from ENGLAND to day, and posted to "A" Coy. 2/Lt W.HARTLEY to U.K. (Sick)	
	6		Relieved by 2nd Bn. Yorkshire Regt. and marched to camp at DAYLIGHT CORNER (N.33.a)	Q 2
	7		Resting and refitting, ironing to moving south the following day.	

← IN THE LINE →

Sheet 39 a

Army Form C. 2118.

WAR DIARY
or
INTELLIGENCE SUMMARY.
(Erase heading not required.) 18th (Service) Bn. Manchester Regt.

Place	Date	Hour	Summary of Events and Information	Remarks and references to Appendices
SWAN CHATEAU	1917 Nov 26/9		Capt. H.G. WATSON transferred to U.K. (Sick) 11.11.17, and struck off the strength of the Battalion accordingly. Capt. E.A. WALKER, M.C., R.A.M.C. attached to the Battalion for temporary duty - 25.11.17 - VICE Capt. T. STANSFIELD. (Wounded.) Lieut. H.P. SAWYER, M.O.R.C. U.S.A. attached to the Battalion from 27th inst. VICE Capt. E.A. WALKER, M.C. Pack train formed, under 2nd Lieut. J.E. LOVE, to draw and carry up R.E. material to Battalions in the line, commencing the 29th inst.	
	30		- Do - Party of 3 Officers and 100 Other Ranks engaged on work for 200th Field Coy. R.E. in forward area.	

A.C. Theobald Major
Comondg. 18th Bn. Manchester Regt.

Q.1   Copy No 7.
OPERATION ORDERS NO. 104   5.11.1917.
BY MAJOR H.C. THEOBALD, D.S.O.
COMMANDING 18th.(S) BATTN.
THE MANCHESTER REGIMENT.

REF. EXPERIMENT. MAP. Sh. 2/10,000.

(1) The 18th. Bn. MANCHESTER REGT. will be relieved in the right sub-sector by the 2nd. ROYAL SCOTS FUSILIERS during the night 5/6th. October, and on relief will move into Brigade support.

(2) "A" Coy. 18th. MANCHESTER REGT. will be relieved by "D" Coy.2nd.R.S.F.
    "B" "   do.   do.   "A"   do.
    "C" "   do.   do.   "C"   do.
    "D" "   do.   do.   "B"   do.

(3) On completion of relief, companies will move as follows :-
    "A" Coy. to LANCASHIRE LODGE   (O.19.d.8/1)
    "B" Coy. to RAILWAY DUMP   (O.20.c.8/3)
    "C" Coy. to HIGH FARM   (O.20.d.1/7)
    "D" Coy. to THE COCOONUTS   (O.19.b.8/1)

(4) Battalion Headquarters will be at ENGLISH FARM (O.20.d.8/3).

(5) Guides (one per platoon and Coy. H.Q.) will report to 2/Lt. ILLINGWORTH at Bn. H.Q. by 10.0 a.m. to-morrow. These men will reconnoitre routes to the new area, so as to be able to guide their Companies back on completion of the relief. Rations for the day to be carried. In addition to these, O.C. "A" Coy. will have 8 guides at his Coy. H.Q. to guide up the relieving Company into position.

(6) Gum boots will be brought down and handed in to the store at ENGLISH HOUSE. Coy. Commanders are responsible for handing in the same number of pairs as were issued to them.

(7) The Transport Officer will arrange for the Maltese Cart to be at DAWN HILL by 5.0 p.m. and one limber at Bn. H.Q. by the same hour. Each Coy's rations will be brought up to the new area it will occupy, and left there in charge of the C.S.M. to be handed over to the Coy. on its arrival.

(8) All trench stores, aeroplane photographs, secret maps, log books, etc., will be handed over to the incoming battalion, and a receipt for same forwarded to Bn. H.Q. by 12 noon on the 6th. inst. Details of work in hand should be passed on to relieving companies.

(9) Completion of relief to be wired to Bn.H.Q. by the code word "H U D S O N" - Coy. Commanders reporting personally at Bn. H.Q. on their way down.

(10) A C K N O W L E D G E.

                                                    H.E. Ogden
                                                    Capt.
                                                    Adjutant,
                                                    18th.(S)Bn.MANCHESTER REGIMENT.

Issued by signals at..6.15 p.m........

Copy No. 1 to O.C.   2 to 2nd. i/c   3 to Adjt.
           4, 5, 6, and 7 to Companies.
           8 to Q.M.   9 to T.O.   10 to M.O.
           11 to S.O.   12 to 90th.Bde.   13 to 2nd. R.S.F.
                     14 and 15 War Diary   16 File.

BATTALION OPERATION ORDERS.
By Major H.C.W. THEOBALD, D.S.O.
Commanding 18th. (S) Battalion,
THE MANCHESTER REGIMENT.

SECRET.

No. 105

Nov. 5th. 1917

1. The 90th. Infantry Brigade will be relieved by the 21st. Infantry Brigade in the Right Brigade Sector, during the nights 6/7th. and 7/8th. instant, relief to be complete by 8-0 a.m. 8th. November.

2. The 18th. Bn. Manchester Regt. will be relieved by the 2nd. Battn. Yorkshire Regt. during the night 6/7th. Novr. and on relief will march to camp at DAYLIGHT CORNER.

3. Companies will move off independently as soon as they are relieved.

4. Route:- Via GORDON ROAD - O.29.b.1.5. - SPY FARM - to LINDENHOEK Cross Roads where guides will be waiting to lead platoons to their billets.

5. Movement east of PECKHAM will be by platoons at not less than 100 yards distance.

6. All Trench Stores, Defence Schemes, secret maps, etc., will be handed over to the relieving Battalion, and a receipt forwarded to Battalion Headquarters by 12 noon the following day.

7. The Transport Officer will arrange for the four Company Lewis gun limbers to be at each Coy. H.Q's. by 6-0 p.m. "B" Coy's. H.Q's. are now at O.20.a.2/2. ESTAMINET CORNER.
Officers' Mess Cart and one Limber will report at Bn. H.Q. by 5-30 p.m. Maltese Cart to be at LANCASHIRE HOUSE at the same hour.
In the event of Working Parties being detailed, more transport
8. will be required. Early notification of this will be sent to Bn.T.O. on the morning of the 6th. instant.

8. Completion of relief to be wired to Bn.H.Q. by the word "EGYPT".

9. ACKNOWLEDGE.

CAPT. & ADJT.
18th. Bn. THE MANCHESTER REGIMENT.

Issued by Orderly at.............

1. 90th. Inf Bde.
2. C.O.
3. 2nd. 1/c.
4. Adjutant
5, 6, 7, & 8 Companies.
9. M.O.
10. T.O.
11. Q.M.
12. O.C. 2nd. Bn. YORKSHIRE REGT.
13, 14 War Diary.
15. File.

Q.3

OPERATION ORDER NO. 100
BY Major E.G.H. TURNBULL, D.S.O.
COMMANDING 18th. (S) BATTALION,
THE MANCHESTER REGIMENT.

WAR DIARY

Reference HAZEBROUCK Sh.Ch. 1/10,000
           Sh.8.G.   1/20,000

1. The Battalion will move by bus to the EPEHY area to-morrow the 8th instant, debussing on the EQUINCOURT-ASIGNE Road - L.25.d.

2. Parade in column of route on the main KEMMEL Road, ready to march off at 6-45 a.m. Head of column to be opposite the entrance to Officers' Quarters facing north.

3. Order of March:- Headquarters, Band, "A" "B" "C" "D" Companies. Dress :- Full marching order. Steel helmets to be worn except whilst actually in the lorries, when soft caps may be put on.

4. Lorries will be drawn up on the main KEMMEL road with the head of the column 100 yards south of KEMMEL cross roads, Lorries Nos. 29 to 46 (inclusive) are allotted to the Battalion. One officer and 24 men to each.

5. In order to facilitate embussing, the following procedure will be adopted :-
    (a) Before moving off Companies will be told off into parties of 24 each, under an officer.
    (b) When on the march, 3 paces will be maintained between each party.
    (c) On arrival at the embussing point, each party will halt opposite its own lorry.
    (d) On the order being given, parties will embus simultaneously.

6. Strict discipline must be maintained on the journey. No men will leave their lorry except with the direct permission of an officer, who will be held responsible that they rejoin as soon as possible.

7. The Transport will move by road under orders of the Transport Officer. Route:- Via LA POMME and EQUINCOURT-ASIGNE.

8. Haversack rations for consumption on the journey will be carried. A hot meal for the men will be served as soon as the cookers arrive in the new area.

9. Blankets will be tightly rolled in bundles of 10, and deposited on the road near the entrance to the Officers' Quarters by 6-0 a.m.. Officers' valises (which must not be more than 60 lbs. in weight) to be there by the same hour.

10. An Advance Party consisting of 2/Lt. W.S. ROLLINS M.C., the four Coy. Orderly Sgts., 1 N.C.O. per Company, a representative from H.Q'rs. Company, Transport, Q.M. Stores, and Orderly Room will parade at the Orderly Room at 7-30 a.m. and proceed by lorry from KEMMEL crossroads at 8-0 a.m. to the new area, where they will report to the Area Commandant, North EPEHY billeting area at VILLAGE GINCHY for instructions.

11. 2/Lt. W.S. TURNBULL will proceed by car from KEMMEL Crossroads at 8-0 a.m. to-morrow to Canadian Corps Headquarters, for instructions as to work to be done by the Battalion. On completion of this duty he will rejoin the Advance Billeting Parties at VILLAGE GINCHY.

12. Two lorries will report at KEMMEL cross roads at 8-0 a.m. to-morrow for the conveyance of blankets, officers' valises, etc., O.C. "A" Company will detail a reliable man to be at the Cross Roads at that hour to guide the lorries to the camp. He will also detail a party of 1 N.C.O. and 12 men for loading.

P.T.O.

13. Company Commanders must ensure that their lines are left scrupulously clean before moving off, and will render a certificate to that effect to the Orderly Room by 9-0 a.m.

14. ACKNOWLEDGE in writing.

H E Ogden
Captain,
Adjutant,
19th. (S)Bn. MANCHESTER REGIMENT.

7.11.1917.

Issued to Signals at...................

```
Copy No.  1 to 90th. Inf. Bde.
          2  " C.O.
          3  " 2nd. i/c.
          4  " Adjutant.
     5,6,7, & 8  " Companies.
          9  " M.O.
         10  " T.O.
         11  " Q.M.
         12  " S.O.
         13  " R.S.M.
    14 & 15  " War Diary.
         16  " File.
```

Q.4

OPERATION ORDER NO. 107.
BY MAJOR H.C.E. McDONALD, D.S.O.
Commanding 18th. (Service) Battalion,
THE MANCHESTER REGIMENT.

24.11.1917.

Reference :- Sheet 28 N.E. 1/20,000.

1. The Battalion will move to SHAB CHATEAU (1.10.c.) to-morrow the 25th. instant, relieving a battalion of the 49th. Division.

2. Companies will move off from present camp at intervals of 5 minutes in the order "A", "B", "C", "D" and "H.Q."
"A" Coy. to move off at 1-30 p.m.
Band will move with Headquarters Coy. DRESS:- Marching Order.

3. Route:- via ST. JEAN CROSS ROADS, HELL X ROADS, (1.2.d.1.7) - YPRES - LILLE G/R. - SHRAPNEL CORNER - WIENNIE CABARET (1.10.4.8/3).

4. At least 200 yards distance will be maintained between companies.

5. Company Commanders must ensure that their lines are left absolutely clean, and will render a certificate to that effect to the Orderly Room before moving off.

6. Three baggage wagons and one lorry will report at the Ration Dump at 9-0 a.m. to-morrow for the conveyance of blankets, Officers' valises, Orderly Room boxes, and Mess kit. Blankets will be tightly rolled in bundles of 10 and deposited at the ration dump by 9-45 a.m. Officers' valises etc., to be there by the same hour. O.C. "B" Coy. will detail a party of one N.C.O. and 12 men for loading these stores.

7. Water cart, maltese cart, three limbers (2 for Lewis guns and one for cooking utensils) and Officers' Mess Cart (for H.Q. Mess and light Mess Box from each company) will be at ENGLISH FARM by 12-30 p.m.

8. Cookers will be sent to SHAB CHATEAU at 2-0 p.m. to be in readiness for arrival of the Battalion at 3-0 p.m.

9. An Advance Party consisting of 2/Lt. TRUSSWILL, the 4 C.Q.M.S's., 1 other N.C.O. per company, and a representative from the band and Headquarters will leave at 8-30 a.m. and proceed to the new area to take over billets. Three cooks will accompany this party.

10. Officers Commanding Companies will report to Battalion Headquarters as soon as their companies have been billetted in the new area.

11. ACKNOWLEDGE.

H E Ogden
...................................CAPT. & ADJT
18th. Bn. THE MANCHESTER REGIMENT.

Issued to Signals at 4.40 p.m.
1. 90th. Infy. Bde.
2. C.O.
3. 2nd. in command.
4. Adjutant.
5. "A" Coy.
6. "B" Coy.
7. "C" Coy.
8. "D" Coy.
9. M.O.
10. T.O.
11. Q.M.
12. File.
13 and 14 War Diary.
15. Copy to..........................

CONFIDENTIAL.

WAR DIARY

for the

MONTH OF DECEMBER.

1917.

18TH.(SERVICE) BATTALION. - THE MANCHESTER REGIMENT.

(VOLUMN XXVI).

In the Field.
31.12.1917.

..................MAJOR,
Commanding.18th.(s).Bn.MANCHESTER REGT.

Army Form C. 2118.

Sheet No 2 R

WAR DIARY
or
INTELLIGENCE SUMMARY.

(Erase heading not required.) 18th (Service) Batt. Manchester Regt.

Place	Date	Hour	Summary of Events and Information	Remarks and references to Appendices
SWAN CHATEAU	1917 Dec 1/10		1. Engaged on working parties in the forward area	
			2. 2nd Lieut L.H.BURROWS rejoined from hospital	
			3. Lieut D.H.ROBERTS relinquished his commission with effect from today, and was granted the honorary rank of Lieutenant.	
			4. Casualty - 1 Other Rank wounded	
			6. Lieut R.DAVIS, M.O.R.C., U.S.R. attached to the Battalion as Medical Officer from today vice Lieut H.SAWYER (admitted to F.A. sick)	
			9. The following officers joined the Battalion for duty and are posted to the companies shown :-	
			2nd Lieut. H.BYROM "A" Cy	
			—do— A.W.RICHARDS "C" Cy	
			—do— A.G.HARMAN "D" Cy	
			—do— W.DOWNIE "C" Cy	
			Draft of 85 Other Ranks joined today from Divisional	

Sheet 41 R.

Army Form C. 2118.

WAR DIARY
or
INTELLIGENCE SUMMARY.

(Erase heading not required.) 18th (Service) Batt. Manchester Regt.

Instructions regarding War Diaries and Intelligence Summaries are contained in F. S. Regs., Part II. and the Staff Manual respectively. Title pages will be prepared in manuscript.

Place	Date	Hour	Summary of Events and Information	Remarks and references to Appendices
	1917			
	Dec 11		Reinforcement Camp	
			Battalion left SWAN CHATEAU to relieve 2nd Bn Bedfordshire Regt in the left front line (POLDERHOEK) Sector, moving via SHRAPNEL CORNER - ZILLEBEKE - and Track "G".	R 1
POLDERHOEK Sector			By 11 p.m. the relief was complete, & the Battalion (which had now come under the orders of the 21st Inf Bde) disposed as under:-	
			Front line	
			On the right "D" Coy	
			In the centre "B" Coy	
			On the left "C" Coy	
			In support "D" Coy	
			Bn. H.Q at THE TOWER (J.14 d 8/4)	
			The 12th & 13th passed fairly quietly, the enemy's activity being mainly confined to trench mortaring of our front line outposts & shelling of back areas. At 2 a.m. on the morning of the 14th however, a message was	

Army Form C. 2118.

Sheet 42.R

WAR DIARY
or
INTELLIGENCE SUMMARY.

(Erase heading not required.) 18th (Service) Batt. Manchester Regt.

Instructions regarding War Diaries and Intelligence Summaries are contained in F. S. Regs., Part II. and the Staff Manual respectively. Title pages will be prepared in manuscript.

Place	Date	Hour	Summary of Events and Information	Remarks and references to Appendices
	19-7		Received from Bde HQ. that the enemy were suspected to be preparing for an attack on the sector held by the Battalion. This warning was at once conveyed to the troops in the front line who stood to in readiness. The enemy's attack was delivered at 6 a.m. & was preceded by a very heavy Trench Mortar bombardment of our front and support line accompanied by vigorous shelling of the back areas, especially round Bn HQ. On the left, the attack was everywhere repulsed, but on the centre & right company fronts, the enemy succeeded in effecting an entrance & finally in occupying the whole of this portion of the front line. A counter attack was immediately organised & met with considerable success but unfortunately owing to lack of bombs it was found impossible to push the attack home, and my brigade	

Army Form C. 2118.

Sheet 43 R.

WAR DIARY
or
INTELLIGENCE SUMMARY.

(Erase heading not required.) 18th (Service) Batt. Manchester Regt

Place	Date	Hour	Summary of Events and Information	Remarks and references to Appendices
	1917		up fresh supplies the enemy was able to drive us back and occupy the whole of his original front. Meanwhile supports had arrived from the 17th Bn Manchester Regt & 2nd Bn Royal Scots Fusiliers, and early on the morning of the 15th, two companies of the latter Battalion took over that part of the Battalion original front line still held by this Battalion. Unfortunately, a few hours later the enemy launched a fresh attack on this part of the line, & owing to lack of bombs it was found necessary to evacuate the whole of the original front line. A detailed account of these operations will be found in the reports to 21st Inf. Bde, dated 16.12.17 a copy of which is attached. At 8 p.m. the 2nd Bn Royal Scots Fusiliers took over the whole of the left sub sector, and this Battalion moved	R 2

Army Form C. 2118.

Sheet 44 R.

WAR DIARY
or
INTELLIGENCE SUMMARY.
(Erase heading not required.) 18th (Service) Batt. Manchester Regt.

Place	Date	Hour	Summary of Events and Information	Remarks and references to Appendices
	1917			
			back to FORRESTER CAMP where it remained for the night moving by train to ALBERTA CAMP RENINGHELST the following afternoon	R 3
			The casualties during the period 12/15th December were as under :-	
			Officers Killed :- 2nd Lieut. J. HOUGHTON	
			Wounded :- Capt. A.V. MICHAELS	
			2nd Lieut. A.W. RICHARDS	
			Missing :- Capt. J.O. McELROY	
			2nd Lieut. H. WHINCUP	
			Wounded (slightly at duty) - 2nd Lieut. W.B. TRUSWELL	
			Other Ranks Killed 11	
			Wounded 39	
			Missing 69	
	Dec. 17.		Spent in reorganising and refitting 2nd Lieut. J. CHAPMAN admitted to F.A. - sick	

Army Form C. 2118.

Sheet 45 R

WAR DIARY
or
INTELLIGENCE SUMMARY.

(Erase heading not required.) 18th (Service) Batt. Manchester Regt.

Place	Date	Hour	Summary of Events and Information	Remarks and references to Appendices
	1917			
	Dec.18/21		Training, and working parties	
	22		Christmas Services were held today in the Y.M.C.A, RENINGHELST and the remainder of the day treated as a holiday. Special Christmas dinners were provided for the men, followed by an entertainment by the "Blue Birds" in the evening. The 2nd Bn. Royal Scots Fusiliers very kindly covered to relieve the Battalion of all working parties for the day, an act which was greatly appreciated by all ranks	
ALBERTA CAMP	23		Training	
	24		Battalion relieved the 2nd Bn. Royal Scots Fusiliers in Brigade Reserve (TOR TOP TUNNELS) moving by rail from FUZEVILLE to MANOR HALT, and thence by march route	R.4
	25/6		In Brigade Reserve, engaged on working parties in the forward area	
	27		Relieved the 17th Bn. Manchester Regt. in the centre subsector	

Sheet 46 R

Army Form C. 2118.

WAR DIARY
or
INTELLIGENCE SUMMARY.

(Erase heading not required.) 18th (Services) Batt. Manchester Regt.

Place	Date	Hour	Summary of Events and Information	Remarks and references to Appendices
	1917		(astride the MENIN ROAD), relief being completed by 8 p.m.	
			Companies disposed as follows:-	
			"D" Coy on the right ⎫ Each with 1 Platoon in	R.S.
			"B" Coy in the centre ⎬ front line and 2 in close support	
			"C" Coy on the left ⎭	
			"A" Coy in support	
			Bn. H.Q. at J.20.b.5/5.	
	Dec 28/30		The town passed quite uneventfully and though for the first twenty four hours the enemy was inclined to be aggressive, our Lewis Guns and snipers very soon obtained the mastery and for the remainder of the tour he showed much less activity. Patrols were out each night and gained useful information. Scarcely but no hostile patrols were encountered, bright nights with snow on the ground rendered the work of patrols carrying parties so very difficult,	

Sheet 47 R.

Army Form C. 2118.

WAR DIARY
or
INTELLIGENCE SUMMARY.
(Erase heading not required.) 18th (Service) Batt. Manchester Regt.

Place	Date	Hour	Summary of Events and Information	Remarks and references to Appendices
	1917			
			but in spite of the bad conditions every party accomplished its allotted task successfully, & with scarcely a single casualty. Wire was put out along the whole sector, and trenches improved in many places.	
			On the night of the 30th the Battalion was relieved by the 17th Bn. Kings Liverpool Regt. and marched back to FORRESTER CAMP.	R.6
			Casualties for the three days were 1 O.R. Killed, 4 O.Rs Wounded Lieut. Col. H.C.W.THEOBALD D.S.O. was admitted to F.A. sick on the 29th inst, and Major J.KELLY M.C. assumed command of the Battalion from that date.	
	Dec 31.		Devoted to resting & cleaning up. The following Officers and men were mentioned in Sir Douglas Haig's Despatch dated the 7th November, 1917.	

Army Form C. 2118.

WAR DIARY
or
INTELLIGENCE SUMMARY.
(Erase heading not required.) 18th (Service) Batt. Manchester Regt.

Place	Date	Hour	Summary of Events and Information	Remarks and references to Appendices
	1917			
			for gallantry in the field :-	
			Capt. H.G.S. BOWER	
			Capt. T. STANSFIELD R.A.M.C. (later attached to Battalion)	
			10826 Pte. P.J. KENNERY — "D" Coy	
			The names of the following Warrant Officers & N.C.O.s were brought to notice in Divisional Routine Orders for gallant and distinguished conduct on the 14th/15th December, during operations at POLDERHOEK :-	
			43865 C.S.M. J. HAYTER "D" Coy	
			10552 Sgt. A. LOYND "C" Coy	
			10769 Cpl. F.E. FREEMAN "D" Coy	

T Mills Major
Commdg 18th (S) Bn Manchester Regt.

(SECRET).   OPERATION ORDER NO. 108.
           By Major. H.C.W. THEOBALD, D.S.O.
              Commanding 18th (Service) Battn.,   Decr. 10th. 1917.
                 THE MANCHESTER REGIMENT.

REFERENCE: Map Sheet - 28.N.W. - 1/20,000 - ZILLEBEKE 1/10,000.

1. No.2. Group (21st Inf. Bde. H.Q.) will relieve No.1. Group (89th.
   Inf. Bde. H.Q.) in the line on the 11/12th and 12/13th December
   1917; relief to be complete by 8.am on the 13th December 1917.

2. The 18th. Bn. Manchester Regiment will relieve the 2nd. Battalion
   Bedford Regiment in the Front Line (Left sub-sector) during the
   night 11/12th December.

3. "A" Coy: 18th.Manchr.Regt. will relieve "C" Coy: 2nd.Bed. Regt.
                                                    (on the right)
   "B" Coy: "   "   "   "   "   "B" Coy: (in the centre).
   "C" Coy: "   "   "   "   "   "D" Coy: (on the left).
   "D" Coy: "   "   "   "   "   "A" Coy: (in support).
   Battn. H.Qs. will be at J.14.d.8.4.

4. Companies will move off at intervals of 5 minutes in the following
   order - "H.Q", "B", "A", "C", "D", Headquarters moving off at 3.0pm.
   Dress: Marching order; packs to be slung.

5. ROUTE: DERBY ROAD - SHRAPNEL CORNER - TRANSPORT FARM - MANOR HALT -
   ZILLEBEKE - DORMY HOUSE, and thence by track "G".

6. 1 Guide per Company (and Battalion Headquarters) from the 2nd. Bedford
   Regt. will be at ZILLEBEKE CHURCH at 3.45pm and will take Companies
   forward as far as PLUMER'S DUMP, where Platoon Guides will be waiting to lead each platoon to its allotted position.

7. Movement will be by Companies at not less than 300 yards distance,
   as far as ZILLEBEKE - thence by platoons at intervals of 200 yards.

8. Lewis Gun Limbers will move with their respective Companies as far
   as ZILLEBEKE where they will be unloaded and sent back.
   The Transport Officer will arrange for two pack mules to be at
   Battn. H.Qs. at 2.15pm to convey Mess Kit, Signalling Equipment, &c.

9. Blankets will be rolled in bundles of 10 and deposited outside the
   Orderly Room by 2.0.pm. Mens' surplus kit (packed in sandbags and
   carefully labelled) and Officers valises, to be there at the same
   hour.

10. Details not proceeding to the Line will be responsible for cleaning
    up the Camp after the Battalion has left, and on completion of this
    task, will march to FORRESTER's CAMP under 2nd.Lieut. J.B.BARKER.

11. All Trench Stores, secret Maps, aeroplane photographs, details of
    work in hand, and proposed, will be taken over on relief and a list
    of these forwarded to Battn. H.Q. within 12 hours of completion
    of relief.

12. Completion of reliefs to be wired to Battalion H.Q. using D.A.B.
    Code.

13. ACKNOWLEDGE.

                                              CAPT. & ADJT.
                                    18th (S) Bn. THE MANCHESTER REGT.

                                                        (P.T.O.

ISSUED TO SIGNALS AT 4.30pm.

Copies to:-

1. 90th. Infantry Brigade.
2. 21st. Infantry Brigade.
3. C.O.
4. 2nd.in.Command.
5. Adjutant.
6. Asst. Adjutant.
7. "A" Coy:
8. "B" Coy:
9. "C" Coy:
10. "D" Coy:
11. M.O.
12. T.O.
13. Q.M.
14. O.C. 2nd.Bedford Regt.
15. R.S.M.
16. War Diary.
17. " "
18. File.

HEADQUARTERS.

21st. INFANTRY BRIGADE.

I beg to submit the following report on the operations at POLDERHOEK on December 14th & 15th. 1917.

At 6.0am. on the morning of the 14th the Battalion was holding the front line with three companies: "A" on the right, "B" in the centre, "C" on the left- "D" Company being in support.

The front line was a continous trench deep and narrow firestepped by sand-bag steps capable of accommodating three men.

The enemy was roughly 30 to 50 yards away in small trenches and posts and appears to have had no connected line.

There was good wire in front of our left Company but very little in the centre or on the right.

The attack began simultaneously along the whole front at 6.0am. A body of the enemy estimated at 50 in number appeared in front of the shell hole which was held by posts of the centre Company, and crossing our trench began to move left and right along the paredos. They threw bombs as they went. The enemy also effected an entrance on the right Company front following the same tactics. On the left front, thanks to the wire which had been strengthened during the night- 40 coils having been put out- the enemy was checked and a heavy fire was brought to bear on him. He failed to enter the left Company's trench at any point and a strongparty of Germans who attempted to rush the left flank post were beaten off.

The enemy pushed home his attack until the whole of the centre and right company fronts were in his possession and then souhht to drive out the remaining by simultaneous attacks on their right flank with bombs and in front where he had, apparently, been reinforced. He was again repulsed, and the Officer Commanding the left company (Capt.J.N.SMART).thenorganised a counter attack in the hopes of regaining the front line. He made good progress for a time but was forced back through supplies of bombs running short and finally established a block 70 yards to the right of his original right flank.

The Company Commander of the right company was in his Headquarters (the pill-box JERICHO) when the attack began and only had with him his Headquarters-the Company Sergt.Major and about 10 O.Ranks. He attempted to reach the front line over the open but was taken in enfilade by a party of the enemy to the S.W. of JERICHO who opened a heavy fire with light machine guns. Concluding that his flank was in danger, this officer took up a position in the communication trench and formed a defensive flank. The Support company sent up a platoon to the left company as soon as the attack commenced and also gave support on the right but they were too few in number to give sufficient weight for a countercounter attack.

Between 10.0am. and noon two companies of the 17th. Bn.Manchester Regt- about 70 in number - reinforced the front line and between 4.0 and 5.0.pm two companies of the 2nd. Batt. Royal Scots Fusiliers also reinforced. A counter attack was then organised. The plan was to attack simultaneously on both flanks and also to move across the open and retake the pill-box JERICHO. Harrassing and protective fire from the field guns had been kept up throughout the day, and a barrage was put down 6.30 to 7.25pm with an interval of ten minutes, on that portion of the front line that the enemy held and also upon his original position in front of the left company. The attack took place at 8.0pm and though the enemy offered stout resistance he was driven back by both attacks until the supply of bombs gave out. "C" Company attacking from their right flank met with strong opposition but 2nd.Lieut.W.E.HARDING who led the bombing attack on the right made very good progress and at one time was within 60 yards of "C" COmpany. His stock of bombs then failed completely and strong reinforcements of the enemy appearing from his rear endeavoured to cut him off but he brought back his party safely after suffering casualties. In this operation we regained one of the Lewis Guns lost during the early morning's operation.

The assault across the open to regain JERICHO was made successfully with few casualties; the enemy had apparently decided not to occupy this strong point at such a stage of the operations for everything was found just as it was left earlier in the day.

Whilst concentrating his attention on 2nd Lieut. HARDING's party the enemy weakened his position aginst "C" Company and they were able to push their attack home until practically the whole of the line formerly held by "B" & "A" had been occupied.

Unfortunately Lieut. Harding had been forced back by this time and found himself utterly unable to co-operate. The enemy again broght up fresh supplies of bombs and pursuing his tactics of the morning got in shell holes in No Man's land in order to cut off "C" Company and began to throw grenades. "C" Company's supply, diminished by the fighting they had done, was soon exhausted by this fresh attack and they too were compelled to their original position. They again established a block where they had made it previously and as the trench at this point was fairly straight for 30 yards they were able to feep the enemy out of bombing range.

In the early hours of the 15th. the men of the 18th. Batt. manchester Regt. greatly exhausted, were replaced at the ombing block in the original front line by a party of the Royal Scots Fusiliers. At 8.0am the enemy, who had by this time ceased to occupy our old front line, established himself in shell-holes some 20yards in front attempting to gt behind the block and take the garrison in the rear. No difficulty was experienced in keeping him back so long as the supply of bombs lasted but when it failed the garrison ~~the garrison~~ were compelled to evacuate the front line and take up their position in the support trench. This trench was then held continuously throughout its whole length as a front line and no further change took place in the situation up to 7.30pm when I handed over command of the left sub-sector to the Officer Commanding the 2nd. Bn. Royal Scots Fusiliers.

There appears to be little doubt that the enemy attacked

a Battalion strong probably about 400 rifles. His men had all been carefully rehearsed in their parts and were thoroughly trained in the tactics of trench warfare. They were all experienced in the use of our bombs, rifles, Vickers and Lewis Guns and all the weapons and bombs which had been captured in the morning were used by the enemy in the subsequent fighting. His men had also been taught several English words of command and frequent shouts of "Retire" "Withdraw" and "Surrender" were uttered. Throughout the enemy showed a most determined front and the many separate parties composing his attacking force collaborated throughout by the use of coloured lights.

His old front line was undoubtedly sketchy and disconnected whereas the line he has taken is a continous trench capable of being turned into a very strong position. It would appear, however, that the retention of the strong point JERICHO and our present front line is a great threat to his new line and it is quite probable in my opinion that he will attempt either to capture them by assault or else to dig a new trench across the angle of the re-entrant

Two position maps are enclosed showing the position at different hours during the attack.

                                          (Sd)   T.J.KELLY.

16.12.17.   MAJOR.

R 3

OPERATION ORDERS.

by MAJOR T.J.KELLY. M.C.
Commanding. V.W.E.

---

1. The 18th. Batt. Manchester Regt. will be relieved by the 2nd. Batt. Royal Scots Fusiliers during the night 15/16th.inst. and on relief will march to FORRESTOR CAMP.

2. One company of the relieving Battalion willbe moving up intothe front line to-night from TORR TOP.
   Each company willdetail an officer to be at the junction of the two "Communication trenches".(leading to "A" Coy.H.Q. and "D" Coy H.Q. respectively) from dusk onwards. As soon as the company of the 2nd. R.S.F. has passed thispoint, these Officers will rejoin their own companies,who will then move off immediately in the order:- "A". "D". "C".

3. Details of "B".Coy. will move out with the companies to whom they are attached.

4. Company Commanders will report personally at Batt. H.Q. on their way down,

5. ROUTE. "E" Track - "Plumers Dump" - "G" Track - "Zillebeke" - "Shrapnel Corner".

6. Arrival in billets to be reported to Batt. H.Q. by runners.

7. Movement as far as ZILLEBEKE will be in parties of 20 at intervals of 50 yds.

8. Acknowledge.

(Sd) W.E.OGDEN. CAPT &ADJT.
V.W.E.

15/12/1917.

Issued at 5-40 p.m.

Copies to:-

1.	90th. Inf. Bde.
2. 3. 4. 5.	Companies.
6. 7.	War Diary.
8.	File.

R 4

Copy No 16

(SECRET). OPERATION ORDER No.109.
By LIEUT COLONEL. H.C.W.THEOBALD. D.S.O.,
Commanding 18th.(Service) Battalion.,
THE MANCHESTER REGIMENT.

Decr.23rd.1917

REFERENCE.Map Sheet 28. N.W. 1/20,000.

1. The 90th.Infantry Brigade will relieve the 89th.Infantry Brigade in the Line, relief to be completed by 10.am. December.25th.

2. The 18th.Bn. Manchester Regt will relieve the 2nd.Royal Scots Fusiliers in Reserve (TORR TOP TUNNEL) during the night 24/25th.

3. Movement will be by rail from FUZEVILLE to MANOR HALT, and thence by march route. Time of parade to be notified later, probably about 2.pm.

4. An advance party consisting of one representative from each company (and Bn.H.Q). two battalion runners, and two Headquarters signallers, will parade outside the Orderly Room at 10.am. under 2nd.Lieut J.ARNOLD and proceed to TORR TOP to take over from the 2nd.Royal Scots Fusiliers and allot accommodation.
One guide per Company and Battalion H.Q. from this party will be at MANOR HALT from 3.pm. onwards to guide companies to their allotted billets.

5. All movement East of ZILLEBEKE will be by platoons at 200 yards distance.

6. Lewis Gun limbers, Maltese Cart and Officers' Mess Cart will leave present camp at 1.30pm. and proceed by road to CANADA DUMP (I.24.d.5/4). where they will be unloaded and sent back to the Transport Lines, MICMAC CAMP.

7. Rations will be conveyed to CANADA DUMP direct. Companies must arrange to send parties to fetch their Lewis Guns and rations from the Dump, immediately on arrival in the new area.

8. Blankets will be rolled in bundles of 10 and stacked in the Sergeants' Mess hut by 10am. Officers' Kits to be there by the same hour. The R.S.M. will detail 1 N.C.O and 1 man (from those remaining out of the line) to be in charge of these stores.

9. Completion of moves to be reported to Battalion Headquarters by runner.

10. Acknowledge.

CAPTAIN,
ADJUTANT

ISSUED TO SIGNALS AT 7.55.pm.   18th.Bn.MANCHESTER REGIMENT.

Copies to:-
1. 90th.Bde H.Q.
2. 89th.Bde H.Q.
3. Commanding Officer.
4. Second in Command.
5. Adjutant.
6. Assistant Adjutant.
7,8,9,10. Companies.
11. Transport Officer.
12. Quartermaster.
13. Medical Officer.
14. O.C. 2nd.Bn.Royal Scots Fusiliers.
15. R.S.M.
16/17. War Diary.
18. File.

OPERATION ORDER No. 110.

by Lieut.Col. H.C.W.Theobald.D.S.O.

Commanding 18th.Batt. Manchester Regt.

1. The 18th. Batt. Manchester Regt. will relieve the 17th. Batt. Manchester Regt. in the right Sub-sector during the night 27/28th. December.

2. "C" Coy. 18th. Manchester's will relieve "D" Coy. 17th. Manchester's on the left.
   "B" Coy. will relieve "A" Coy. in the centre.
   "D" Coy.   do.   "C" Coy. on the right.
   "A" Coy.   do.   "B" Coy. in support.
   Batt. H.Q. will be at J20, b 5/5.

3. Company's will move off at intervals of a quarter of an hour in the following order:- "C". "D". "B". "A". "H.Q.". commencing at 4.30.p.m.
   At least 300 yds. to be maintained between platoons.

4. ROUTE. Via Track "A". to Western end of PERTH AVENUE where guides from the 17th. Manchester Regt. (4 per Coy.) will be met.
   Guides for each post will be provided at Company H.Q.

5. Rations will be issued to each man before moving off from TORR TOP. In addition 6 petrol tins of water per Coy. and 2 of tea will be issued and carried up.
   Water bottles will be filled before moving off.

6. All trench stores, maps, aeroplane photographs, barrage rations &c. will be taken over and a list forwarded to Batt.H.Q. by 9.a.m. on the 28th. inst.

7. Completion of reliefs to be wired to Batt.H.Q. by the code word STARLING.

                                      (Sd) W.E.OGDEN. Capt.
                                            Adjutant.
27/12/1917.   18th.(S) Batt. Manchester Regt.

Issued at 10.a.m.
Copies to:-
1.   90th. Inf. Bde.
2. 3. 4. 5. Companies.
6.   C.O.
7.   17th. Manchester Regt.
8. 9.   War Diary.
10.   File.

R6

OPERATION ORDER No. ???

by MAJOR T.J.KELLY. M.C.

Commanding 18th. Batt. Manchester Regt.

1. The 18th.Batt. Manchester Regt. will be relieved in the right sub-sector by the 17th. Batt. Kings Liverpool Regt. tomorrow night.

2. Guides (4 per Coy.) will report at Batt. H.Q. at 4.30 pm. to act as guides tp each platoon and each Coy. H.Q. of relieving Batt.

3. Company Commanders will be careful to obtain receipts for all Stores, Maps &c handed over

4. In coming out Companys will move by twos and threes across the open and use communication trenches as far as possible.
On relief Coys. will proceed tom FORRESTOR CAMP via "A" track GLOUCESTER DRIVE- ZILLEBEKE- SHRAPNEL CORNER.
Movement east of ZILLEBEKE will be by Platoons, and Company Commanders will take steps to ensure that Companys are formed up WEST of this point and marched back to Camp as a formed body. Strict attention will be paid to march discipline and an Officer or a Senior N.C.O. must be left to bring on stragglers at the pace of the slowest. No man is to be allowed to fall out but must come with the slow party.

5. Each Company will report relief complete by the words "NOT KNOWN" over the telephone, Company Commanders reporting personally n the way out.

6. Lewis Gun Limbers will be at CANADA DUMP from 8-30 onward and L.G. teams will take their guns there. The Limbers will proceed independently to FORRESTER CAMP as soon as the Senior L.G. N.C.O. of each Company informs the driver that everything is loaded

7. The Quatermaster will arrange to take over FORRESTER CAMP and will have men in the vicinity of SWAN CHATEAU to guide Companys to their billets.
A Hot Meal will be provided for the Batta on its arrival in Camp.

8. The Quater master will arrange to take over all stores &c. from ALBERTA CAMP and O.C. Details will arrange with him regarding transport of mess and orderly room baggage. O.C. Details will also arrange for Senior N.C.O. to march Details to FORRESTOR CAMP during the day.

9. Acknowledge.

(Sd) W.E.OGDEN. CAPTAIN
ADJUTANT
18th.Batt. Manchester Regt.

29.12.1917.

Index........................

SUBJECT.

18th Manchester Regiment.

No.	Contents.	Date.
	January 1918.	

CONFIDENTIAL.

WAR DIARY

for the

MONTH OF JANUARY.

1918.

18TH. (SERVICE) BATTALION. - THE MANCHESTER REGIMENT

(VOLUME XXVII).

In the Field.
1-2-1918.

..........J. Bacon.......... Lieut.Col.
Commanding. 18th. (s). Bn. MANCHESTER REGIMENT.

Sheet. 40. R.

WAR DIARY
or
INTELLIGENCE SUMMARY.

Army Form C. 2118.

(Erase heading not required.)

18th Service Batt. Manchester Regt.

Place	Date	Hour	Summary of Events and Information	Remarks and references to Appendices
	1918			
FORRESTOR CAMP	Jan 1st		Training	
	5		Battalion moved to billets at EBBLINGHEM entraining at DICKEBUSCH at 11 a.m.	R 1
	6		Training. Lieut. Col. H.C.W. THEOBALD, D.S.O. reported from Field Ambulance to-day	
EBBLINGHEM	7		Battalion left EBBLINGHEM at 7.30 p.m. and marched to STEENBECQUE entraining there at 12 midnight.	R 2
	8		Arrived at LONGUEAU at 8 a.m. where detrained and marched to billets at VAIRE-SOUS-CORBIE arriving at 1 p.m. Capt. J.E. SMART awarded the Military Cross for distinguished and valuable services in the Field. (New Years Honours Gazette)	
VAIRE-SOUS-CORBIE	9/12		Training 10th 2nd Lt. J. ARNOLD admitted to Field Ambulance (sick) Major F. WALTON, M.C. (6th Bn. Durham L.I.) assumed command of the Battalion on the 11th inst.	

VICE Lieut Col. H.C.W. THEOBALD. D.S.O.

Army Form C. 2118.

WAR DIARY
or
INTELLIGENCE SUMMARY.

(Erase heading not required.) 18th (S) Bn Manchester Regt

Sheet No 1 R

Instructions regarding War Diaries and Intelligence Summaries are contained in F. S. Regs., Part II. and the Staff Manual respectively. Title pages will be prepared in manuscript.

Place	Date	Hour	Summary of Events and Information	Remarks and references to Appendices
	1918			
	Jan 13		Battalion marched to billets at HARBONNIERES, via HAMEL – WARFUSEE – ABANCOURT – BAYONVILLERS arriving at 1 p.m. 2nd Lt A. LUCAS rejoined the Battalion today from Divl. Burial Party.	R.3
	14		Marched to billets at NESLE, via LIHONS – CHAULNES – PUZEAUX arriving at 4 p.m. The following Officers struck off the establishment:- Capt. C. RISSIK Lieut. C.N. GREEN Lieut. W.M. BARRATT Lieut. T.R. ESSÉ Lieut. J.E. SHANAHAN	R.4
NESLE	15/18		Training. Draft of 98 O.Rs. joined the Battalion on the 16th inst. from Divl Reinforcement Camp (ex "H" Depot.) Lieut A.V. MICHAELIS and 2nd Lt A.W. RICHARDS transferred to U.K. (wounded) and struck off the strength of the Battalion accordingly	
	19		Battalion marched to billets at LIGEMONT via CRESSY – ERCHEU, arriving at 1.30 p.m.	R.5

Sheet No 2. R.

Army Form C. 2118.

WAR DIARY
or
INTELLIGENCE SUMMARY.
(Erase heading not required.) 18th Service Battalion Manchester Regt

Instructions regarding War Diaries and Intelligence Summaries are contained in F. S. Regs., Part II. and the Staff Manual respectively. Title pages will be prepared in manuscript.

Place	Date	Hour	Summary of Events and Information	Remarks and references to Appendices
	1918			
LIBERMONT	Jany 24/25		Training. The Army Commander Sir H. de la P. GOUGH K.C.B. K.C.V.O (Commanding Fifth Army) visited Brigade Area on 22nd inst: Captain H.G.S. BOYER proceeded on leave to the 21st inst and Captain (Adjutant) N.E. OGDEN M.C. on 23rd inst, 2nd Lieut A.E. WAKEFIELD returned from Field Ambulance 25th inst.	R.6
BEHERICOURT	26		The Battalion marched to billets in BEHERICOURT via MUNRANCOURT - BUSSY - GENVRY - NOYON arriving about 2 p.m.	
CHAUNY	27		Marched to Billets in CHAUNY SUD	R.7
	28		Training	
In the Line	29/30		The Battalion left CHAUNEY SUD and proceeded to the trenches to relieve the 15th FRENCH CAVALRY REGIMENT on the night of 29/30th inst. Disposition of Battalion was:- Battalion Headquarters in dugouts at H9 b 55 "D" Company - Right Front Line - BAILLON Sector H15 d 25 "A" Company - Left Front Line at L'ERMITAGE H16 c 51 "C" Company - Right Support. "B" Company - Left Support.	R.8

Sheet 3R

Army Form C. 2118.

WAR DIARY
or
INTELLIGENCE SUMMARY
(Erase heading not required.) 18th Service Battalion Manchester Regiment

Place	Date	Hour	Summary of Events and Information	Remarks and references to Appendices
	1918			
In the line	Jany 29/31	Contd.	This Sector was very quiet and trouble to visit all the lines in daylight. The following appeared in the Supplement to LONDON GAZETTE of 21.12.1917 dated 22.12.1917:- Quartermaster & Hon Lieut T.C. PIERCE to be Hon. CAPTAIN. 2.12.1917. J. Warren Lieut Colonel Comdg 18th Service Battalion Manchester Regt.	

R.1.

(SECRET). OPERATION ORDER No.111.   Copy No. 14
          By MAJOR.T.J.KELLY, M.C.,
          Commanding 18th.(s)Battalion.,
          THE MANCHESTER REGIMENT.   3rd.January.1918.

REFERENCE:- Sheet.28. 1/40000.
             36a. N.W. 1/20000.

1. The Battalion (less Transport) will move by rail and road to billets in the BLARINGHEM Area on the 5th.January, entraining at DICKEBUSCH at 11am.

2. Movement will be by rail from DICKEBUSCH to EBBLINGHEM and thence by march route.

3. Parade in column of route on the SHRAPNEL CORNER – KRUISSTRAATHOEK Road ready to march off at 9am. Head of column to be opposite H.Q.Mess, facing S.W.

4. Order of March:- H.Q., Band, A, B, C, D Coys. Dress Full marching order, soft caps to be worn, leather jerkins outside packs. 100 yards to be maintained between Companies on the march.

5. Transport will move by road under the orders of the Transport Officer, leaving present area on the morning of the 4th inst., and rejoining the Battalion the following day at BLARINGHEM

6. An advanced billetting party, consisting of 2nd.Lt. D.TRUSDALE the 4 C.Q.M.Ss and Cpl Glynn, will travel on the same train as the Battalion, and on arrival at EBLINGHEM will proceed on in advance to allotted billets.

7. Blankets will be rolled in bundles of 10, and deposited outside the Shoemakers hut by 7am; Officers' valises to be there at the same hour. O.C. "B" Coy will detail a party of L.N.C.O and 10 men for loading these stores.

8. Company Commanders must ensure that all their huts are left scrupulously clean, and will render a certificate to the Orderly Room to that effect by 8.30am.

9. Lewis Gun Limbers, Officers' Mess Cart, and Maltese Cart must be packed ready for moving this afternoon.
    As much kit as possible must be taken on the Battalion transport, and this will be dumped outside the Shoemaker's hut and collected this afternoon.

10. Acknowledge.

                                          CAPTAIN,
                                          ADJUTANT,
ISSUED TO SIGNALS AT 2.3 pm. 18th.Bn. MANCHESTER REGIMENT.

Copies:to:-
1. 90th.Bde H.Q.
2. Commanding Officer.
3. Adjutant.
4. Assistant Adjutant.
5,6,7,8.Companies.
9. Transport Officer.
10. Quartermaster.
11. Medical Officer.
12. R.S.M.
13.14. War Diary.
15. File.

(SECRET). OPERATION ORDERS No.113. Copy No. 15
By. LIEUT COLONEL.H.C.A.THEOBALD, D.S.O.,
COMMANDING.18th.(s).BATTALION,
THE MANCHESTER REGIMENT.

Reference:- (HAZEBROUCK. 1/100,000.
(AMIENS. 1/100,000.

1. The Battalion will move by rail and road to billets at LA NEUVILLE on the 7/8th.January, entraining at STEENBECQUE at 12 midnight.

2. Detraining station will be LONGUEAU.

3. Parade in column of route ready to move off at 7.30pm; head of the column to be at the Cross Roads 100 yards N.E. of the Chateau, facing East.

4. Order of March:- H.Q, Band, A,B,C & D Coys. 100 yards to be maintained between companies when on the march.

5. Route:- WALLON CAPPEL - BOIS DES HUIT RUES - MORBECQUE.

6. Dress:- Full marching Order. Soft caps to be worn; leather jerkins outside the tunic.

7. Transport will move to STEENBECQUE Station under orders of the Transport Officer, leaving at 6.30pm.

8. Blankets and Officers valises will be stacked outside each billet by 8.pm, whence they will be conveyed to the station by lorry; mess boxes will be taken on the last load, and must be ready by 4.pm, at the latest.

9. Special care must be taken that all billets are left clean, and Company Commanders will render a report to that effect to the Orderly Room by 6pm.

10. Tea will be served on arrival at LONGUEAU. Men must be warned to have their mess-tins ready, so that no delay occurs.

11. O.C. "C"Coy. will detail a party of 1 Officer & 10.ORs. to report to the R.T.O. LONGUEAU on arrival for the purpose of cleaning out the carriages.
    Name of Officer selected to be notified to this office by noon tomorrow.

12. Special attention must be paid to train discipline. No man will leave his carriage without permission and each company will detail an Officer to ensure that this order is carried out.

13. Guides will be provided at destination to conduct companies to their billets. Arrival to be reported to Battalion Headquarters by runner.

14. Acknowledge.

ISSUED TO SIGNALS AT 8.10 pm.

.... CAPTAIN,
ADJUTANT,
18th.Bn.MANCHESTER REGIMENT.

Copies to:-
1. 90th.Bde H.Q.
2. Commanding Officer.
3. Second in Command.
4. Adjutant.
5. Assistant Adjutant.
6,7,8,9. Companies.
10. Transport Officer.
11. Quartermaster.
12. Medical Officer.
13. R.S.M.
14,15. War Diary.
16. File.

18th Battalion, Manchester Regt.
OPERATION ORDER NO. 114

(SECRET)   Copy No..........
                                                                                              12/1/18.

Reference :- Sheet AMIENS 1/100,000

1. The Battalion will march to billets at HARBONNIERES tomorrow the 13th inst.

2. Parade in column of threes on the main road, ready to march off at 7.45.a.m. Head of column to be opposite the Orderly Room - facing S.E.

3. Order of March -- Band, H.Q., "D", "A", "B", "C", Companies, Transport.

4. Route- HAMEL - VILLERS BRETONNEUX - MARCELCAVE -- GUILLAUCOURT.

5. One blanket per man will be carried. The remainder will be rolled in bundles of ten and dumped at the Q.M.Stores by 6.30.a.m. O.C."B"Coy. will detail a party of 1 N.C.O. and 10 men for loading these stores and if necessary this party will remain behind and follow on with the blanket waggons.

6. Officer's valises to be at the Q.M. Stores not later than 7.0.a.m.

7. A "slow party" consisting of those men likely to be unable to keep up with the battalion will parade at 7.30.a.m. under 2nd Lieut. S.L. Heyhoe and proceed direct to destination by the shortest route. This officer will report to the Adjutant tonight for further instructions.

8. All billets must be left scrupulously clean, latrine buckets emptied, refuse burnt and a certficate to that effect rendered to the Orderly Room by 7.30.a.m.

9. Particular attention must be paid to March Discipline, and the instructions issued on this subject complied with in every respect.

10. Acknowledge.

ISSUED TO SIGNALS AT 7.42.p.m.
                                                                  .... CAPTAIN,
                                                                                ADJUTANT,
                                                                  18th Bn.Manchester Regt.

Copies to:-
1. 90th Bde.
2. Commanding Officer,
3. Second in Command,
4. Adjutant,
5.,6.,7.,8., Companies,
9. Transport Officer,
10. Quartermaster,
11. Medical Officer,
12. R.S.M.
13.,14., War Diary,
14. File.

SECRET.

R 4

18th. SERVICE BATTALION. MANCHESTER REGIMENT.
---ooo---
OPERATION ORDER. No. 115.

Copy No.... 13
13/1/18

Reference:- Sheet AMIENS 17. 1/100,000.

1. The Battalion will march to billets at NESLE tomorrow 14th inst.

2. Parade in column of threes on the LIHONS Road, ready to march off at 9.15am. Head of the column to be opposite "D" Coy. Office - facing S.E.

3. Order of March:- H.Q, "C", "D" Coys, Band, "A", "B" Coys, Transport.

4. Route:- LIHONS - CHAULNES - PUZEAUX.

5. Dinners will be served at the 1 o'clock halt.

6. One blanket per man will be carried, and remainder dumped at the Q.M.Stores not later than 7.30am. O.C. "C" Coy will detail a party of 1 N.C.O and 10 men for loading these stores.

7. Officers' Valises to be at the Q.M.Stores by 8.15am.

8. Slow party will parade outside the Orderly Room at 8.45am, under 2nd.Lieut S.L.HEYHOE. This Officer will report to the Adjutant, tonight, for instructions.

9. All billets must be left in a clean and sanitary condition and a certificate to that effect rendered to the Orderly Room by 8.30am. The Commanding Officer wishes Company Commanders to pay special attention to the points brought to notice today.

10. ACKNOWLEDGE.

.... CAPTAIN,
ADJUTANT,
ISSUED TO SIGNALS AT....pm. 18th.Bn.MANCHESTER REGIMENT.

Copies to:-
1. 90th.Bde.
2. Commanding Officer.
3. Second in Command.
4. Adjutant.
5,6,7,8. Companies.
9. Transport Officer.
10. Quartermaster.
11. Medical Officer.
12. R.S.M.
13, 14. War Diary.
15. File.

R5.

SECRET.   18th. (S) Battn. MANCHESTER REGIMENT.   Copy No..... 14

OPERATION ORDER NO. 116.

18.1.18.

Reference Sheet AMIENS 17 - 1/100,000.

1. The Battalion will march to billets at LIEKRMONT tomorrow the 19th. instant.

2. Parade in column of threes on the CRESSY Road ready to move off at 10.25am. Head of the column to be 300 yards South of H.Q. Coy. billet, facing S.E.

3. Order of march:- H.Q., "B", "C" Coys, Band, "D", "A" Coys., Transport.

4. Route: CRESSY - ERCHEU.

5. Slow party will parade outside the Orderly Room at 9.45am under 2nd.Lieut. J.E.LOVE. This Officer will report to the Adjutant at 9.30am for instructions.

6. All blankets will be dumped at the Q.M. Stores by 8.0am. Officers' valises to be ready not later than 9.0am.

7. Billets must be left in a clean and sanitary condition and a certificate to that effect rendered to the Orderly Room by each Company before 10.0am.

8. Arrival in billets to be reported to Battalion Headquarters by runner.

9. Attention is drawn to the instructions issued regarding inspection of feet both before and after the march.

10. ACKNOWLEDGE.

Capt. & Adjt.
Issued to Signals at .2.19.p.m.   18th.Bn. THE MANCHESTER REGIMENT.

Copies to:-
1. 90th. Brigade.
2. Commanding Officer.
3. Second-in-Command.
4. Adjutant.
5.6.7.& 8. Os.C. Companies.
9. Transport Officer.
10. Medical Officer.
11. Quartermaster.
12. R.S.M.
13. Band.
14.15. War Diary.
16. File.

SECRET.   18th (S) Bn. MANCHESTER REGIMENT.   25.1.18.

Operation Order No.117.

Reference Maps: AMIENS Sheet 17.   1/100,000.
                ST.QUENTIN " 18.   1/100,000.
----

(1)   The Battalion will march to billets in BEHERICOURT tomorrow the 26th. instant.

(2)   Parade in column of threes on the FRENICHES Road ready to move off at 7.30am. Head of column on FRENICHES Road to be 300 yards from RUE DE CALVIARE facing South East.

(3)   Order of march: H.Q. Coy: "C" Coy: Band: "D", "A" and "B" Coys: Transport.

(4)   Route: MUNRANCOURT - BUSSY - GENVRY - NOYON.

(5)   Slow party will parade outside Headquarters Mess at 6.45am under 2nd.Lieut. L.S. Illingworth. This Officer will report to the Adjutant at 7.pm tonight for instructions.

(6)   All blankets will be rolled in bundles of 10 and dumped inside the gates of the Guard Room not later than 6.0am. Officers' valises and mess boxes must be at the same place by 6.30am.

(7)   Billets will be left in a clean and sanitary condition and a certificate rendered to that effect to the Orderly Room by each Company before 6.30am.

(8)   Arrival in billets to be reported to B.H.Q. by runner.

(9)   Dinners will be served on arrival in billets.

(10) Attention is drawn to the instructions issued regarding inspection of feet both before and after the march.

(11) ACKNOWLEDGE.

Issued to Signals at: 5.0pm.

Copy No.1. 90th.Bde.HQ.
       2. Commanding Officer.
       3. 2nd.in.Command.
       4. Adjutant.
       5.6.7.8. Companies.
       9. T.O.
      10. M.O.
      11. Q.M.
      12. R.S.M.
      13. Band.
      14.15. War Diary.
      16. File.

                                    2nd.Lieut.
                                    A/Adjutant.
                                    18th.Bn. Manchester Regt.

SECRET.   18th. SERVICE BATTALION. MANCHESTER REGIMENT.   26.1.1918.

OPERATION ORDER No. 118.

Reference Maps :- St. QUENTIN.   1/100,000.
                  70D.   1/40,000.
                  70E.NE.   1/20,000.
                  70D.NW.   1/20,000.

1. The battalion will march to billets in CHAUNY SUD and ARBLINCOURT tomorrow the 27th instant.

2. Parade in column of threes. Head of column opposite Headquarters (Chateau) facing South. at 9.30 a.m.

3. Order of march :- H.Q, "D", "A" Coys, Band, "B" & "C" Coys.

4. Route :- CHAUNY.

5. Slow party will parade at/8.30am. ready to move off under 2nd.Lieut. L.H.BURROWS.   *ORDERLY ROOM*

6. All blankets will be rolled in bundles of 10 and dumped at Q.M. Stores, not later than 8.15am. Officers Valises and mess boxes will be dumped at the same place by 8.45am.

7. Billets will be left in a clean and sanitary condition and a certificate rendered to that effect to the Orderly Room by each Company before 9.0am.

8. Arrival in billets to be reported to B.H.Q. by runner.

9. Dinners will be served on arrival in billets.

10. Attention is drawn to the instructions issued regarding inspection of feet both before and after the march.

11. ACKNOWLEDGE.

                                              2nd. LIEUT,
Issued to Signals at 6.30pm.   .... A/ADJUTANT,
                                  18th. Bn. MANCHESTER REGIMENT.

Copy 1. 90th. Bde H.Q.
     2. Commanding Officer.
     3. 2nd. in Command.
     4. Adjutant.
     5,6,7,8. Companies.
     9. T.O.
    10. M.O.
    11. Q.M.
    12. R.S.M.
    13. Band.
    14.15. War Diary.
    16. File.

(SECRET)   18th. (S) Bn. MANCHESTER REGT.   Jan. 29. 1918.

Ref. Sheet 70^D N.W. 1/20,000.   Operation Order No. 119.

1. The 18th. Bn. Manchester Regt. will relieve a Battalion of the 5th. French Cavalry Division in the Centre Sub-Sector during the night 29/30th. instant.

2. "D" Coy: 18th.Bn.M.R. will relieve the Coy. at present holding the Right half Sub-Sector.
   "A" Coy: ,,   ,,   ,,   the Coy. at present holding the Left half Sub-Sector.
   "C" Coy: ,,   ,,   ,,   the Coy. at present in Right Support.
   "B" Coy: ,,   ,,   ,,   the Coy. at present in Left Support.
   Battn. Headquarters will be at H.9.b.5.5.
   Other details as arranged at Conference 28.1.18.

3. Companies will move off from present billets at intervals of five minutes in order "D", "A", "C", "B" and H.Q. Coy. First Company to move off at 4.30pm.

4. Companies will maintain at least 250 yards interval West of SINCENY; thence platoons will move at 50 yards interval.

5. Guides (1 per Company) will be met at the road junction G.11.a.8.3. Platoon Guides will be met at Bn. H.Qs.

6. Lewis Gun Limbers will move off with their respective Companies.

7. Rations, Water and Cookers as arranged with the Transport Officer.

8. Blankets (1 per man) will be carried; remainder will be rolled up in bundles of 10 and deposited at the Q.M. Stores by 3pm.

9. Officers' Mess Cart and Maltese Cart will be at present Battn. H.Q. at 4.0pm.

10. TRENCH STORES Lists of all stores, secret maps, aeroplane photographs, log books, defence schemes etc. handed over to Companies by the French will be rendered so as to reach Battn. H.Q. by 12 noon on the 30th. inst.

11. Completion of relief to be wired to Bn. H.Q. by runner.

12. ACKNOWLEDGE.

Issued to Signals at 12 noon.

                                              2nd. Lieut.
                                              A/Adjutant,
                                              18th.Bn. MANCHESTER REGT.

Copies to:
1. C.O.
2. 2nd.in.Command.
3. Adjutant.
4.5.6.7. Coys.
9. T.O.
10. M.O.
11. I.O.
12. Q.M.
13. R.S.M.
14. File.
15.16. War Diary.
17. H.Q. 90th. Brigade.

Index..........................

SUBJECT.

18th Manchester Regiment

No.	Contents.	Date.
	February 1918	

Confidential

War Diary

for the

Month of February.

1918

18th (Service) Battalion, The Manchester Regiment

(Volume XXVIII)

In the Field
25th Feby 1918

J E Ogden
Capt
adjt for.
Lieut.-Col.
Commanding 18th Bn. Manchester Regt.

WAR DIARY or INTELLIGENCE SUMMARY

Army Form C. 2118.

Sheet No. N

(Erase heading not required.) 16th (Service) Bn Manchester Regt

Place	Date	Hour	Summary of Events and Information	Remarks and references to Appendices
	1918			
	Feb 1/2		In the line holding the FORET D'EPINOIS Sector	
		9	Relieved during the night 9/10 by 6th Bn London Regt 3 on completion of which marched to billets in CHAUNY	N 1
		10	Marched to GUISCARD via NEUFLEUX - QUAY arriving at 1.30 p.m. Capt. M. BRUNTON transferred to 16th Bn Manchester Regt. & struck off the strength immediately	N 2
		11	Marched to billets at GRANCOURT	N 3
		12	2/Lt A.S BURGESS rejoined Battalion from 30th Divisional Depot & 2/Lt J CHAPMAN from 10th Mayo LIBERMONT	
		13	Party of 50 O.R.s of 'A' Coy under command of 2/Lt A.E WAKEFIELD detached on working party at HAM	
		14	2/Lt N SEDGWICK transferred to 16th Bn Manchester Regt & struck off the strength from today	
		15	Detachment at HAM moved to ROVE	
		17	Battalion carried to billets at MATIGNICOURT at 2 p.m	N 4

Army Form C. 2118.

WAR DIARY
or
INTELLIGENCE SUMMARY.
(Erase heading not required.) 18th (Service) Bn. Manchester Regt.

Sheet 45 N

Place	Date	Hour	Summary of Events and Information	Remarks and references to Appendices
	Feb 19		Moved by train to HAUT ALLAINES (VIIth Corps)	
	20		Amalgamation Bulter forming "C" & "D" Coys of 17th Eventing Battalion	

W.E. Ogden Capt.
for Lieut.-Col.
Commanding 18th Bn. Manchester Regt.

SECRET

18th Bn. Manchester Regt.

OPERATION - ORDER No. 121

8.2.1918.

Ref - Sheet 70D 1/40,000

1. The 18th Bn. Manchester Regt. will be relieved in the CENTRE sub-sector during the night 9/10th Feby by the 6th Bn LONDON Regt and on completion of relief will march to billets at CHAUNY.

2. Companies will be relieved in the following order - C, B, A, D Coys, moving off as soon as each company relief is complete.

3. Guides as detailed in this office AQ 239 will report at the Orderly Room at 5 p.m. and proceed under 2nd Lt J ARNOLD to the BUTTES DE ROUY - H I c 8 4, to meet the relieving unit.

4. East of the line PIERREMANDE - SINCENY - CHAUNY a minimum distance of 250 yards will be maintained between Companies.

5. One Officer per Battn HQ, One Officer per Coy HQ, and one NCO per platoon relieved will remain behind for 24 hours after the completion of relief. This party will collect at Bde. HQ, SINCENY at 10.30 a.m. 11th inst, and will be conveyed thence by lorry to the ERCHEU area.

6. All French stores will be handed over to the relieving battalion and receipts for same forwarded to Battn HQ by 12 noon, 10th inst.

7. The Transport Officer will arrange for Lewis Gun limbers to report at Coy HQ, as soon as possible after dusk. Cookers and Watercarts will move off as early as possible to CHAUNY, and the Quartermaster will arrange, if possible, to provide hot tea for the Battalion on its arrival in billets.

8. Completion of reliefs to be wired to Bn HQ by the name of the Senior Platoon Commander in each Coy.

9. ACKNOWLEDGE

H E Ogden
Captain
Adjutant.
18th Bn. Manchester Regt.

Issued to Signals at 9.20 pm

Copies to :-
No 1 C.O.
2 Adjt
3 A Coy
4 B
5 C
6 D
7 QM & TO
No 8 I.O.
9 File
10 9o Bde.
11 6th Bn London Regt
12) War Diary
13)

18th. (S) Bn. MANCHESTER REGT.

SECRET.   OperationOrder No. 122.   9.2.18.

Ref: ST. QUENTIN Sheet 18 - 1/100,000.

1. The Battalion will march to billets at GUISCARD tomorrow the 10th. instant.

2. Parade in column of threes ready to move off at 9.50am. Head of column to be opposite H.Q. Mess facing West.

3. Order of march: H.Q., "D", "C" Coys: Band, "B" "A" Coys. Transport.

4. Route: NEUFLIEUX - GUIVRY.

5. Slow party as already detailed will parade at the Orderly Room at 8.30am under 2/Lieut. A.G. HARMAN. This Officer will report to the Adjutant for instructions before moving off.

6. Blankets will be rolled in bundles of 10 and deposited at the Q.M. STORES not later than 7.30am. Officers' valises to be ready by 8.30am.

7. All billets must be left clean and a certificate to that effect rendered to the Orderly Room by each Company before moving off.

8. Arrival in billets to be reported to Battalion H.Q. by runner.

9. ACKNOWLEDGE.

Capt. & Adjt.
18th.Bn. MANCHESTER REGIMENT.

Issued to Signals at 12.45am.

Copies to:-
1. Commanding Officer.
2. Adjutant.
3.)
4.) All
5.) Coys.
6.)
7.) T.O.
8.) M.O.
9. Q.M.
10. I.O.
11. R.S.M.
12. Band.
13. File.
14. War Diary.
15. "   "
16. Copy to 90th. Brigade.

N3

SECRET.   18th (S) Bn. MANCHESTER REGT.   Feby.10/1918.

OPERATION ORDER NO.123.

Reference ST. QUENTIN Sheet 18 - 1/100,000.

1. The Battalion will move to billets ~~xxxxxxxx~~ at GOLANCOURT tomorrow the 11th. instant.

2. Parade in column of threes on the RUE DE HAM ready to move off at 9.50am.
Head of the column to be opposite "D" Coy: office, facing north.

3. Order of march: H.Q., "C", "B" Coys: Band: "A", "D" Coys: Transport.

4. Blankets will be deposited at the Quartermaster's Stores not later than 7.30am. Officers valises to be ready by 8.30am.

5. The usual certificates will be rendered to the Orderly Room certifying that all billets are left in a clean and sanitary condition.

6. Arrival in billets to be reported to Battn. H.Q. by runner.

7. ACKNOWLEDGE.

Issued to Signals at 9.30pm.

Copies to:-

1. Commanding Officer.
2. Adjutant.
3. "A" Coy:
4. "B" Coy:
5. "C" Coy:
6. "D" Coy:
7. T.O.
8. M.O.
9. Q.M.
10. File.
11. War Diary.
12. "   "
13. Copy to 90th. Bde. H.Q.
14. Band.   15. R.S.M.

Capt. & Adjt.
18th.Bn. MANCHESTER REGIMENT.

(SECRET).   18th (S) Bn. MANCHESTER REGT.   Feby. 16th. 1918.

Operation Order No.124.

Ref:) ST. QUENTIN 18. 1/100,000.
) AMIENS   17.   "

1. The Battalion will march to billets at LANGUEVOISIN tomorrow the 17th Feby.

2. Parade in column of threes ready to march off at 9.30am. Head of the column to be at junction of main HAM Road and ESMERY - HALLON Road facing south.

3. Order of march: H.Q., "B", "C" Coys - Band - "D", "A" Coys - Transport.

4. Route: ESMERY - HALLON - HOMBLEUX - QUIQUERY.

5. Slow party will parade at the Orderly Room at 8.30am under 2/Lt. PLATT. This Officer will report to the Adjutant for instructions before moving off.

6. Blankets will be rolled in bundles of 10 and deposited at the Q.M. Stores by 7.30am. Officers valises to be ready not later than 8.30am. The R.S.M. will detail a loading party of 1 N.C.O. and 10 men of H.Q. Coy. to report to the Q.M. at 7.30am.

7. Certificates will be rendered to the Orderly Room by 9.0am that each Company's billets have been left in a clean and sanitary condition.

8. Advance party for the move to CHAULNES on the 18th instant will probably leave GOLANCOURT early tomorrow morning. This party will consist of 2/Lt. J. ARNOLD, 2/Lt. E.L. CAPPER, 4 O.Rs. per company and Battalion H.Qs. and 2 pioneers. Detailed instructions regarding this party will be issued later.

9. An advance party consisting of 2/Lt. Truswell and the four Coy. Q.M.S's will move off at 8.30am and proceed in advance to take over billets at LANGUEVOISIN.

10. Arrival in billets to be reported to Battalion H.Q. by runner.

11. ACKNOWLEDGE.

Issued to Signals at 8.0pm.

Copies o:-
                                        Capt. & Adjt.
                            18th. Bn. MANCHESTER REGIMENT.

1. Commanding Officer.
2. Adjutant.
3,4,5,& 6. Coys.
7. T.O.
8. M.O.
9. Q.M.
10. R.S.M.
11. Band.
12. File.
13,14. War Diary.

Copy to 30th. Div. "G".
 "   " 90th. Inf. Bde.